C000203920

63/2

First published 2018 by Phillimore & Co. Ltd

The History Press
The Mill, Brimscombe Port
Stroud, Gloucestershire, GL5 2QG
www.thehistorypress.co.uk

British Library Cataloguing in Publication Data.
A catalogue record for this book is available from the British Library.

ISBN 978 0 7509 8758 5

Typesetting and origination by The History Press
Printed and bound in Europe by Imak

VICTORIAN BRACKLEY

Brackley Top Station, Great Central Railway, 1899

SIGILLVM · BVRGI · DE · BRACKLEY

Helen with love from Celia & John

VICTORIAN BRACKLEY

JOHN CLARKE

John Clarke

CONTENTS

ACKNOWLEDGEMENTS

The Brackley and District History Society acknowledges the support of the following sponsors, without whom publication of this volume would not have been possible:
Brackley Town Council
South Northamptonshire Council
Faccenda Foods
Borras Construction Limited
Macintyers Estate Agents
The Old Hall Bookshop
J.C. Clarke
Tesco plc

Illustrations have been included with the permission of Northamptonshire Record Office (NRO) and Brackley Library (A.A. Green Collection). All others from Professor John Clarke's own collection.

Brackley Town Council

This, the final volume of the trilogy dedicated to the history of Brackley, provides a unique and interesting record of the town's history.

From the Iron Age, the Saxon '*Bracca*', through to jousting, the wool trade and now into the Victorian era, bringing Brackley right into the twentieth century and thus providing an insight into the people and events that moulded the town you see today.

The town's deep and wonderful history is, at long last, exposed through the meticulous and dedicated work of one team … Professor John Clarke.

Having worked in publishing myself for many years, I know the amount of work required to produce such a publication and cannot leave this foreword without mention of the members of the Committee of the Brackley and District History Society, who have worked so hard to get this historical record published.

Councillor Don Thompson
Brackley Town Mayor
September 2017

Chapter One

DEAR OLD BRACKLEY

Even today, I still meet people who talk of 'dear old Brackley'. The same expression was used, rather more frequently, in my childhood in the 1950s. Somehow, it cheers me up and I always love to hear it. 'Dear old Brackley' strikes a chord in me and has been a crucial motif in my life and career. Yet, what does it mean? Curiously, I have never received a satisfactory answer. The normal response goes something like this: 'You know John, *real* Brackley; you're Brackley too; you must understand.'

In part, this book represents a voyage of self-discovery. I want to work out what I mean by 'dear old Brackley'. But I know that 'dear old Brackley' is part of a heritage I share with others. With this book, I hope that I can help some of my readers to 'bring back' the half-forgotten stories they heard as children. In short, I shall consider myself well rewarded if my thoughts assist others to develop their own personal visions of 'dear old Brackley'.

I offer two suggestions to guide my readers. The first is that, behind the idea of 'dear old Brackley' there lies a mixture of buildings, loyalties and values – above all, that sense of place and intimacy which comes from knowing everyone in a small community. It may add up to a kind of 'Spirit of Place'. Yet, as readers of my earlier works will appreciate,[1] Brackley has changed a good deal over the centuries; to get a 'fix' on 'dear old Brackley' we need an element of time as well. This leads on to my second and more important suggestion – that, to all intents and purposes, 'dear old Brackley' should be identified with Victorian Brackley, which in the narrowly academic sense is the subject of this book.

But why should 'dear old Brackley' and 'Victorian Brackley' be treated as identical? Let us consider the words 'dear' and 'old' more carefully. 'Dear' obviously implies affection, but 'old' is more difficult. Brackley has existed in some form or other since Roman times, so nineteenth-century Brackley is hardly 'old' in the overall context of the history of the town. But it is 'old' in the personal context; it refers to the Brackley of our parents, grandparents and great grandparents. When we express our affection for 'dear old Brackley', many of us are expressing our love, not only for the town, but also for members of our own families.

1   Clarke, John, *The Book of Brackley* (Buckingham, Barracuda Books, 1987) and *Yesterday's Brackley: From Restoration to Reform* (Buckingham, Barracuda Books, 1990).

In part, when we say 'dear old Brackley', we are being nostalgic for our childhoods, even if these were not themselves actually Victorian.

Furthermore, Victorian Brackley is the earliest Brackley to which most of us can make significant visual reference. When we see 'dear old Brackley' in our mind's eye, we are probably thinking of Victorian photographs. Of course, there are many pre-Victorian buildings in Brackley – such as the Church or the College Chapel – but we tend to visualise them in their Victorian form. 'Our' College Chapel is not that of the Middle Ages, or the tumbledown ruin of the eighteenth century; rather, it is the Chapel as restored by Buckeridge and furnished with elegant gasoliers by Clarke the ironmonger. 'Our' Church is the Church as restored by Thicknesse and Egerton.

The visual power of Victorian Brackley is so strong partly because it had no successor until the middle of the twentieth century. In the 1950s, the physical appearance of Brackley had changed little since 1914. Despite some modern housing and the survival of buildings from the eighteenth century and earlier, the overall 'tone' was Victorian. The two railway stations were Victorian, as were the interior of St Peter's Church, many of the buildings of Magdalen College School, the Congregational and Methodist Chapels, the enormous Manor House, the flamboyant Church School, the 'black and white' Vicarage, the Cottage Hospital, 'hunting boxes' like the Red House in the High Street, the middle-class villas in the Banbury Road, the 'artisans' dwellings' erected by William Judd, the police station, the gasworks and the brewery all dated from this period.

The image was even more compelling because every building had associations with figures of major local importance. There were the 'classic' Vicars (Thicknesse and Egerton), the local boy made good and brilliant Headmaster (Isaac Wodhams), the local boy who married money and bought a brewery (Walter Norris), the complete gentleman (the Earl of Ellesmere), the Station Master (Mr Taylor), the medical men (Dr Parkhurst and 'old' Dr Stathers), the Squire (John Locke Stratton) and – for those with a taste for such things – the Radical (Thomas Judge). The list goes on and on.

The 'characters' seemed larger than life and, in some quarters, they still provide a standard against which their successors can be measured and found wanting. Of course, it was not perfect. It could be petty and intolerably snobbish; even the wives of successful traders expected to be curtsied to. There was much poverty and most people prefer to forget the awful Workhouse. Yet at least those in authority knew how to behave and most of those beneath them knew how to be properly thankful.

To misquote Matthew Arnold, this was the Brackley that was still 'whispering the last enchantments of the Victorian Ages' to me in my childhood. It was not so much history but more of a living presence. It seemed a Golden Age, the culmination of earlier epochs of greatness and romance. No doubt, I viewed the stories about Mr Thicknesse and the Earl of Ellesmere like those of King Arthur and the Knights of the Round Table.

But are golden ages ever more than illusions, the product of childish imagination? Many years later, I had a shock. In 1982, when I opened Barrie Trinder's otherwise excellent *Victorian Banbury*, I was horrified to read:

Some market towns remained 'sleepy hollows', small agglomerations of shops, visited by a mere handful of carriers, with infrequent and declining markets, only one or two weak dissenting causes, and a few voluntary societies. Many such towns lost their parliamentary representation, if they ever enjoyed it, in the 1832 Reform Act. They were places which had declined, relative to larger centres in the 18th century, and, except in special circumstances, this decline continued in the 19th. Such towns, the Brackleys, the Bishop's Castles and the Beaminsters, may be defined as 'immature' market towns.[2]

2   Trinder, Barrie, *Victorian Banbury* (Chichester: Phillimore & Co., 1982) p.2.

My first reaction was one of incredulity; how could a town which achieved so much be called a 'sleepy hollow', or a place whose first Charter had been issued in 1260 be described as 'immature'? I was not deceived by the references to Bishop's Castle and Beaminster. I suspected they had been included to lull readers into accepting *Victorian Banbury* as a work of dispassionate and fashionable 'urban history'. It seemed to me that, in reality, Trinder's book was nothing less than an attack by a Banbury man on Brackley and the version of Brackley history I had revelled in as a child. I saw it as a challenge, almost a declaration of war.

But calmer reflection soon prevailed. Trinder is a good historian and I remembered that others – Brackley people themselves – once called the town 'Sleepy Hollow'. I realised that Victorian Brackley must be set in a wider context, which may not be to its advantage. In other words, this book has to be something more than a votive offering to the cult of 'dear old Brackley'. I must try to untangle the reality from romantic nostalgia. But I refuse to go 'the whole hog' with Trinder. I remain convinced that, as with the Kingdom of Heaven, there is much to be said for approaching history 'like a little child'.

It is perhaps too easy to talk of 'Victorian Brackley'; should we regard it as a whole or as no more than a succession of several very different periods? Here, I confess a debt to a 'national' historian, GM Young, whose *Portrait of an Age: Victorian England* (first published in 1936) remains the best overall study of the period. Young asked himself whether there had ever been such a thing as 'Victorian England'? Young thought not; the period had been too varied and changing to be viewed as a coherent whole. That encouraged me to ask the same question about Victorian Brackley and I found my answer was similar to Young's.

Of course, there were a few constant features. One was that Brackley was overshadowed by its larger neighbour – Banbury. Of course, Brackley remained in Northamptonshire. Administratively, it continued to look to Northampton; ecclesiastically it looked to Peterborough; educationally it looked to Oxford. But for most economic purposes, the best way to describe Brackley is as part of an area unofficially known as 'Banburyshire'. 'Banburyshire' was made up of those parts of Oxfordshire, Northants, Bucks, Warwickshire and even Gloucestershire which were nearer to Banbury than to their own county towns.[3] By the 1840s, Banbury was one of the most flourishing market towns in England. Brackley is only 9 miles from Banbury and, as the *Banbury Guardian* of 6 July 1843 put it, 'To the 140 places within a circuit of ten miles, it [Banbury] may be said to be a metropolis'. The opening of the Buckinghamshire Railway (later London & North Western, LNWR) from Bletchley to Banbury, via Buckingham and Brackley, in May 1850 only served to strengthen Brackley's orientation towards its powerful neighbour. Significantly, Brackley never had a direct rail link to Northampton – inconvenient for anyone who was engaged on official business or who wanted to visit relations in the County Lunatic Asylum at Berrywood.

By the 1840s, there was an increasing tendency to read Banbury papers, a development likely to encourage Nonconformist and Radical ideas. Only the 'county-orientated' gentry continued to take the *Northampton Mercury* or the *Northampton Herald*.

The arrival of the Great Central Railway (GCR) at the end of the century may have diminished the 'pull' of Banbury. The GCR gave Brackley a direct link to London as well as to other towns like Leicester and Aylesbury. The new line led to a late-Victorian version of the old distinction between Brackley St James and Brackley St Peter: 'Bottom End' and 'Top End'. The two stations were over a mile apart; those living closer to the new 'Top Station' now tended to do their shopping in Aylesbury, while those nearer to the old 'Bottom Station' continued to go to Banbury. But Banbury's loss of influence was only

3   Ibid., pp.16–17.

temporary. Neither station was very convenient, involving a long walk for most people. The position was transformed in the 1920s and 1930s with the appearance of motor buses. The buses, which stopped at the Greyhound and the Market Square, were more convenient and cheaper than the trains. Most of the services went to Banbury and thus Brackley's westward orientation was reinforced once more.

Another constant was the survival of the traditional Brackley dialect. Despite Banbury's economic dominance, its influence made little headway in patterns of speech. Perhaps this was due to the lack of significant numbers of 'immigrants'. Someone from Banbury would immediately announce themselves as 'I be Bambry', but I doubt if anyone ever said, 'I be Brackley'. 'Bambry', with its rising note at the end of sentences, carried the first hints of the speech patterns of Birmingham and the West Midlands. 'Buckingham', on the other hand, with its slight glottal stop, belongs to a family of dialects culminating in Cockney. But 'Brackley' and 'South Northants' is unlike either.

Of course, 'Brackley' had its enemies. Especially during the Mastership of Rev Robert Ashwin (1910–29), one of the prime missions of Magdalen College School was to produce pupils who 'spoke nicely'. The campaign had some success, but only with a minority. The rest continued to say 'yourn' for 'yours', 'hisn' for 'his', 'unkhed' for 'unhappy' and 'chimbley' for 'chimney'. It is notoriously difficult to reproduce dialect sounds using ordinary letters. In this area, the man who did it best was Rev Jack Linnell, author of *Old Oak*. Linnell wrote mostly about Syresham and Silverstone. Even there the dialect is not quite the same as in Brackley, but it is very close. Linnell gives a marvellous account of a sermon given by a Methodist lay preacher in the Chapel at Silverstone:

> Well, here I be, but I thought o' one time as us'd never get here. Afoore us set out the missus wur as akhud as could be, an' comin down Gulliver's Hill, the britchin' bruk, an' us settled down as nice as could be on the grass by the side o' the rooad. 'Bwoy', sez I 'Old Sca-aper [the Devil] dooan't mean us shall goo to Silson to-day, but us'll see if us keeunt dish the old chap!' and so here us be, but for all the good I'm a-gooin' to do you, I might just as well a'stopped up in Bucknell's 'ood an' hollered 'Cookoo'; for you Silson folk never did know nothin, and never 'ull, and I reckon nuthen'll ever be required an ye![4]

Yet the search for constants does not get us very far – as Young found in his investigation of Victorian England. This may come as a surprise and points to an important difference between popular impressions and historical reality. The Victorian period is often seen as a time of stability, certainty and lack of change – perhaps not in the great towns and cities but at any rate in the countryside. This is quite untrue as far as Brackley is concerned. Although it remained a small community throughout, it experienced tremendous changes between the Reform Bill of 1832 and the outbreak of World War I. I would go so far as to claim that these changes were actually greater than those that have occurred since 1914. Some of the features of Victorian Brackley, which people imagine lasted for centuries, were actually very short-lived. One of the supposed characteristics of a traditional society is the presence of a resident Lord of the Manor. In reality, Brackley only acquired such a figure in 1878 and it 'lost' him in 1915. Thus a 'traditional' arrangement lasted for less than forty years.

In order to make sense of Victorian Brackley, there is no alternative but to break it up into shorter periods. GM Young believed there had been three Victorian Englands and I believe there were three Victorian Brackleys. I do not adopt Young's chronology. His early-Victorian England ended in 1847 and

4   Linnell, JE, *Old Oak* (Northampton: The Burlington Press, 1984) p.72.

14

his mid-Victorian England in 1868, but Young was looking at things from a London perspective and it would hardly be surprising if Brackley lagged behind somewhat. From the way I look at things, early-Victorian Brackley lasted from the 1830s to the late 1860s. Then there was mid-Victorian Brackley which lasted from the late 1860s until the mid-1880s and, finally, there was late-Victorian Brackley which lasted until World War I – although its 'ghost' survived until the 1950s.

Each of these Brackleys has a distinct aura or zeitgeist. There is little to admire about early-Victorian Brackley and its story must be told in largely negative terms. But mid- and late-Victorian Brackley were very different places compared to the town between 1832 and 1868; together they make up the real 'dear old Brackley' beloved of our grandparents. In some ways it was a 'sleepy hollow', yet in other respects it showed great energy and dynamism; it certainly possessed considerable charm and style.

But how to explain the turning points of Victorian Brackley – the *Wendepunkten* as it were? I am not normally an enthusiast for the 'great man' theory of history, but here it is inescapable. The great change from early- to mid-Victorian Brackley came with the arrival of Rev Francis Thicknesse in 1868. This year began the 'High Noon' of Victorian Brackley and here the tone must be overwhelmingly positive.

The second and lesser change, from mid- to late-Victorian Brackley is linked with the arrival of 'democracy' in local and national government. Much was achieved between the late 1880s and 1914, but there are worrying trends, sometimes reminiscent of the 'bad' early period, so that positive and negative features are more or less equal. For those inclined to Hegelian dialectic – I confess I know not how many Hegelians there are in today's Brackley – we may postulate early-Victorian Brackley as the Thesis, mid-Victorian Brackley as the Antithesis, and late-Victorian Brackley as the Synthesis.

The 'bad' early period, the 'good' middle and the 'mixed' late are reflected in changes in population patterns. It may be premature to condemn early-Victorian Brackley. At least the town was growing. When the first National Census was taken in 1801, Brackley's two parishes were found to have a total population of 1,495. Numbers grew rapidly in the next thirty years, reaching 2,107 by 1831 – an increase of 41 per cent. But population growth does not necessarily indicate prosperity or harmony. It can be more of a curse than a blessing – more poor loudly demanding charity and relief, more social tensions, bad and insanitary housing, more potential criminals.

It is true that from the 1830s the rate of increase began to abate. The 2,383 inhabitants recorded in 1861 represent an increase of only just over 13.1 per cent since 1831. Between 1861 and 1891 numbers grew to 2,614, or by 9.7 per cent. After 1891, apart from a short period of growth between 1901 and 1911, Brackley experienced forty years of contraction.

Some people had always taken off elsewhere but, at the end of the nineteenth century, the trickle became a flood. As early as the 1851 Census, there were thirty-five people in Banbury who claimed to have been born in Brackley; by 1871 there were sixty. Later emigrants went further afield. Some went abroad, others to London or to an industrial city. Around the turn of the century, there seems to have been something like a concerted emigration movement to Coventry, seen by many as a place of wealth and opportunity. The gains of earlier years were wiped out and, with 2,373 people in 1921, Brackley was back to its 1861 size. The decline accelerated in the 1920s and, with the 2,097 recorded in the 1931 Census, numbers were lower than a century earlier. If the downward trend had continued, Brackley's future would have been bleak indeed.

There was no census in 1941 – due to World War II – but an upward trend was visible once more in 1951. At 2,531 Brackley's population was higher than at any time between the wars. Thereafter the rate of expansion was rapid, faster even than during the 'population boom' of 1801–31.

The 1961 Census showed that Brackley had passed the 3,000 mark for the first time in its history. Only twenty years later, in 1981, numbers had more than doubled to 6,535.

Brackley's Population 1801–1981

1801	1,495		1901	2,487	(-4.9%)
1811	1,580	(+5.7%)	1911	2,633	(+5.9%)
1821	1,851	(+17.2%)	1921	2,373	(-9.9%)
1831	2,107	(+13.8%)	1931	2,097	(-11.6%)
1841	2,121	(+0.7%)	1941	No Census	
1851	2,277	(+7.4%)	1951	2,531	(+20.7%)
1861	2,383	(+4.7%)	1961	3,208	(+26.7%)
1871	2,351	(-1.3%)	1971	4,612	(+43.8%)
1881	2,504	(+6.5%)	1981	6,535	(+41.7%)
1891	2,614	(+4.4%)			

The pattern at Towcester – 2,031 in 1801 – is similar to Brackley's; Towcester's 2,775 in 1891 fell to 2,252 in 1931. But things were different in larger communities like Banbury. In 1801, with a population of 4,070, Banbury was already more than two and a half times bigger than Brackley. By 1901, however, Banbury's population had reached 13,026, or more than five times the size of Brackley's. Banbury grew most rapidly between 1841 and 1871, when Brackley's growth was already slowing. But even Banbury grew only slowly between the 1870s and the 1930s, its period of relative stagnation coinciding with Brackley's absolute decline.[5]

In the late nineteenth century, the major growth points were the big cities. Norman Stone's idea of 'Metropolis' sums up the process well.[6] The other side of the coin was that the smaller the place the more likely it was to lose population. Thus, the decline in numbers in the villages around Brackley and Banbury started earlier and was proportionately greater than in Brackley itself. The population of the rural parishes in the Banbury Poor Law Union fell from 21,231 in 1841 to 15,527 in 1901.

I do not claim that my version of Victorian Brackley is the only way to approach the subject. At any given moment the population is made up of the young, the middle aged and the elderly; hence there is always a diversity of outlooks and values. All I suggest is that my scheme of things may help to achieve an understanding of what was really a very complex historical process. It is up to my readers to decide if it works.

5   Stacey, Margaret, *Tradition and Change: A Study of Banbury* (London: Oxford University Press, 1960) pp.5–7.

6   Stone, Norman, *Europe Transformed, 1879–1919* (Glasgow: Fontana, 1983) pp.13–15.

Town Hall from the High Street. Note the building in the middle of the road. (NRO)

People's General Supply Stores. Note the thatched roof.

Westbury carrier, outside the Master's Lodgings on the corner of Buckingham Road.

Chapter Two

IT DON'T HURT 'EM

We must now turn to early-Victorian Brackley, in many ways a troubled and divided community. The loss of the Parliamentary seats in 1832 removed the chief reason why the Bridgewater Trustees, preoccupied with canals and coal mines, had previously taken some interest in the town – at least at election times. Now the age-old problem of absentee Lords of the Manor threatened to become worse than ever. On 1 July 1837, James Lock, Chief Agent to the Bridgewater Trustees, wrote to Lord Francis Egerton (later Earl of Ellesmere) to remind him that no head of 'the most noble family' had even visited Brackley 'since the Duke of Bridgewater [died 1805] drove there in his coach and four when a young man'. Fifty years had elapsed since an Estate Manager had given the Halse farms a proper inspection. Most of the farm buildings were inconveniently placed and run down.

The old Church of St Andrew at Halse had not been used since the seventeenth century and was now a total ruin. A leading Trustee, Mr Hains, visited the Church and proposed its demolition. The proposal caused much distress to at least one of the tenants. In an undated letter – probably written in 1837 – Mr Thomas Bannard asked for reconsideration. He wanted the Church to be restored, pointing out that the long walk – 2½ miles – to Brackley St Peter's deterred many of the sixty inhabitants of Halse. As a result, many developed 'a carelessness for divine duties' or attended 'Conventicles held at neighbouring Hamlets to the prejudice of the Established Church'. If restoration was impossible, at least the Church should be made secure. Bannard was appalled at the thought that soon 'swine and cattle' might be grubbing among the bones of the illustrious dead buried there. Failing that, Bannard appealed to 'the prevailing taste for antiquity'. Hains's proposal was particularly shocking because another Trustee was none other than the Archbishop of York. Bannard concluded:

> Think, oh think for a moment and let it not be said that Lord E[gerton] and Mr L[ock] have no interest in the spiritual wellfare for their Vessells while it is so amply in the power of both to provide for them. Mr Hains, I have no doubt, is fully qualified as a Projector in modern improvements, but as an admirer of Antiquity he has proved that it is not his element or he could not have sat under the well turned Arch and meditated its destruction.[1]

1   Letter shown to me by the late Mrs Olive Harding.

The demolition went ahead and Lock seemed eager to extend the same policy into Brackley itself. One of the Bridgewater houses in the town, 'occupied by a person of the name of Lathbury', was in a ruinous condition and 'I would say that the best thing would be to pull it down and not to rebuild it'.[2]

Francis Egerton had authorised some repair work to the chancel of St Peter's but the work was not yet complete and the overall condition of the church was disgraceful. Lock reported:

> One of the windows is in so rotten a condition that I am afraid it will require new stone mullions which will cost about £10. I hope your Lordship [Egerton] won't think this wrong; it is the only thing of the sort which has been done since the Duke of Bridgewater's death.[3]

The Trustees certainly did nothing to save St James's Church, demolished in 1836. When Baker saw it in the 1820s, it had already been in 'a very dilapidated state'.[4]

It was not all gloom, and *Whellan's Directory* for 1849 mentions no fewer than 110 traders, shopkeepers and innkeepers. Some had several occupations; perhaps they were very enterprising or – more likely – none of their various jobs provided sufficient business on its own. Thomas Bannard, landlord of the Cross Keys was also a carpenter. Charles Thomas Rudkin of the George was also an auctioneer and appraiser. John Hatwell of the Horse and Jockey was also a cooper. Edward Bowerman of the Reindeer was a plasterer and slater and Joseph James of the Wagon and Horses was a butcher.

Representative Brackley Traders, 1849

Joseph Barrett	Bookseller & Binder; Printer & Stationer; Newsagent and Circulating Library; Agent to the Norwich Union Fire & Office
Edward Bartlett	Linen & Woollen Draper
James Bartlett	Currier & Leather Cutter
John Blackwell	Blacksmith
Timothy Blencowe	Brazier & Tinman
William Blencowe	Brewer & Maltster
Frederick Cave	Ironmonger & Seedman
William Cave	Maltster
John Chatwell	Boot & Shoe Maker
Elizabeth Dix	Ironmonger, Brazier, Gunsmith and Whitesmith
Thomas Course	Baker
Robert East	Grocer and China & Glass Dealer
John French	Miller
Alfred Hayward	Agent to County Fire and Provident Life Offices
Robert Howard	Basket Maker
James Jelleyman	Rope & Twine Maker

2   Northamptonshire Record Office (NRO), Ellesmere Papers, X 9637, Vol. 16.

3   As Note 2.

4   Baker, George, *The History and Antiquities of the County of Northampton*, two volumes (London: John Bowyer Nichols & Son, 1822–43) Vol. 1, p.579.

Benjamin Judge	Grocer
Elizabeth Judge	Butcher
Richard Judge	Butcher
Thomas Judge	Butcher
Richard Kendal	Baker
William Knibbs	Saddler and Harness Maker
George Lathbury	Butcher
Francis Layton	Cabinet Maker
William Mee	Perfumer, Stationer, Jeweller & Toy Dealer
John Nichols	Coach Maker
William Norris	Painter, Gravestone Cutter and Bird Preserver
Frederick William Rudkin	Grocer & Tea Dealer
Robert Russel	Auctioneer, Land Surveyor and Agent to the Atlas Fire & Office
Henry Sirrett	Chymist and Druggist
Smith & Blackwell	Fishmonger and Orange Dealers
William Walford	Watch & Clockmaker
Samuel Walters	Linen and Woollen Draper
James Wootton	Stonemason
Henry Wright	Slop Seller and Shoe Dealer

But the compilers of the *Directory* had not kept their information up to date – perhaps a sign that they did not regard Brackley as a place of any importance. Thus, Elizabeth Dix had ceased trading as an ironmonger in 1841. In January of that year, Mrs Dix had issued a handbill thanking her customers for their patronage since the death of her husband (1837) and announcing that she had disposed of her business to Mr Joseph Clarke – who had actually managed the concern for the previous twenty years. Thus began the firm of Clarke's the Ironmongers, which was to remain an important feature of the commercial life of Brackley until 1948.

Many of the traders mentioned in the 1849 Directory were the direct heirs of men – often with the same name and in the same trade – who figure in the Purefoy Papers, the Court Rolls and the correspondence of John Welchman over a century earlier. Even then, the Lathburys had been butchers, a Timothy Blencowe was trading as a tinman and a James Wootton as a stonemason. While there were a few newcomers, 'trading Brackley' had not changed much since the 1730s.

Some of these early-Victorian tradesmen were elected to the Corporation, a body with virtually nothing to do since the changes of the 1830s. The Corporation functioned – if that is not too strong a word – in a bizarre 'time warp'. Well into Queen Victoria's reign, new burgesses were required to subscribe to complicated declarations about the political and theological disputes of the seventeenth century now long forgotten by most people. Thus:

I *A.B.* do declare that I hold that there lies no obligation upon me or any other from the Oath commonly called the Solemn League and Covenant and that the same was in itself an Unlawful Oath and imposed upon the subjects of this Realm against the known laws and liberties of the Kingdom.[5]

5   NRO, Ellesmere Papers X9637, Vol. 16.

Gradually the traders came to dominate the Corporation, as their forefathers had done before the 'invention' of absentee burgesses in the 1760s.

The sole purpose of the absentee burgesses had been to return the Duke of Bridgewater's nominees as Members of Parliament. The loss of the Parliamentary seats in 1832 rendered the absentees' role redundant and no more were chosen. But existing absentees retained a life interest and it took a long time for the group to disappear. Augustus Hill Bradshaw (Burgess 1803, Alderman 1803, Mayor 1805, 1808, 1815, 1822 and 1828) died in 1846. Samuel Meacock (Burgess 1805) survived until 1852. The last of the absentee burgesses, Robert Augustus Bradshaw (Burgess 1824) did not die until 1871 – almost forty years after the Reform Bill.

Among the tradesmen who became burgesses, the most prominent were the auctioneer, Robert Russel (Burgess 1834, Alderman 1843, Mayor 1843, 1847, 1852 and 1858; died 1860) and John Cave, landlord of the Red Lion (Burgess 1843, Alderman 1861, Mayor 1865, 1870, 1873 and 1876; died 1880). Other mayors included the Halse farmers, John and Edward Butterfield, and Alfred Hopcraft, son of the Enclosure Commissioner. The tradition of clerical mayors was maintained in the person of Rev Charles Arthur Sage. Born in 1786, Sage was the third son of Joseph Sage, Assay Master at the Royal Mint and Sarah, daughter of John Shakespear, Alderman of the City of London.

Sage was educated at Trinity College, Cambridge (BA 1810) and ordained Deacon (Peterborough) in 1811. The Bridgewater Trustees presented him to the living of Brackley in 1825 – in succession to Rev TB Woodman.[6] Sage probably had earlier connections with the Trustees; he became Burgess in 1818, seven years before he was presented to the Living. In 1826, Sage was appointed Rural Dean and Bishop's Surrogate. He was an active magistrate, a Poor Law Guardian, and, from 1839, Chaplain to the Workhouse – although he later gave up this 'ungentlemanly' post to Rev HW Smith. Sage became an Alderman in 1825 and was Mayor in 1826, 1829, 1831, 1832, 1833, 1836, 1839, 1844, 1848, 1850, 1853, 1856 and 1861. He died on 20 December 1867.

The Corporation 1818–81[7]

Name	Burgess	Alderman	Mayor	Died
Rev C A Sage	1818	1825	1826, 1829, 1831, 1832, 1833, 1836, 1839, 1844, 1851, 1853, 1856, 1861	1867
William Cave	1819	–	–	1829
Joseph Nichols	1820	–	–	1855
John Butterfield	1821	1842	1842, 1846, 1850	1850
William Collison	1822	–	–	1834
Robert Bradshaw	1824	–	–	1871
Rev Anselm Jones	1824	1835	1835	1838
Benjamin Lansdale	1825	–	–	1862
William Tripp	1826	–	–	1829

6   For details of Sage's career, see Henry Isham Longden, *Northamptonshire and Rutland Clergy from 1550* (Northampton: Archer Goodman, 1938–52), Vol. XII (1941), p.31.

7   Constructed from Pearson, B.E., *Local Gleanings, No. II*, 'The Town Hall or Corporate Brackley' (Brackley: James Smart, 1881) pp.35, 41 & 42.

Edward Butterfield	1828	1851	1851, 1859, 1868	1881
James Pendlebury	1829	–	–	1863
Robert Weston	1829	–	–	1841
Edward Taylor	1829	–	–	1849
John Goodman	1830	–	–	1867
John French	1834	–	–	1844
Robert Russel	1834	1843	1843, 1847, 1852, 1858	1860
Edward Bartlett	1835	–	–	1843
Benjamin Wesson	1835	–	–	1858
William Dix	1835	–	–	1837
Frederick Runkin	1836	–	–	1876
Robert East	1837	–	–	1848
James Bartlett	1838	1852	1855	1874
Alfred Hopcraft	1840	1853	1854, 1860, 1864, 1869	1872
Joseph Barrett	1841	–	–	1855
Isaac Bartlett	1842	1868	1874, 1878	Alive
Joseph Clarke	1843	–	–	1851
John Cave	1843	1861	1865, 1870, 1873	1880
William King Malins	1844	–	–	1870
Edward Taylor	1844	1873	1877	Alive
David Hearn	1846	–	–	Alive
John Anstee	1848	–	–	1851
Henry Walsh	1849	–	–	1865
Thomas Stuchbury	1851	–	–	Alive
George Taylor	1851	–	–	1879
Robert Bartlett	1851	–	–	1865
Henry East	1852	–	–	1855
Robert Roper	1852	–	–	1862
William Tibbetts	1852	–	–	1861
Rev HW Smith	1852	1853	1857, 1862, 1866	Alive
Richard Jones	1853	1874	–	1878
John Nichols	1853	–	–	1878
John Collier	1853	1878	1880	Alive
Thomas Pratt	1855	–	–	1864
John Richardson	1855	–	–	Alive
Henry Hawkins	1855	–	–	Alive
Robert Weston	1858	1860	1863, 1867, 1871	1872
Robert Russel	1860	1872	1872, 1875, 1879	Alive
Henry Holton	1861	–	–	Alive
William Blencowe	1861	1880	–	Alive
Thomas Slatter	1862	–	–	Alive
Walter Moore	1862	–	–	Alive

John G. Clarke	1862	–	–	Alive
William Ellis	1863	–	–	Alive
Clement Blencowe	1863	–	–	Alive
John Farmer	1864	–	–	Alive
Robert Anstee	1865	–	–	Alive
William Tucker	1865	–	–	Alive
James Goodman	1867	–	–	Alive
Robert Hawkins	1868	–	–	Alive
John Walsh	1870	–	–	Alive
Edward Bartlett	1871	–	–	Alive
John Hopcraft	1872	–	–	1874
Richard Judge	1873	–	–	Alive
Arthur Nichols	1874	–	–	Alive
Robert Hocter	1876	–	–	Alive
Alfred Hopcraft	1878	–	–	Alive
William Cave	1878	–	–	Alive
Joseph Nichols	1879	–	–	Alive
William King	1880	–	–	Alive

There are clear signs that membership had become virtually hereditary in a few families. In many instances a burgess was elected shortly after the death of his father. Thus, Edward Bartlett died in 1850 and Robert Bartlett became Burgess in 1851. Alfred Hopcraft died in 1872 and John Hopcraft became Burgess the same year.

After the Enclosure Act of 1829, it was logical to proceed to an arrangement on Tithe Commutation. The agreement was drawn up by the Local Surveyor, Robert Russel, on 22 February 1840 and confirmed by the Tithe Commissioners on 19 December of the same year. The former Rectorial Tithes became an annual payment of £167 10s to the Bridgewater Trustees and the Vicarial Tithes an annual payment of £238 6s 10¼d to Rev Sage. The largest payments were due from the Halse farmers, all tenants of the Bridgewater Trustees. Thomas Bannard was to pay £34 to the Vicar on 338 acres, the representatives of the late Robert Bartlett £46 on 335 acres, Mary Butterfield £32 on 247 acres, Alfred Hopcraft £74 on two farms totalling nearly 400 acres. Payments on the Magdalen properties were significantly lower, with the Vicar receiving only £17 10s on just over 200 acres. The measure probably helped to prevent the regular bickering over tithes, once such a feature of local life. Yet both sides were taking a gamble. The agreement was based upon current prices; if they went up the occupiers would benefit and the former tithe owners would suffer; but if prices fell – as they were to in the late nineteenth century – it would be the other way around.

As well as his membership of the Corporation, Sage also presided at Vestry Meetings – which had a more important role in the running of the town. But neither the Vestry nor the Corporation did much for ordinary people. Sage was not a popular figure; he seemed more interested in punishing the poor as a magistrate and a Guardian than in caring for their physical and spiritual welfare as their Vicar. In Sage's time, the Church in Brackley was at a low ebb and the Methodists were the most vital force in the town. An article in the *Methodist Recorder* of 4 February 1904 – admittedly hardly an unbiased source – says of these years, 'But for the Methodists, there would have been neither education or piety in the town. In those days, alas, the Church was deserted, the Grammar School scarcely known.'

In his last years, John Wesley had visited Brackley on several occasions when staying with his friends, the Padbury family of Whittlebury. The Padburys were related to the Burmans of Brackley and Samuel Burman, then 'a prosperous trader' (actually a shoemaker), was the first active Methodist in the town. At first, the Methodists were unpopular and Burman's shoes were boycotted. His business seemed on the brink of collapse, but he saved it by walking to Northampton to secure orders. One morning, when Burman opened his front door, he found a great heap of stones had been piled against it during the night; of course, the stones fell into the house. The Vicar, Thomas Woodman, sent for Burman's son and urged him to give up his connection with the Methodists; the young man refused. Although the tactics used against the 'Methodies' were essentially 'horse play', they could be distinctly unpleasant.

> About this time, a preacher took his stand in the Market Square, but soon the alarm was given and some of the baser sort brought a heap of straw to the place, set light to it and began to cry, 'Fire! Fire!'. The engine was brought, water procured and they played pretty freely on the straw, not forgetting the people who were assembled to hear the preacher. They were compelled to retire to a friend's house, but thither the engine and its friends followed and continued to annoy them.[8]

Initially, the Methodists met in a small room but then moved to a larger one near to St James's Church. A Brackley Methodist Circuit was established in 1799. This was amalgamated into the Banbury Circuit in 1804 but was re-established as a separate Circuit in 1809. The new Circuit had thirteen preaching places and 240 members and was headed by Rev John Sydserff and Rev Jarvis Shaw.

A number of prominent Methodists, including Rev Joseph Gostick, visited the community in Brackley. Gostick discovered a prayer meeting for 'Single Females of the Society' from which married women were rigorously excluded. Gostick was moved to write a poem, dated 21 April 1816, urging a more liberal attitude:

> Reject, then, good sisters, this foolish condition,
> And at least grant your sisters, though married, permission,
> In that sacred temple with you to appear,
> And yet in devotion may join you without fear.
>
> Imitate those assemblies before the bright throne,
> Where idle distinctions shall never be known,
> Then Angels and Saints your praises shall join,
> Who with heart and with voice in your service combine.[9]

By 1830, the Methodists were strong enough to erect a purpose-built Chapel in Hill Street (formerly Tinkers' Lane). When the author of the article in the *Methodist Recorder* came to Brackley, he met an old lady, Dinah Fennimore, who could remember playing on the building site when she had been a little girl. On the day the Chapel was opened, there was flooding in the 'Bottom End' and some of the men who attended had to walk through the flood carrying their wives on their backs. Later a gallery was added. The

8   *Methodist Recorder*, 4 February 1904.

9   Ibid.

Methodists were so delighted with their new Chapel that they gave the builder more than he had asked for, 'an act of surprising generosity, of which only a poor and pious people could be capable'.

Arrangements in the services were informal. One elderly shepherd, who normally sat in the gallery, would always stroll down, accompanied by his dog, to sit on the pulpit steps so that he could hear the sermon better. The Trustees eventually widened one of the steps so that shepherd and dog could be more comfortable.[10] The Chapel profited directly from the demolition of St James's Church in 1836. John Tibbetts acquired the Communion table and a chandelier from St James's and gave them to the Chapel. The table eventually found its way back into Anglican hands and is now in St Peter's Church.

By the 1840s, the Methodist community contained a number of families who were to be pillars of the Chapel into the twentieth century, although a few, such as the Garretts and the Kendals, returned to the Church in the 1870s. The *Methodist Recorder* mentions: Thomas and James Gaskins, Robert Buckley, Robert Freeman, Mr Jones of Hethe, old Mrs Archer (the Chapel Keeper), Mrs Whitten, Mrs French, Mrs East of Hinton, Mr and Mrs Sirett, John Osmund of Westbury, Robert Blackwell (the leader of the choir for forty years) and Billy Jakeman. Although the article does not say so, Billy Jakeman was a little 'simple', but he used to carry 'good old Mr Tibbets'' base viol in its green baize cover up to the gallery at every service, come down to the door to await the minister's arrival and 'then take the hymns triumphantly up to the leading singers, Mr Richard Kendal and Mr Richard Garrett, both Masters of song'.

It is unlikely that the author of the article was told what happened to Billy Jakeman. Although admirable in many ways, the Methodist community failed to look after its poor simpleton. The *Brackley Observer* of 19 November 1873 contains this sad report:

William Jakeman, so long and familiarly known to our readers, died on Sunday last in the Workhouse. The Deceased, on being received into the House was, we are informed, literally in a state of starvation and, although Dr Farmer immediately rendered him all the assistance that could be afforded, he was unable to cope with the effects of previous neglect, want and misery.

In the early days of Methodism, the element of 'enthusiasm' was strong and there are accounts of experiences bordering on the ecstatic. In 1832, Rev James Penman died at Brackley after a few days' illness, 'unspeakably happy in God'. Even more extraordinary was the deathbed of John Osmund of Westbury:

It was related of this good man that his departure was signalised in a remarkable manner. He had endured great domestic opposition and trouble and in his last hours was attended, in the absence of every member of his family, by two kind neighbours. These persons declared that, as they watched the dying man, they suddenly were aware of strains of music which seemed to come nearer and nearer until they filled the room and at the same time a bright unearthly light shone upon the countenance of the old saint. The music gradually passed away as it had come and he was gone. They declared that they never would forget this scene and the token God had given to the sincerity and fidelity of his Servant as long as they lived.[11]

All accounts of the Chapel agree that most of the early members were 'in lowly circumstances'. The

---

10   Ibid.

11   *Methodist Recorder*, 4 February 1904.

cost of the new Chapel proved a heavy burden and the debt was not cleared until 1859. In view of their poverty, the Methodists' efforts in education – to be discussed later – seem all the more praiseworthy.

The religious census of 1851 shows that, for Northamptonshire as a whole, 56 per cent of regular worshippers went to Church as against 44 per cent who went to some kind of Chapel. But the Nonconformists were not united. The 1851 Census also reveals that no fewer than fifty-one rural communities in Northamptonshire had more than one Chapel. There was least likely to be a Chapel of any description in villages where the living was in the gift of an Oxford College; thus, any Dissenters from Evenley, a Magdalen living, had to worship in Brackley. In places with two Chapels, however, one was likely to be Methodist, the other Baptist or Independent. This was the normal pattern where a town had either lost or was narrowly holding onto its market. In Brackley the 'second' Chapel took the form of an Independent or Congregational community. There had been Independents in Brackley in the late seventeenth century, but they seem to have died out well before the rise of Methodism. Thomas Coleman's *Memorials of the Independent Churches in Northamptonshire* (1853) suggests that Brackley Congregationalism was a recent development.[12]

There were many Congregational Chapels in Northamptonshire, but the one in Brackley had closer links with Buckinghamshire. In the early 1830s, the North Bucks Association, which had an academy at Newport Pagnell, obtained a room to hold services but this soon proved inadequate for the large congregation.[13] In 1836, however, the present Chapel was erected in the Banbury Road at a cost of £650; unlike the Methodists, the Congregationalists seem to have been able to raise the necessary money with comparative ease. According to Coleman, the Chapel could seat 300 people, but that must have been a very tight fit. By 1838, there were twenty full members with a resident minister – Mr G Smith; it was Smith who 'first administered the Ordinance of the Lord's Supper' on 24 June 1838.[14] But Smith did not stay long and the community was left 'destitute of a pastor' for extended periods.

When Coleman was writing, the minister was Mr T Roberts, 'late student at Newport Pagnell'. Roberts had accepted the invitation to become pastor in August 1852, 'under somewhat pleasing [though unspecified] circumstances'. Coleman hoped that Roberts's ministry would be 'rendered truly useful, that the Church may be increased, and the name of the Redeemer glorified'. In 1853, the Chapel had thirty-three communicant members and ran a Sabbath School which drew more than fifty pupils.[15]

But if Coleman is right about the late start of the Congregational community in Brackley, how did it manage to gain a foothold in a small town? Some of the members may have been Congregationalists elsewhere but, to make converts, they needed to project an image distinguishing them from both Anglicans and Methodists. The Church in Sage's time was hardly appealing but not all those dissatisfied with the Established Church were drawn to the Methodists. In the event, the Congregational Chapel found a 'niche' of its own. Although never rivalling the Methodists or the Church of England in numbers, the 'Congies' came to possess a distinct, rather middle-class tone. This probably explains why the money for the Chapel was raised so quickly. It is certainly significant that the Congregational Chapel is in the Banbury Road, opposite some smart Victorian villas.

12   Coleman, Thomas, *Memorials of the Independent Churches of Northamptonshire* (London: John Snow, 1853) p.369.

13   For the Newport Pagnell Academy, see Lewis, Marilyn, *A Tale of Two Bridges: Searching for God in Newport Pagnell* (Newport Pagnell: printed privately, 1999).

14   Coleman, op. cit., p.370.

15   Ibid.

Well into the twentieth century, it was considered 'more polite' to attend the Congregational Chapel than the Methodist one. From an Anglican point of view, the Congregationalists were seen as people with whom one could have a rational debate – unlike the 'enthusiastic' Methodists. Indeed, some claimed that Congregational Ministers delivered sermons of a higher intellectual calibre than those issuing from either Anglican or Methodist pulpits. One of the rules of Methodism was that ministers should move after three years; Congregational Pastors, like Anglican Vicars, tended to stay much longer. The two systems had their advantages and disadvantages. The Methodist pattern meant that there was no danger that a minister would become 'stale'; sheer human curiosity meant that there was a strong incentive to go the Chapel in Hill Street 'to see what the new Minister was like'. Yet the rapid 'turnover' of Methodist ministers meant that few could become really influential figures in the community. Congregational Pastors, such as Mr Jeavons in the late nineteenth and Mr Martin in the twentieth century, stayed for many years and became important local figures.

In Brackley, Congregationalism displayed none of the 'enthusiasm' characteristic of the early days of Methodism. The stalwarts of the Chapel tended to be successful shopkeepers, cottage landlords and even a few professional men. The Chapel gained an advantage when arrivals from Scotland, such as the Smart family, hitherto members of the Kirk, decided that Congregational worship was more to their taste than the Book of Common Prayer and surpliced choirs.

There was little direct antagonism between Congregationalists and Methodists. Methodists needing legal advice tended to consult a Congregational solicitor – such as Mr Fairthorne or later Mr Law – rather than an Anglican lawyer; there was no Methodist one. But Congregational children later attended the Church, not the Chapel School. As late as World War I, however, the children of the Congregationalist cooper, Mr Jones, complained that when Vicar Broughton boxed their ears – and Broughton was a great ear boxer – he always hit them harder than the Church children.

If the Church of England had not put its house in order in the 1870s, Brackley might have followed the distinctive socio-religious pattern of its neighbour Banbury. There, even in the 1950s, a significant proportion of the professional and commercial middle classes still preferred the many Chapels to St Mary's.[16] But perhaps it could never have been like that. Despite its promising start and the high quality of its ministers, the Congregational Chapel never quite 'took off'. In the last resort, Brackley's middle class was too small and, apart from the Congregational minority, too much in awe of the gentry and its values to be capable of acting on its own.

There may have been an element of the 'upwardly mobile' in the Congregational Chapel, but the opportunities for such mobility were few in early-Victorian Brackley. For the poor, the chief occupations were domestic service and lacemaking for girls and women and farm labouring for men and boys. The Victorian ruling class was so committed to the view that 'an Englishman's home is his castle' that no formal enquiry was ever made into domestic service. Yet Inquiries, both formal and informal, were made into lace and agriculture and tell us much about conditions and attitudes in Brackley and its hinterland.

Even in the 1840s, the local handmade lace was facing competition from the machine-made sort produced in Nottingham. Evidence about the trade can be found in the Report of Major JG Burns to the Children's Employment Commission of 1843, in the Report of Mr JE White to the Children's Employment Commission of 1863 and in Thomas Mozley's *Reminiscences, Chiefly of Towns, Villages and*

16 Stacey, *Tradition and Change*, p.66.

Schools, 1885. All agree that lace schools were crowded and sometimes insanitary; ventilation and lighting were extremely poor and wages low. Mozley, Perpetual Curate of Moreton Pinkney in the 1830s, noted that, in a typical lace school, some thirty girls and women were packed into a small room. After dark, groups of four or five gathered in around a single candle, 'about which water bottles were so fixed as to concentrate the light on the work of each child'.[17] Medical men expressed concern; Dr Collier of Towcester told Burns:

> Much injury ensues to young girls from the habit they have of wearing a strong wooden busk in their stays to support them when stooping over their lace pillows, this being worn when young and the bones soft, acts very injuriously to the sternum and ribs, causing narrow chests.[18]

Many of the girls suffered from constipation and dyspepsia and, sadly, 'consumption is rife among them'. There was little sign of improvement when White reported in 1863:

> The general appearance of all regularly employed in lace work is unhealthy. There is a general want of colour and also of animation; as described by one person, 'they look that white'. The worn and frequently early-aged faces and frequently failing sight show unmistakable marks of the labour they have gone through and the anxiety they still suffer from the alterations of high pressure and the absolute want of work. Even the youngest of them often beg to work over hours as that gives them the only money as a rule they ever get for themselves. One little girl of nine works so hard as even to frighten her mistress for her health and till she has to stop working.[19]

These observations are supported by the testimony of lacemakers themselves, including several from Brackley. Ann Freeman, aged 52, told Burns that she had begun lace work in her sixth year. Children normally worked a nine-hour day and were very tired at the end of it. Lace work was not inherently unhealthy – 'If they bean't set too hard a task, it don't hurt 'em.' Yet Ann agreed that lacemaking was harmful for girls under 8, stunting their growth and weakening their backs. Work now was definitely harder than when she was a girl. Sarah Figg, aged 17, felt much more tired after work than she used to be.

Caroline Chatwell, aged 13, worked at Mrs Buffin's Lace School in Brackley. Sometimes Caroline felt faint from lack of food and had recently been treated for 'water on the brain', which the doctor attributed to bending so long over the lace pillow. In winter, Caroline's hands and feet were very cold and she found it difficult to work by candlelight. Her wages were only 2d or $1\frac{1}{2}$d per day. Her family was in poor circumstances, eating meat only once a week. Caroline was hardly exaggerating when she said, 'We live very hard'. Mrs Buffin was a strict disciplinarian who occasionally gave her girls a slap with her hand or a knock with her stick. Caroline did not blame her; she was a 'very good mistress and I like her very well'. Perhaps Caroline feared that if she said anything else she might encounter Mrs Buffin's stick once Major Burns had gone.

---

17 Mozley, Thomas, *Reminiscences, Chiefly of Towns, Villages and Schools*, two volumes (London: Longmans, Green & Co., 1885), Vol. 2, p.223.

18 BPP 1843, Second Report of the Children's' Employment Commission, Vol. XIV. Report of Major J.G. Burns, A13.

19 BPP 1863, First Report of the Children's Employment Commission, 1863, Vol. XVIII. Mr J.E. White's Report.

Complaints about the effects of lacemaking on the health of girls appear to be substantiated by the unusual pattern of mortality in children and young people. Elsewhere, death rates among male children and teenagers were normally considerably higher than among their female counterparts. Between 1838 and 1844, however, the teenage female death rate in the lacemaking districts of South Northamptonshire was 85 per cent higher than for corresponding males. It was almost double that found in the Peterborough area, where no lace was made.[20]

Compared to lacemaking, agricultural work was relatively healthy. In 1868, Frederick Norman reported to the Royal Commission on the Employment of Children, Young Persons and Women in Agriculture. He noted that the system of working in private gangs, which caused such serious social problems in the Eastern Counties, was rare in Northamptonshire as a whole and virtually unknown in the south of the county. There were few women farm workers, especially in the lacemaking areas. Many boys were employed; some started as early as 7, but they did not work throughout the year. Full-time employment began at 10. Statute fairs were still held in market towns like Brackley but were falling into disuse.[21] Norman describes the work performed by 'Women, young persons and children':

Spring: Picking weeds, gathering stones and hoeing.

Summer: Spudding thistles, haymaking; in harvest, they rake, make bands and help to tie the corn up, when their husbands or fathers are engaged in reaping, besides gleaning on their own account.

Autumn: After harvest, women and young children (under ten) are very seldom employed; they are occasionally employed in storing root crops.

Winter: Women are sometimes employed in picking stones and in cleaning turnips for the stock. Children are very seldom employed.

Young children were often employed to scare birds, especially from about 20 February till the first week in May, again for three weeks before the corn was cut and again for three weeks in autumn after the wheat was sown. They were also engaged in 'dibbing' beans and, occasionally, wheat in the spring. At the age of 10 or 11, boys started to go out with the plough team, although few farmers thought they were much good until they reached 12. Adult male wages were 13 or 14 shillings a week in the north of the county; around Brackley they were lower – usually 11 shillings. Women received between 8d and 10d per day and boys under 10, 3d or 4d. Accidents were comparatively rare and mostly arose 'from children playing carelessly with machines'.[22]

Although there was genuine concern about the health of the lower classes, particularly women and children, there was also a feeling that the poor were the authors of their own misfortunes. Their deplorable

20 BPP 1849, Appendix to the Ninth Annual Report of the Registrar General of Births, Deaths and Marriages, Vol. XXI, p.46.

21 BPP 1867–68, First Report of the Royal Commission on the Employment of Children, Young Persons and Women in Agriculture, Vol. XVII. Report of Mr FH Norman, p.xxvi.

22 Ibid., p.xxxvi.

moral state was revealed by their improvidence, their truculent and disrespectful behaviour towards their betters and their sad propensity to vice. Thus, Dr Collier told Burns that 'the moral condition of the lacemakers seems as low as that of the straw plaiters [of Buckinghamshire] and prostitution is rife among them for the same reasons – scanty earnings, love of finery and an almost total absence of early moral culture'. Their priorities were all wrong; most seemed to prefer vain clothes to a good meal – 'indeed their fondness for dress is proverbial'. According to Rev HJ Barton, Rector of Wicken, lace schools were 'little dens of iniquity, in which not only vile talking was heard, but vile books were read aloud'.[23] There are even hints that lace itself, after all a product intended to enhance female sexual allure, would somehow contaminate those who made it.

But concern about the behaviour of women and children paled into insignificance compared to the alarm about adult males. A member of the 1833 Select Committee on Agriculture asked a witness from Potterspury whether he thought local farming had improved during the previous ten years. The witness replied that, far from improving, farming had deteriorated; yields of grain, previously about 3 quarters per acre, had declined by around one-sixth. The decline reflected tenant farmers' inability to cultivate their land properly. The problem was really caused by insufficient profits. In a few instances, the low rate of return could be attributed to high rents and tithes, but excessive wages and exorbitant Poor Rates were usually to blame. The availability of generous Poor Relief (this is pre-1834) put an artificial 'floor' under wages and gave labourers no incentive to hard work. Their efforts were visibly declining – 'I know of no other cause than that they can obtain money without work, and consequently they cease to endeavour to obtain by work'.

The 'superabundance' of the poor had not meant lower wages. Farmers were frightened by the 'almost general discontentment in the labouring population' and thus, 'the men are paid more money for the same work performed in consequence of the intimidation arising out of fears of fires'. This is a clear reference to the Swing Riots of 1830. Although there was no trouble in Brackley itself, there was violence in Banbury, Kings Sutton, Tadmarton, Upper Boddington and Bodicote. Excessive drinking was a major evil:

> Compared with five or six years ago, the demoralisation of the people is increasing – due to the Beerhouses; I consider them the principal cause of it; there is a facility and an increased inducement for the labourers to spend money, and they have no provident habits whatsoever.[24]

There are times when upper-class attitudes to the poor seem close to hatred. Hostility is particularly marked among the clergy, although, even among this group, the views of Thomas Mozley of Moreton Pinkney seem extreme. A newcomer to the area, probably imbued with the aesthetic values of the Lake Poets, Mozley found the South Northamptonshire landscape as unattractive as its people:

> The valleys and villages of Northamptonshire are very like one another. There is nothing great or distinctive; no hills, nor rivers, no plains of any size. The ash is the weed of the county. 'You've come to a very cold field' was one of my first greetings – field being the usual term for parish or like district.[25]

23   Ibid., p.460.

24   BPP 1833, Select Committee on Agriculture, Vol. V (1). Evidence of John Cooper, pp.446, 448, 451.

25   Mozley, op. cit., Vol. 2, p.206.

To Mozley, the local poor were a race apart, no better, indeed, if as good as the savages of heathen lands. He had never encountered 'so primitive a society' elsewhere in England and thought he might have had a better welcome if he had 'been cast in an island of the Pacific among rude and generally inoffensive savages'.[26] The people Mozley encountered around Moreton Pinkney may have been savages, but inoffensive they were not. His typical parishioner was a lazy, drunken lout:

> Here is a fellow, big, handsome, strong of limb, ready spoken and with brains that answer his purpose, who finds there are people who will care for his wife and children. He has married, very probably, the prettiest woman in the village and her children are like her. Whatever he may do, or fail to do, he knows that they will not entirely want for food and clothing. Night after night, day after day, early and late, earlier still and later still, he is sotting at the public house, neglecting his employment, disqualifying himself for it, and losing his employers or his customers.[27]

Of all the faults of the lower orders, however, Mozley found their impertinence hardest to take. He tells what he clearly regards as a truly shocking story; a lady ordered a Gypsy woman out of a field, but the Gypsy replied, 'I walked this field before you were born and I shall walk across it when you are dead.'[28] [29] While the Gypsies, whom Mozley described as 'English Bedouins', may have been an extreme case, the rest of the poor were dangerously like them. It was almost too much for a delicately brought up young clergyman to bear. Mozley was writing in the 1880s, over forty years after he had left South Northamptonshire, but the lapse of time had done nothing to soften his sense of outrage and horror.

So, what was to be done? One answer would have been to welcome the rise of Methodism, which seemed to encourage sobriety, morality and hard work. Yet the Anglican clergy persisted in regarding Methodism as a dangerous and subversive force. Mozley gives the clearest summary of what we may call 'the upper-class solution' to the shortcomings of the local poor. Mozley believed that the most urgent task was to deal with 'the worst plague of Christian civilisation: the foul dragon to be crushed or chained, the scandal of charity'.[30]

26 Ibid.

27 Ibid.

28 Mozley described the Gypsies as 'English Bedouins'.

29 Mozley, op. cit., Vol. 2, p.235.

30 Ibid., p.239.

Northamptonshire Militia outside the Town Hall.

Brackley Town Hall viewed from the south. Note the open arches.

The Most High, Puissant and Noble Prince, FRANCIS, EGERTON,

Duke of Bridgwater, Marquis of Brackley, Earl of Bridgwater, Viscount Brackley, and Baron of Ellesmere

Above: Brackley Church in the 1840s; a minor restoration was undertaken at this time.

Left: Egerton Arms.

Below: Billy Jakeman, the Methodist boy. (NRO)

Chapter 3

A DEATH AT THE WORKHOUSE

Colonel William Cartwright and Rev Francis Litchfield of Farthinghoe saw themselves as the St Georges in the forthcoming contest with the 'foul dragon of charity'. I have said something of Cartwright in my *Yesterday's Brackley*.[1] Born in 1792, five years before Cartwright, Litchfield was the son of a successful Northampton doctor. He had been educated at Rugby and at Merton College, Oxford. He then entered the Church and became Curate of Farthinghoe.[2] Litchfield and Cartwright were both Tories although, at least in terms of national politics, the Cartwrights were to the Left of Litchfield. In all conscience, they would have been hard put to it to be to his Right. Colonel Cartwright's father, William Ralph Cartwright, MP for Northamptonshire, was a supporter of George Canning; in 1829 he voted for Catholic Emancipation.[3]

WR Cartwright remained a Tory (unlike some other 'Canningites', such as Palmerston, who went over to the Whigs in 1830), but his opposition to Parliamentary Reform was lukewarm. Litchfield, however, denounced both Emancipation and Reform in the most uncompromising terms. Later, he objected to legislation giving legal recognition to weddings conducted in Nonconformist Chapels because such blasphemous ceremonies could never be valid in the sight of God. Those who 'married' in this way were simply living in sin and, hence, the government was guilty of encouraging fornication and 'concubinage'.[4] Litchfield was also an anti-Semite who reacted angrily to proposals that Jews be accorded full civil rights:

1   Clarke, John, *Yesterday's Brackley*, pp.158–65.

2   Greenall, R.L., 'Parson as a Man of Affairs: the Rev Francis Litchfield of Farthinghoe (1792–1876)', *Northamptonshire Past and Present*, Vol. VIII (2), 1990–91, p.121.

3   Cartwright later regretted his vote for Emancipation, describing it as the greatest blot on his political career. *Northampton Mercury*, 24 July 1841.

4   The Dissenters Marriage Act 1837.

Who ever heard, in a Christian country, of political liberty being extended to a sect of men whom Heaven has branded with a curse, men who have shed the blood of our Blessed Saviour, and continuously and impiously to glory in that stupendous crime.[5]

So far as is known, Colonel Cartwright expressed no views either on Nonconformist marriages or 'The Jew Question'. Yet, for many years, Litchfield and Cartwright agreed on most issues of social policy. As early as 1822, Litchfield wrote a series of letters to the *Northampton Mercury* attacking the operation of the Old Poor Law as leading to extravagance, idleness and the destruction of natural affection. It should be felt a disgrace to receive Poor Relief, and women with illegitimate children should be sent to prison. The government should also introduce legislation to compel the poor to attend Church every Sunday.[6] This fitted in well with the programme the Cartwrights had devised for Brackley.

Mozley describes Litchfield as an 'inspiration' to his fellow clergy – 'the most prominent, most amusing and, in some ways, the most useful man in my neighbourhood'. A big man, Litchfield liked 'a good pace' and was 'always looked for at the Northampton Races'. He was not often at Farthinghoe; he would gallop into the village just in time for the service on Sunday and then ride away again. But Litchfield must have paid some visits to his parish and made good use of them, 'for it was the best ordered village in the neighbourhood, the single exception to the universal tidiness being the parsonage'.[7] Mozley remembers Litchfield as 'a furious Conservative, supplying weekly inspiration in a Northampton paper in a deadly struggle with its Radical contemporary'.[8] It is an indication of Mozley's own stance that the 'Radical contemporary' was the respectably Whiggish *Northampton Mercury*, sometimes considered the mouthpiece of the Spencer family.

Litchfield wanted the Tories to have their own 'voice'. In 1834, along with William Ralph Cartwright, William Willes of Astrop, Sir Charles Knightley of Fawsley and Sir Robert Gunning of Horton, he helped to found the *Northampton Herald*. But the country gentlemen were too grand to take an active part in determining editorial policy. Here, Litchfield's influence was paramount and it was he who devised the *Herald*'s slogan – 'For King, the Church and the Farmer we are prepared to brave every battle – with them we stand – with them we fall'.[9] In passing, it is worth noting that, while in the twentieth century, the *Daily Herald* supported the Labour Party, in Litchfield's time, the word 'Herald' in a newspaper title indicated High Tory views. The *Bucks Herald*, founded in 1832, enjoyed the financial support of the Duke of Buckingham and took an editorial line very similar to that of the *Northampton Herald*.[10]

Although the *Herald* criticised the Whig Government, Litchfield and Colonel Cartwright acknowledged that it had passed one excellent piece of legislation – the Poor Law Amendment Act of 1834. The Act was based upon four central propositions. First 'Out-Relief' was to be abolished wherever possible; the

5   A reference to the unsuccessful Jewish Disabilities Bill of 1836. *Northampton Herald*, 20 August 1836.

6   *Northampton Mercury*, 12 October 1822. Litchfield wrote under the pseudonym of 'Rusticus'. Greenall, 'Parson as a Man of Affairs', p.121.

7   Mozley, Thomas, *Reminiscences Chiefly of Towns, Villages and Schools*, Vol. II p.281.

8   Ibid., p.282.

9   *Northampton Herald*, 13 September 1834; Greenall, 'Parson as Man of Affairs', pp.125–26.

10   Lineham, L, 'The *Bucks Herald*, its Politics, Supporters and Finances, 1832–1866', *Records of Buckinghamshire*, Vol. XL (2000), pp.1–14.

able-bodied poor would cease to receive assistance in their own homes. To be given support of any kind, applicants would have to enter the Workhouse. Second, poverty must be regarded as a disgrace, almost a crime, deserving virtual imprisonment – just as Litchfield had argued in 1822. Third, conditions in the Workhouse must be based upon the principle of 'Less Eligibility'; the living standards enjoyed (or rather endured) by the inmates must be worse than those obtainable from the lowest-paid employment outside. Fourth, inside the Workhouse there must be strict segregation of the sexes, extending even to married couples, to prevent any increase in 'the surplus population'.

The Act had important local associations. It was widely known as 'Althorp's Act', having been introduced into Parliament by Viscount Althorp, MP for South Northamptonshire and later 3rd Earl Spencer. At the 1831 Election, the Whig candidates, Viscount Althorp and Viscount Milton, were returned for the County seats, defeating the Tories, William Ralph Cartwright and Sir Charles Knightley of Fawsley. The 1832 Reform Act gave two members to the new constituency of South Northamptonshire, where the first elections under the new franchise were held in December 1832. Cartwright returned to Parliament, alongside Althorp, but was joined by Knightley at the end of 1834, when Althorp moved to the Lords on inheriting the Spencer earldom.[11]

Litchfield and Colonel Cartwright believed that enormous benefits would ensue if the principles behind Althorp's Act could be enforced. Little would be achieved, however, unless those in authority could harden their hearts against misplaced indulgence and sentiment. Then, and only then, would the burden on respectable ratepayers be diminished – because the poor would be forced to work hard, to 'save for a rainy day', and generally arrange their lives to ensure that they would never need to enter the dreaded portals of the Workhouse. In modern parlance, the Act provided the means to break the 'dependency culture' which many identified as the root cause of 'Pauperism'.

Thus, Litchfield and Cartwright saw the new Brackley Workhouse as a prime instrument in the transformation of the character of the lower orders. True, the Act appeared unkind to the poor, but it was precisely this group who would be the ultimate beneficiaries. In a typically forceful contribution to the *Northampton Herald* of 28 March 1835, Litchfield asserted, 'when workhouses are once erected, the best generally will be those in which there are fewest inmates. It is in the disinclination (*properly created*) on the part of the poor to enter workhouses, that the efficiency of such establishments is to exist'. Sadly, the Brackley poor seemed to be too stupid to be capable of reaching this blindingly obvious conclusion.

Unfortunately, it was proving difficult to put theory into practice. At the new Workhouse, construction costs had gone over budget and thus ratepayers were denied the anticipated savings. Worse still, there was a danger that the 1834 Act might be frustrated if paupers continued to obtain Out-Relief. It was accepted that total abolition of Out-Relief was impossible because some paupers were either too old or too sick to be moved from their cottages.

Cartwright, now Chairman of the Board of Guardians, decided to crack down on any 'marginal cases'. Of course, when dealing with requests for Out-Relief, medical opinion was crucial. Some practitioners, like Dr Lever of Culworth, were suspiciously liberal in giving 'certificates'. It may not be a coincidence that, in 1838, Lever was accused of performing an illegal abortion. Although acquitted, he was no longer consulted by the Guardians. Where possible, applicants for Out-Relief were examined by the Workhouse Medical Officer, Dr Frederick Gee of Brackley. Gee seldom issued certificates. On 16 November 1836,

11   Greenall, 'Parson as a Man of Affairs', pp.125–26.

he was instructed to examine Joseph Rubbra of Brackley who had asked for Out-Relief on grounds of sickness and infirmity; Gee reported that Rubbra was well enough to enter the Workhouse.[12]

The Guardians considered applications for Out-Relief at their weekly meetings in the boardroom of the Workhouse. Cartwright's tough views usually prevailed. In April 1837, however, requests for Out-Relief for John Giffen of Evenley and Sophia Claridge of Steane received strong minority support from a group of elected Guardians headed by Peter Hopcraft of Evenley. In general, ex officio Guardians opposed Out-Relief more often than elected Guardians, although Rev Clarke of Eydon, Rev Causton of Turweston, Philip Pierrepoint of Evenley and Samuel Severne of Thenford sometimes wavered. Elected Guardians usually supported requests for Out-Relief from people in their own parish while opposing it for others. Yet some elected Guardians representing 'Open Parishes' in the North of the Union (Helmdon, Culworth, Sulgrave, Syresham and Moreton Pinkney) supported virtually all requests and openly rejected the principles behind the New Poor Law.

It was thus difficult enough to persuade the Guardians to stick to a tough policy, but the debate could not be confined to the Workhouse Board Room. Applications for Out-Relief were often accompanied by vociferous campaigns by paupers themselves. Those who had once enjoyed a modest standing in their communities were especially prone to challenge adverse decisions. In November 1838, John Carter, Parish Clerk of Thenford, was denied Out-Relief and told to enter the Workhouse. Carter had the effrontery to complain directly to the Poor Law Commissioners in London. For good measure, he appended the tale of Mrs Middleton, a Thenford widow, who had been evicted from her cottage. Mrs Middleton's request for Out-Relief had also been rejected but she refused to enter the Workhouse and now faced starvation.

The Commissioners required explanations. Robert Weston Jr, the Cartwrights' Agent and Clerk to the Union, replied that, Parish Clerk or not, Carter had been dismissed from his main employment for using bad language – hardly a reason for special treatment. Mrs Middleton's family was of low repute. Her three daughters had had six illegitimate children between them and the real reason for her eviction had been 'commitment to gaol for non-payment of a fine levied for selling beer without a licence'. The Commissioners were satisfied with these explanations.

But the biggest problem of all was that some of the early enthusiasts for the New Poor Law, notably Francis Litchfield, were having second thoughts. Despite his harsh words, Litchfield was beginning to fear that the New Poor Law was being applied too rigidly and blamed the influence of the Poor Law Commissioners. Writing in the *Northampton Herald* on 10 June 1837, he expressed 'extreme regret at the manner in which the [Poor Law] Commissioners are every day rendering the New Poor Law more and more unpopular … we certainly never contemplated such a grinding system'. Colonel Cartwright, however, thought the system was not 'grinding' enough. The growing division between the two men who had once been the strongest supporters of the Workhouse System threatened the entire strategy of reforming the character of the lower orders in the Brackley Union.

The issue that divided Litchfield and Cartwright concerned the role of central government. In the last resort, Cartwright was a centraliser, believing that the poor could only be tamed and improved if the authorities in London intervened to support the efforts of the local gentry and clergy. One of Cartwright's favourite watchwords was 'efficiency'. He used it so often in the 1830s that one is tempted to suspect that he was really a 'closet' Benthamite. In contrast, Litchfield believed that the parsons and the squires could effect

---

12   The main source for the working of the New Poor Law in the Brackley area and for 'Workhouse Scandal' are the Guardians' Minute Books in the NRO. Dates of meetings are given the text.

the necessary reformation of manners without much assistance from outside. He regarded uniformity and centralisation as profoundly un-English, equating such ideas with the dreaded French Revolution. If local magistrates surrendered too much power to Whitehall, they would ultimately destroy their own position.

Litchfield did not like the way central government was coming under the influence of middle-class, urban and industrial interests which viewed the gentry, agriculture – even the Church – with distaste. There might indeed be common ground between these new elements and the clergy and gentry in that both wanted to reduce the burden of the Poor Rates, but there, agreement ended. The new forces, represented in the views of the Poor Law Commissioners, did not understand the importance of hierarchy and deference. They were not real gentlemen and the prospect of an England not controlled by gentlemen was an abomination. In short, Cartwright was too ready 'to sup with the Devil'. Much as Litchfield wanted to transform the poor, he was unwilling to invite sinister outside forces into the previously 'independent' worlds of the English counties. To forestall this danger, he was prepared to make the New Poor Law a little less 'grinding'. The clash between these diametrically opposite views explains much about the 'Great Brackley Workhouse Scandal'.

From Cartwright's point of view, even if Out-Relief could be reduced, little good would be achieved unless the Workhouse became a place of real dread. He was horrified by reports from the Workhouse Chaplain that the Master, Charles Sumpter, had been absent for extended periods. While Sumpter was away, the unsupervised inmates got up to all kinds of mischief. If the principle of sexual segregation was breached, there might be additions to 'the surplus population'. The last thing that Cartwright wanted was for people to conclude that life in Brackley Workhouse might be quite fun. There was probably never much danger of that, but Cartwright was determined to tighten policy. On 6 July 1837, the Guardians resolved that Sumpter's absences 'prevented the Exercise of that Salutary discipline upon which the moral improvement of the Inmates principally depends'.

Sumpter would have to go and he resigned early in 1838. His successor was chosen by Cartwright with minimal consultation with the other Guardians. Joseph Howe had been a sergeant in a Guards Regiment and served in the early days of the Metropolitan Police. He had recently been Master of the Workhouse at Dartford in Kent. Cartwright, who was interested in police matters, may have known Howe already. Equally, the new Master could have been suggested by Vicar Sage, who had relations in the Dartford area. Howe was physically impressive and was later described as 'a gigantic man, over six feet tall, with a correspondingly muscular frame'. Perhaps his mere appearance would overcome problems of any indiscipline. It would take a bold pauper indeed to cheek the likes of Joseph Howe. Cartwright was to develop a high regard for Howe; although often critical of Sumpter, he was to support the new Master through thick and thin.

Litchfield made no public comment on Howe's appointment but probably disapproved of the 'get tough' policy it represented. Although he resigned as an ex officio Guardian, he retained a close interest in the affairs of the Union. He was anxious not to be seen leading a campaign against Cartwright whose family was still linked to him as backers of the *Northampton Herald*. Litchfield needed an 'agent', connected with the Workhouse, whose letters could be published in the *Herald*. Ideally, while avoiding direct criticism of the colonel, these letters might still make his position impossible by destroying the reputation of his protégé, Joseph Howe. Although there is no certain proof, I suspect that Litchfield's 'agent' was the Workhouse Chaplain, Rev Pryce Jones.

From the start, the Guardians had seen the Chaplain as vital to the success of the Workhouse, hoping that his ministrations would strike at the improvidence and moral laxity which were the prime causes of pauperism. The obvious Chaplain would have been the Vicar of Brackley, but Sage considered the post beneath his dignity – and the advertised salary was only £40 a year. No other beneficed clergyman was interested and, eventually, the chaplaincy was offered to Jones.

Pryce Jones was of Welsh descent, although his father, John Jones, had been Vicar of Abthorpe. John Jones died young and Pryce and his many brothers and sisters were brought up by an uncle. Pryce received only a modest education and was lucky to be accepted for ordination without a university degree. In 1819, he became Curate of Helmdon and in August 1822 married a local girl, Mary Anne Edmunds, the daughter of a tenant farmer. With little money, influential contacts or obvious abilities (his command of grammar and syntax sometimes fell below the standards of most nineteenth-century clerics), Pryce Jones's career in the Church progressed no further. He was never to have a parish of his own; he died, aged 68, in December 1855, still Curate of Helmdon.

Jones's fellow clergy seem to have regarded him with a mixture of pity and contempt; a Workhouse chaplaincy was a kind of ecclesiastical booby prize. Not surprisingly, Jones had a chip on his shoulder. When offered the Workhouse job, his first reaction was to refuse unless the salary was increased to £50 a year. The Guardians were surprised, supposing Jones would have accepted with alacrity. Since no one else would take the job, however, they had no choice but to pay him his £50. To begin with, Jones did everything to please Cartwright, providing the Chairman with information to discredit Sumpter. He seemed the ideal Chaplain, walking in from Helmdon and visiting the Workhouse daily. In June 1837, the Guardians showed their confidence in Jones by giving him a full set of keys to enable him to enter all wards whenever he wished.

But Jones was becoming discontented, perhaps thinking his services deserved more recognition. He probably turned to Litchfield for sympathy. After all, Litchfield had also been a Curate for many years, working hard to transform the character of Farthinghoe while the incumbent, Rev Edmund Milward, was a total recluse, 'seldom seen by anyone, even by his domestics, and never paid any visits'. But Litchfield and Jones were not really in the same position. Litchfield was a magistrate, an influential figure in the county and never short of money. When Milward finally died in 1838, Litchfield was presented to the living of Farthinghoe and, shortly after, received the rectory of Great Linford, Bucks. His two parishes gave him an income of more than £800 a year – many times Jones's meagre salary.

It is unlikely that Jones was motivated solely by disappointed ambition. His own impoverished childhood may have given him a genuine sympathy for the poor. He knew too that the New Poor Law was especially unpopular in Helmdon. He began to complain that children and old people in the Workhouse, who hardly deserved to be punished for the 'crime' of poverty, were being neglected and were 'frequently left in a dirty and miserable state'. These complaints were not acted upon.

The early months of 1838 saw serious sickness and Jones later complained that the inmates were denied proper medical attention. Dr Gee had not attended in person as regularly as his contract stipulated and he had delegated his responsibilities to a series of assistants, including a Mr Morrison and a Mr Segitmeir. These assistants were unsatisfactory and had often moved on when the Guardians sought to investigate their conduct. Jones was already contemplating resignation but, for the time being, felt he must stay on to protect elderly inmates from Sumpter's neglect.

Jones expressed initial approval of Howe. On 5 February 1839, he reported that he had 'found the old people as well provided for and as well arranged as could be' and on 21 February observed that 'the purity of the House compared to what has been is remarkable'. He could now resign with a clear conscience and later explained:

I should have left the office helpless and despairing of the welfare of the poor creatures who might have been reduced to the necessity of becoming inmates of the Brackley House, had not the intervention of the present master convinced me that there was some hope.

Unfortunately, the circumstances of Jones's resignation and the problem of finding a successor only served to sharpen his worries and resentment. Again, few clergymen were interested, but Sage (notoriously unsympathetic to the poor) was finally persuaded to take the job – but on two conditions. He was to remain as an ex officio Guardian (some thought he should resign if he took a paid position from the Union) and the salary must be increased to £60 a year. Cartwright agreed, although the Commissioners only accepted the arrangement with hesitation. Jones was furious when he heard about the increase in salary and demanded to be paid at the higher rate for the period of his notice. The demand was refused. Jones's anger at Cartwright and Sage soon led him to revise his views on Howe.

On 12 March 1839, Jones left a note at the Workhouse 'seeming to imply some censure upon the Visiting Committee'. The complaint was discussed at the Guardians' Meeting on 20 March, but the charges were rejected and the Guardians recorded their 'express thanks and approbation of the Conduct of the Committee'. Jones then alleged that Dr Gee had been negligent in his treatment of George Wilkins, a young Helmdon boy living in the Workhouse. He also drew attention to the case of 'the child of Harriet Barnes of Helmdon which was brought out of the Workhouse by its Mother rather than remain there destitute of Medical Aid in the season of sickness'. The Guardians investigated, interviewing both Gee and Howe. The unanimous verdict, delivered on 17 April, was that there had been no negligence. Gee admitted that he had not kept accurate records, but still the Guardians declared themselves 'perfectly satisfied with the attention paid by him generally to the inmates of the Workhouse'. Jones was just raking up an old story and should have made any complaints back in the spring of 1838.

But the Guardians were worried. Helmdon people were drawing up a petition to the Commissioners protesting about Gee. To appease their critics, the Guardians voted to allow the Barnes family Out-Relief. By the summer of 1839, however, the Guardians had recovered from their fright. On 14 August, they dismissed another letter from Jones on behalf of Harriet Barnes as 'quite frivolous and vexatious'. They also voted to stop Out-Relief for Alice Cadd, Harriet's mother and grandmother of the former Workhouse child. Mrs Cadd had been taking a petition around the neighbourhood protesting about conditions in the Workhouse and begging alms for her grandchild. If Mrs Cadd was well enough to travel the length and breadth of the Union, she could hardly be sick enough to merit Out-Relief. She would either have to support herself and her family or enter the Workhouse.

Elections to the Board of Guardians were held in the spring of 1840 and Jones was returned by the ratepayers of Helmdon. As a Guardian himself, he could wage his campaign with greater effectiveness. Jones soon discovered that Joseph Howe was already unpopular with some Guardians. The Master's troubles had begun in September 1839 when he fell out with the Workhouse porter, Thomas Jones. Thomas Jones was not related to the Curate of Helmdon, but was a cousin of William Jones, an elected Guardian from Kings Sutton, another village where the 1834 Act was extremely unpopular. Although William Jones supported his relation, Cartwright persuaded the Guardians to back Howe and to dismiss Thomas Jones. Against Cartwright's wishes, however, a majority of Guardians insisted on calling Howe into the Board Room to admonish him for his part in the dispute. Of course, the 'malcontents' needed a leader and Pryce Jones was their man.

After his trouble with the porter, Joseph Howe became more dependent upon Cartwright than ever. He had to go along with the Chairman's desire for a harsher regime, although there is no evidence that he disagreed. Furthermore, the policy was encouraged by Assistant Commissioner Henry Parker and may have been suggested by him. Parker held a 'watching brief' over the affairs of the Brackley Union on behalf of the Poor Law Commission. Cartwright and Parker were pressing for the establishment of a 'Punishment Room' where 'refractory paupers' could be confined and kept to a bread and water diet. The Commissioners accepted the scheme, but reminded the Brackley Guardians that the physical punishment of adult paupers was prohibited. The reminder is interesting in the light of later developments and could even imply that the Commissioners had already heard rumours about Howe's ideas about punishment.

The creation of the Punishment Room and Parker's involvement worried Litchfield. He had always been suspicious of London bureaucrats, protesting earlier at the way the Poor Law Commissioners were bombarding Unions with circulars and instructions. Such interference was sure to provoke 'ill blood' and resentment against 'the numerous endeavours at making business for London Commissioners which are every day being developed'.

When Jones attended his first meeting as an elected Guardian on 1 April 1840, he raised a lone voice against the customary vote of thanks to Cartwright for his services as Chairman. Within a few weeks, however, Jones had created a sizeable party. A group of elected Guardians criticised Howe, and by implication Cartwright, at every turn. Apart from Jones, the group included Thomas Taylor of Whitfield, George Smith of Radstone, Thomas Coleman of Sulgrave, Thomas Watkins of Moreton Pinkney and, on occasion, William Blencowe and Edward Taylor of Brackley St James.

One Guardian and then another would raise an issue directly or indirectly calling Howe's honesty into question. Was there any truth in rumours that Mr and Mrs Howe had taken tea and sugar intended for the inmates? Investigation showed the rumour to be groundless. Would the Guardians call Howe into the meeting and warn him not to give Workhouse supplies to his niece? Of course, the Guardians agreed – even though when Howe came into the boardroom, he insisted that he had never misappropriated supplies of any kind. On one occasion, the Master was solemnly accused of giving away cabbages grown in the Workhouse garden; he countered that the Workhouse had more cabbages than it knew what to do with and that the surplus vegetables had been exchanged for other things.

The account of these questions, as recorded in the Guardians Minute Book, make them seem so absurd that it is tempting to sympathise with Howe and to question Jones's judgement and motives. Yet if this was nothing more than a vendetta by a disappointed and limited man, why did so many other Guardians support him? It is even more remarkable that Cartwright, of all people, should have been 'rattled' by ridiculous questions about cabbages. But Cartwright now announced his impending resignation, both from the Chair and from the Board. He said that he wanted to resume an active military career, although in the event he did not do so. Perhaps Cartwright hoped that his announcement would occasion a show of approval for his policies. If the approval was sufficiently impressive, he might resume his old position once Jones had made himself totally idiotic. But there is another possibility. Perhaps Cartwright knew that, if Jones continued with his investigations, he would uncover serious abuses.

At first, things went Cartwright's way. A public subscription was launched to buy a piece of silver to be given to the Chairman in recognition of his services. The subscription raised £130, on the face of it impressive testimony to the popularity of the New Poor Law among the ratepayers. A handsome tureen, appropriately inscribed, was presented to Cartwright at a dinner in Brackley Town Hall. The dinner commenced at 4 p.m. on Wednesday, 3 June 1840 – nicely timed for the convenience of farmers attending

Brackley Market. According to the *Northampton Mercury* of 6 June, the function had been attended by 'about one hundred and twenty of the most respectable inhabitants of the Union'. The particularly memorable wines had been a credit to the caterer, Mr William Stutchfield, landlord of The Crown.

At the conclusion of the meal came the speeches and the toasts. PS Pierrepoint (Deputy Chairman) thanked Howe and the other officers:

> … not for doing their duty, for that they were bound to, but for having done it with such zeal and energy as made the duties of the Chairman and the Guardians infinitely less onerous than they must have otherwise been.

Speaker after speaker praised Cartwright and the New Poor Law. Sage said that he could not understand how any clergyman valuing the health and comfort of the poor could do otherwise than welcome recent changes – no doubt a dig at Jones. Rev Bennet of Croughton agreed, adding that the Poor Law Commissioners themselves often held up the Brackley Union as a model for more benighted places to follow. Mr Alfred Hayward described the New Poor Law as 'the only safeguard of the landed interest' and was appalled at any suggestion that the Commission should be abolished. Mr William Malins, representing Brackley St Peter's, declared that no parish had been more in need of the Act and no ratepayers more indebted to it. Even William Blencowe, who had sometimes wavered towards Jones, joined in the chorus of praise, predicting that the new system would soon 'effect a remarkable change in the moral character of the Poor'. In reply, Cartwright modestly disclaimed any personal contribution; the credit was due to the Act and the wise principles it embodied.

All the speakers were Tories and this was why the Whig *Northampton Mercury* gave such prominence to the dinner. The *Mercury* of 13 June stressed that the various speeches provided non-political testimony to the benefits of a Whig Act. But there were further implications. Unless specifically renewed, the Poor Law Commission was due to be disbanded in 1841. Parliament would soon have to take a decision and some misguided Tories advocated non-renewal. Yet the happy collaboration between the Brackley Guardians and the Commissioners suggested the wisdom of continuing the present arrangements. Finally, the *Mercury* predicted that, wherever else 'Poor Law agitators' might try to cause trouble, they would be wise to avoid Brackley, a town where the merits of the 1834 Act were so widely and rightly appreciated.

Of course, it may have been somewhat insensitive to celebrate the triumph of the New Poor Law – 'Less Eligibility', 'The Punishment Room' and the rest – with a slap-up feast for the well-to-do. Perhaps some contrasted Stutchfield's memorable wines with the bread and water diet now the lot of 'refractory paupers' in the Banbury Road. But that was not the half of it. The real story behind the 'Cartwright Dinner' is a tragic one. While the toasts were being proposed and the fine wines consumed, a 7-year-old boy was dying in Brackley Workhouse. According to the *Northampton Herald*, he expired on Sunday, 7 June 'after a week of excruciating agony'. Ironically, the *Mercury*'s edition of 13 June – which lauds the Brackley dinner – also carries an account of the Inquest into the death of William Hirons of Farthinghoe.

The *Mercury* explained that Workhouse boys were given a weekly 'tepid bath', an occasion of innocent fun. The Master, Joseph Howe, was usually present and – at the boys' request – sometimes threw cold water over them in the tiled bathroom. On 30 May, the bath water was found to be leaking and Howe told the boys to put hot water into the bath so that the wooden plug would swell. This was done, but Howe assumed that further pails coming from the kitchen would contain cold water. His assumption was wrong; he picked up a pail of what was actually boiling water and threw it over Hirons and another boy:

Upon their screaming, he said to the boy from whom he had received the pail, 'Good God, why did you not tell me it contained hot water?' And the boy said that he was not aware that the master intended to throw it upon the boys.

Medical assistance was summoned at once and everything possible done for William Hirons. Although in Hirons's case the scalds proved fatal, it was gratifying to learn that the other boy was recovering well. At the Inquest, a 'respectable jury of fifteen men resident in that town' returned a verdict of 'Accidental Death'. No effort had been spared to investigate the incident and no criticism could be made about the Inquest procedure. The Brackley Coroner, Robert Weston – also the Clerk to the Union – had properly declined to preside and, in the event, the Northampton Coroner, George Abbey, conducted the Inquest. A magistrate from Hirons's own village (presumably Litchfield) had expressed his satisfaction with the propriety of the verdict. Despite the tragedy of William Hirons, Howe was a good man: 'nothing could be stronger than the testimony given to the general kindness and humanity of the Master'. Dr Gee had stressed Howe's fondness for children and Rev Sage insisted 'the health and care of children have been the particular subjects of the Master's solicitude; one trait above all predominates in his character and that is his kindness to children'.

But was Howe really such a good man? Although Litchfield may have expressed public satisfaction with the Inquest verdict, he was willing to open the columns of the *Herald* to those who took a different view both of the Inquest and of the Master's character. The tone adopted in the *Herald*'s account of the Inquest is markedly less complacent than that found in the *Mercury*. Unlike its rival, the *Herald* uses emotional, even sensational language. Its account is headed 'Violent Death of a Child in a Workhouse', and refers to Hirons as 'the poor thing' and to the accident as 'the melancholy event'. It dwells on the boy's fearful sufferings, adding that the tragedy is particularly distressing because the boy's mother, cruelly deserted by her husband, is also an inmate of the Workhouse. It draws attention to the 'great and painful sensation' felt by the people of Brackley. Ostensibly, the *Herald* tries to be fair to Howe, mentioning the favourable testimony given by both Gee and Sage. It refuses to give credence to 'unjust rumours' to the discredit of the Brackley Workhouse and its Master'. But this could be just a ploy to arouse interest in those very rumours. Unlike the *Mercury*, the *Herald* mentions evidence showing Howe to have been 'somewhat exact in the discipline which he enforces at the establishment'. At least one obvious lesson could be drawn:

> We take this opportunity of suggesting to Unions generally that attention should be paid to the manner in which the bathing of children in Workhouses is conducted, and to Masters of Workhouses that they should on no account permit themselves to let little children have access to boiling water.

Whereas the *Mercury* takes the lengthy Inquest as proof of a desire for a proper inquiry, the *Herald* suspects that the Jury was out so long because some jurors doubted whether this really was a case of 'Accidental Death'. The *Herald* concludes with some awkward questions. After this tragedy, could the Brackley Workhouse still be held up as a model of its kind and were all the Guardians satisfied with the way things had been handled?

The time had come for Pryce Jones to play a larger part. A letter from him, under the signature of 'A Guardian of the Parish of Helmdon', appeared in the *Mercury* of 20 June. Jones objected to the paper's treatment of the story of William Hirons – 'scalded to death by the Master'. Jones denied the suggestion that all Guardians approved of the 'management and discipline of the Workhouse' or had been properly informed about the accident and the timing of the Inquest. In fact, only seven or eight of the thirty-two Guardians had attended; most only heard of the accident after the Inquest had taken place. Readers must have sensed a suggestion of a cover-up, at least until after the Cartwright Dinner. Jones had 'anything but a feeling of satisfaction on the management and (misnamed) efficient discipline which has hitherto pervaded the institution'. He claimed that a majority of his fellow Guardians agreed with him. It is striking that, in this letter, Jones's prose style reads remarkably like Litchfield's.

The letter was followed by a reply from the editor of the *Mercury*, questioning Jones's claim that other Guardians were discontented; surely they would have voiced any criticisms at the dinner? The *Herald* of 27 June comes to Jones's rescue, pointing out that at the time of the dinner, most of the Guardians had no knowledge of the accident. The *Mercury*'s comments were 'a base perversion of the truth'. It made too much of the Brackley dinner, reporting it 'out of the common way, in order to make it the ground work for a party article'. It was no surprise that the Guardians who spoke at the dinner stressed 'the benevolent and merciful operation of the Poor Law'; people usually take a favourable view of their own labours, 'particularly on an occasion when they meet for no higher purpose than to lavish praise upon themselves'. In support of Jones, the *Herald* printed a letter from an anonymous Guardian who attended the Inquest – but only after hearing of the death indirectly. This correspondent was unhappy about the way the Inquest had been conducted and denied 'any responsibility for that proceeding'.

The trouble with the *Herald*'s campaign – as orchestrated by Litchfield – was that it failed to take a clear line on the New Poor Law. Rather lamely, the paper declared itself 'not hostile to the Poor Law generally' but only to particular parts of it. The *Herald* tried to blame the tragedy of William Hirons upon 'the accursed *centralising tendency* of the New Poor Laws' – that is, upon the Poor Law Commissioners in London. The logic is not clear. The *Herald* warned 'educated and upright country gentlemen' (people like the Cartwrights) not to associate themselves 'with democratic orators and republican assemblies – assemblies alike hostile to liberty and the comforts of the poorer classes of society'. Of course, if there was a link between the Commissioners and the death of William Hirons it went through Colonel Cartwright, but the *Herald* could not say so. By the end of June 1840, the rival Northampton papers concluded that the story had run its course and found other issues to quarrel over. By now, the names of William Cartwright, Pryce Jones and Joseph Howe were probably quite well known in Northamptonshire but were hardly 'national news'.

All this was to change in January 1841. A national newspaper, *The Times* itself, turned its attention on Brackley, deploying more sophisticated journalistic skills than those evidenced in either the *Northampton Mercury* or *Herald*. Now there were no constraints on attacking Cartwright. On 9 January 1841, *The Times* devoted almost an entire page to a case recently heard by magistrates at Eton. A pauper woman, Elizabeth Wise, complained about her treatment in Eton Workhouse. She claimed that, on 27 December 1840, she had gone to the Children's Ward to bandage the feet of her daughter who was suffering from severe chilblains. The Master appeared, told her she had no business in the Children's Ward and ordered her to leave. Wise begged to be allowed to comfort her child, but her pleas only enraged the Master, who seized her roughly and carried her bodily to the Punishment Room, known to the inmates as the 'Black Hole'.

In the depth of winter, Wise was kept in a cell, which had no glass in the window, for over twenty-four hours. She was denied heat, light, food, or drink, even a chamber pot. Such treatment undoubtedly contravened Workhouse Regulations but the Master was unabashed and told the magistrates that, regulations notwithstanding, Wise thoroughly deserved her spell in the Black Hole. The magistrates were shocked by the Master's demeanour and his behaviour and imposed a fine of £10 for wilful assault.

The Master was an unpopular figure in the neighbourhood; when he left the Court, he was 'saluted with the hisses and groans of persons who assembled on the spot'. *The Times* revealed that the Workhouse Master's name was Joseph Howe.

The Times demanded to know why such a brute had been appointed as a Workhouse Master. The paper noticed that, in Court, Howe had been represented by Assistant Poor Law Commissioner Henry Parker. On 21 January, *The Times* carried a letter from WG Cookesley (1802–80), an Eton Master and a rising Classical scholar. Cookesley explained that Howe had been appointed on the strength of recommendations from Parker and Colonel William Cartwright, 'Chairman of the Brackley Guardians'. Parker had described Howe as 'a kindly and well-disposed man' while Cartwright praised his professionalism and efficiency. But Cookesley had heard other things about Howe; he feared that the savage treatment of Elizabeth Wise would have come as no surprise to the inmates of Howe's former Workhouse at Brackley. *The Times* of 1 February carried a letter from Jones confirming Cookesley's suspicions.

The Times provides the main source of information about Howe's last weeks in Brackley. The Guardians' Minute Book is uninformative and Jones specifically questioned its reliability, claiming that the sole merit of Robert Weston's Minutes was that they had been 'so arranged as to appear formal and well-shaped on paper'. Jones had a point. The Minutes contain references to 'an accident in the Bath House' but nowhere are we actually told of a death. On 10 June, Cartwright refused to allow a debate on the tragedy but yielded on 1 July. Weston's Minutes read strangely and imply that the Guardians were more concerned about the absurd cabbage business than with the death of a young boy:

> The Board proceeded to consider Mr Jones's proposal of 10 June last as to the Accident to the Boy, William Hirons, which led to a further inquiry as to the Master having disposed of vegetables from the Workhouse garden and ended by a Motion being made by Mr Bennet and Mr Clarke that he be called in and reprimanded accordingly.

The Times was getting interested in Parker's role in Howe's move from Brackley to Eton. According to Jones, Parker had been a frequent visitor to Brackley in June and July 1840. Even more than Cartwright, Parker had been willing to go to any lengths to protect Howe. He had insisted that the Inquest should be held in the Workhouse Board Room rather than in one of the usual places – The Crown or the Town Hall. Parker's influence had been behind the Accidental Death verdict, a verdict which had been received with 'total incredulity' in the Brackley area. If Jones was right, did people think the correct verdict should have been Manslaughter or even Murder? Did they believe that Howe knew that the water in the pail was boiling? Whatever Sage and Gee said about Howe's kindness to children, could he have been a sadist who enjoyed making women and children suffer? In the light of the Eton case, one is bound to wonder what really happened in the Workhouse bathroom. Was the Inquest a 'fix'? Cookesley clearly thought it was:

> The inmates of a workhouse be so much at the mercy of the master, particularly when he is backed up by an Assistant Poor Law Commissioner, that no wonder need be felt if, in the most palpable and outrageous case of cruelty, much truth adverse to Master cannot be elicited, whereas there is hardly a Master of a Workhouse in England who cannot get some pauper under his care to say what he wishes in his favour.

There were also some strange aspects to the story of Howe's eventual departure from Brackley. Jones claimed that he had proposed a motion to dismiss Howe at the Guardians' Meeting on 1 July 1840.

The motion had been duly seconded and was generally supported by other Guardians. A number had made speeches attacking Howe's general want of humanity and questioning his integrity. Jones had been sure of a majority but, before a vote could be taken, Cartwright intervened to say that, if the Guardians insisted on sacking Howe, the Poor Law Commission would overrule them. In other words, Brackley would be 'stuck' with Howe. This warning must have been 'cleared' with Parker who sat at Cartwright's side throughout. Cartwright suggested another course: if the Guardians contented themselves with a mild reprimand, Howe would soon move on and find another job. The Guardians agreed. A few days later, Howe resigned and, on 11 July, local newspapers carried an advertisement for a new Master.

Cartwright gave his own account in a letter to *The Times* of 5 February 1841. Whatever may have happened later, Howe had been a success at Brackley, whose paupers owed him a 'considerable debt of gratitude'. There had actually been fewer punishments of 'refractory paupers' than under Sumpter. There was no mystery about Joseph Howe's departure; the poor man had been so upset by Hirons's death that he had decided to leave the town as soon as possible. But Cartwright made no attempt to explain how the kindly Master of the Brackley Workhouse had become the monster revealed in the Eton case. Cookesley responded by mocking any suggestion of a 'character change':

> That the same man who was guilty of the deliberate and malignant cruelty which Howe practised against Elizabeth Wise should be of so delicate and sensitive a frame that he could not bear to stay in a place where he had in perfect innocence occasioned the death of a child, is a prodigy in the history of human nature.

When Howe applied for the Eton job, no mention was made of Hirons's death – and to that extent the Eton Guardians were misled. The unanswered question is whether Cartwright and Parker 'fixed' the post at Eton for Howe because they genuinely believed in him and were surprised by his subsequent conduct, or whether they had no illusions about him and cynically passed a sadist onto another Union to save themselves further embarrassment? Of course, 'The Brackley Workhouse Scandal' became hopelessly embroiled in wider issues, particularly those concerning the renewal of the powers of the Poor Law Commissioners, but for three weeks Brackley was national news.

The shady story revealed first by the *Northampton Herald* and then by *The Times* damaged Cartwright's influence in Brackley, but it did not destroy it. The colonel resigned from the Board of Guardians and removed himself to Flore, but Brackley had not heard the last of Colonel Cartwright and his crusade to bring discipline, obedience and morality to the lower orders of South Northamptonshire.

Brackley Workhouse, Banbury Road, the scene of a great scandal.

Colonel Cartwright in old age, former Chairman of Brackley Poor Law Guardians.

Chapter Four

FAST ASLEEP?

When addressing a political meeting in Brackley on 17 December 1866, Mr JB Langley of London recalled earlier visits to the town and said that he had found it 'fast asleep'. Langley was not far wrong. On occasion, the sleeper stirred, perhaps brought close to consciousness by the whistles of the trains that came in 1850. But that was all; for the most part, the stirrings were those of a man in the grip of a nightmare that never seemed to end. It was a nightmare of decay and stagnation.

One might have thought that the Workhouse Scandal would have absorbed all of the energies of Rev Litchfield and Colonel Cartwright, yet the pair busily engaged in other disputes also involving the vexed question of 'centralisation'. Cartwright viewed the traditional system of law enforcement much as he regarded the Old Poor Law. As the Old Poor Law produced more poverty, so the old system of law enforcement produced more crime. Although potential wrongdoers were supposed to be deterred by the ferocious punishments on the Statute Book, too many criminals were never caught or brought to trial. For many, crime *did* pay.

Cartwright despaired of the old Parish Constables. He had a point. Richard Cowley's *Policing Northamptonshire, 1836–1886* describes the typical old-style constable as 'normally of the lowest intelligence, semi-literate, and as criminal as the thieves he was in duty bound to catch'.[1] Cartwright believed that the solution was to establish 'an efficient police force', which would prove that crime did not pay. The criminally inclined poor of Brackley would mend their ways when they saw wrongdoers being caught and punished. But, as with the Poor Law, central government would have to take a hand, preferably by extending the system of the Metropolitan Police – established in 1829 – to the entire country.

Anxiety about crime had produced local initiatives in the 1820s. The leading citizens of several Northamptonshire towns formed 'Catch Criminal Societies', which offered rewards for the recovery of members' stolen goods.[2] In 1836, police forces were established in Northampton, Banbury and

1   Cowley, R., *Policing Northamptonshire, 1836–1886* (Studley, Warwickshire: Brewin Books, 1986), p.6.

2   Warwick, L., 'Legal lore of Northamptonshire, 2 – The Catch Criminal Societies', in *Northampton and County Independent*, February 1980.

Buckingham, but their jurisdictions were strictly limited to the boundaries of the boroughs concerned. In the same year, however, a Royal Commission was appointed 'for the purpose of inquiring as to the best means of establishing an efficient constabulary in the counties of England and Wales'.[3] The Commission was headed by Edwin Chadwick, the arch 'centralist' whose 1832 Report had led to the New Poor Law of 1834. In 1839, Chadwick's Commission reported in favour of 'rural police forces'.

Because of fears of Chartist violence, the Whig Government acted quickly and passed the County Police Act. The Act stipulated that the new police forces, funded from the County Rates, were to operate in accordance with regulations issued by the Home Secretary. This provision alarmed Litchfield with his hatred of centralisation. But there was a crucial difference between the New Poor Law and the County Police Act. The New Poor Law applied everywhere but the Police Act was 'permissive'. County magistrates were given discretion either to 'adopt' the Police Act or to ignore it. If Litchfield could persuade the Northamptonshire magistrates to shun the County Police Act, he would save his county from another dose of London interference and control – and take the Cartwrights down a peg or two in the process. Encouragingly for Litchfield, magistrates in neighbouring Buckinghamshire and Oxfordshire had no intention of setting up police forces. Indeed, in the seventeen years following 1839, only twenty-eight of the fifty-six counties of England and Wales actually 'adopted' the County Police Act.[4] It was not until 1856 that the law was changed to make police forces compulsory everywhere.

As Litchfield probably suspected, however, many in Northamptonshire were delighted with the County Police Act and were determined to adopt it as soon as possible. In the autumn of 1839, the *Northampton Mercury* ran a campaign for a police force. Litchfield mobilised the *Herald* to argue the opposite case, asserting that a rural police force would do as much 'to enslave this free country as any measure that was carried into effect during the dictatorship of Oliver Cromwell'.

But Litchfield's campaign was of no avail. In December 1839, magistrates meeting at the Quarter Sessions in Northampton began discussions on the issue. On 4 January 1840, a proposal for a county police force was introduced by William Ralph Cartwright and seconded by P.S. Pierrepoint of Evenley – later Colonel Cartwright's successor as Chairman of the Brackley Poor Law Guardians. Opponents included Sir Charles Knightley, Cartwright's colleague as MP for South Northamptonshire, and – of course – Rev Francis Litchfield. The proposal was carried by twenty-six votes to eight. Welcoming the decision, the *Mercury* of 11 January 1840 scorned the 'utter futility of the arguments employed against it by the Rector of Farthinghoe'.

Then Cartwright and Litchfield clashed over the appointment of the first Chief Constable. Litchfield suggested Major Robert Law of the Madras Army but Cartwright secured the appointment of a Bow Street Runner named Henry Goddard, who was regarded as one of the best detectives in England. Cartwright insisted that his colleagues should not be looking for 'a person of high military rank … but [for] one who would look after [seek out] criminals and suppress crime'.[5] Litchfield saw Goddard as a symbol of centralisation. He had supposed that members of the new police force would be appointed and dismissed by the magistrates; now he found that appointments were to be made by the Chief Constable. The magistrates' only means of influencing police proceedings would be through their control over

3   Critchley, TA, *A History of Police in England and Wales* (London: Constable, 1967) p.69.

4   Ibid., p.89.

5   Cowley, *Policing Northamptonshire*, p.15.

the purse strings. When the Northamptonshire Constabulary came into existence, Litchfield habitually referred to it as 'the gendarmerie' in order to stress its foreign and oppressive character.

By December 1840, it had been decided that the force was to consist of one Chief Constable, seven Superintendents and forty-three Constables. The county was to be divided into seven divisions; one division would be based at Brackley and headed by a superintendent. There were to be constables at Brackley, Byfield, Charlton, Culworth, Middleton Cheney and Syresham. Goddard had already issued his first Police Order. Constables were required:

> To go on duty from 5 o'clock in the morning until 10, commencing again at 7 o'clock in the evening and patrol until the beer houses are closed, or longer if necessary, and report to the Superintendents any beer house conducted in a disorderly manner and found open after the hours regulated by the magistrates. Also pay particular attention and remove all vagrants encamping or pitching tents wherever found.[6]

But Litchfield had not given up. The police force turned out to be more expensive than anticipated and crime rates did not go down to begin with. Litchfield prepared a standard petition – with the name of the parish left blank – demanding abolition. Whatever the *Northampton Mercury* might say about his reasoning, Litchfield's ideas had some support. In July 1844, eighteen Northamptonshire parishes sent 'Litchfield petitions' to the Quarter Sessions. A further twelve such petitions were presented between 1845 and 1849. As late as March 1856, the Brackley Poor Law Guardians petitioned the Quarter Sessions 'against any increase in the county police'.

But a new spirit was dawning. The police force became less controversial under Goddard's successor, Henry Lambert Bailey, Chief Constable between 1849 and 1875. Bailey came from an Irish gentry background, which probably made him more acceptable to the squires and parsons than the Cockney Goddard had been. The Quarter Sessions of April 1850 agreed to erect purpose-built police stations at Brackley, Towcester and Kettering. The original estimate for the handsome stone police station at Brackley was £600, but this had to be revised to £800.[7] The police station was located in the Banbury Road which represented the 'new face' of Brackley, with the police station, the Workhouse, the Congregational Chapel and some rather grand villas for the better-off townspeople. It was the nearest thing Brackley had to a 'Victorian suburb'. If it had been any larger, they would surely have called it 'Cartwrightville'.

The coming of the railway also favoured the development of the Banbury Road and the Bottom End. When the London & Birmingham Railway Company was formed in the early 1830s, the Secretary, Richard Creed – backed by George Stephenson – favoured a route through Buckingham and Brackley. Had this scheme been adopted, the town's future would have been completely different. But the plan encountered furious opposition from local landowners led by the Duke of Buckingham and, as a result, a more easterly route via Bletchley was chosen.[8]

Brackley would have to wait for half a century before it obtained direct rail access to London. In the meantime, the best it could hope for was a branch line – and even that was a while in coming. For a few years, coach operators survived by providing services which fed into the embryonic railway network.

---

6   NRO, Box X 304.

7   Cowley, *Policing Northamptonshire*, p.34.

8   Simpson, Bill, *The Banbury to Verney Junction Branch* (Oxford: Oxford Publishing Company, 1977) p.10.

In April 1840, John Drinkwater and C W Fowler – landlords of the White and Red Lion public houses in Banbury – invested in a new coach. The coach was called *The Union Railway* and ran 'every afternoon, Sundays excepted, at 2.45, through Brackley, Buckingham and Winslow, and Whitchurch, to the Aylesbury Station, to meet the seven o'clock train to London. Returns from Euston Square at 3 o'clock in the afternoon'.[9]

But the days for the coaches were coming to an end as proposals for cross-country railways were placed before Parliament. These lines were designed to give towns to the east and west of Bletchley access to the main London and Birmingham route. The line from Bletchley to Bedford was opened in October 1846. Acts of Parliament were then secured to build one line from Bletchley to Oxford and another from a junction (later known as Verney Junction) near Claydon on the projected Oxford line, to Buckingham and Brackley.

In 1847, the Oxford & Bletchley Junction and the Buckingham & Brackley Railways amalgamated to form the Buckinghamshire Railway. Powers were acquired for the Buckingham and Brackley line to be extended to Banbury.[10] Local backers of the scheme included Mr Pierrepoint of Evenley and Mr Horewood of Steane Park. Work on the line to Brackley commenced at Buckingham on 20 April 1847. Financial problems delayed construction and forced economies.[11] The bridges were wide enough to take two tracks; only one was installed, although there were passing loops at some stations, including Brackley.

The line was completed early in 1850. The contractor, Thomas Brassey took an experimental trip along the route on 25 April and the first public train ran on the 1 May. The train, covered with flags and bunting, carried the local celebrities to open each station in turn. A telegraph system had been installed and the first message to come across the wires was the happy news of the birth of Queen Victoria's third son, Arthur, later Duke of Connaught.[12]

The railway was expected to boost the rather stagnant local economy. Mr Pierrepoint made his first railway journey a few days after the opening. On alighting at Brackley Station, he was received by 'tradesmen and other respectable inhabitants'. They gave him three hearty cheers and he expressed his hopes for the prosperity of the town. The arrival of the railway brought the price of coal in Brackley down from 22 to 15 shillings per ton. It had been calculated that Winslow, Buckingham, Brackley and Banbury and their surrounding villages consumed about 65,000 tons of coal per annum and it was expected that most of this would now be carried on the Buckinghamshire Railway. Unfortunately, the opening of the Great Western Railway station at Banbury, by far the largest town on the branch, forced a downward revision of the estimated traffic. The line did not prove a great commercial success and was soon leased to the London & North Western Railway (LNWR, successor to the London & Birmingham). The LNWR instituted a policy of cost cutting; trains were infrequent and slow. The timetable remained unchanged for many years. The *Bicester Advertiser* of 21 July 1855 announced it as:

9   Taylor, AM, *Gilletts: Bankers at Banbury and Oxford* (Oxford, Clarendon Press, 1964) p.48.

10   Simpson, *The Banbury to Verney Junction Branch*, p.10.

11   Ibid., p.17. The station at Brackley cost £3,994, with an extra £1,050 for turntables and machinery.

12   Ibid., p.24.

	A.M.		P.M.		Sundays
Banbury	6.55	9.45	2.30	6.15	2.30
Farthinghoe	7.05	9.52	2.40	6.25	2.41
Brackley	7.18	10.05	2.53	6.38	2.52
Buckingham	7.32	10.18	3.06	6.51	3.12
Winslow	7.52	10.35	3.21	7.06	3.29

	A.M.		P.M.		Sundays
Winslow	8.59	11.56	5.30	8.21	12.02
Buckingham	9.14	12.10	5.52	8.38	12.17
Brackley	9.39	12.25	6.10	8.53	12.34
Farthinghoe	9.52	12.38	6.25	9.06	12.50
Banbury	10.05	12.50	6.35	9.15	01.00

Some young men joined the railway service to take employment elsewhere. Sadly, the rather clumsy youths were often involved in accidents. The *Bicester Advertiser* of 2 May 1857 reported the serious accident that had befallen Frederick Stranks 'belonging to Brackley'. Stranks was employed as a porter at Euston Square; he had run to shut the door of a moving train but had collided with another official and fallen under the train. The wheels had passed over his limbs and 'it is feared that his injuries are such as will prove fatal'. James Smith had a lucky escape at Brackley in October 1855. Smith, a carter employed by Mr Edward Taylor, was taking a wagon containing salt from the station. But Smith was seriously injured 'about the back' when he fell against a cartwheel; and 'but for the timely assistance of a boy who was with him he might have received fatal injury'.

Accidents and Court cases arising from them figure prominently in local newspapers in the 1850s, although most seem to have been quite trivial affairs. The *Bicester Advertiser* of 25 October 1856 contains an account of a case brought by Mr W Mansfield against Rev W D Ryland of Hinton-in-the-Hedges. Ryland's dog had attacked a horse and gig driven by the plaintiff. Mansfield submitted a hefty bill for a total of £29 17s; items included £3 11s 6d paid to John Nichols for repairing the gig, £3 7s 6d to Thomas Morton for 'farrying' the horse, £2 10s 6d to Mr Thomas Dawson for 'attendance on the plaintiff', £10 for damage done to the horse by 'deterioration in value', 8s for damage to the harness and £10 for 'loss of time, injuries sustained by the plaintiff and expenses incurred by him in consequence of such injuries'.

Despite the accidents and tragedies, there was a slight recovery in Brackley's economic fortunes in the mid-1850s. In January 1856, a Corn Exchange commenced on the ground floor of the Town Hall, then still open to the elements. All the stands were soon let at an annual rental of 10s 6d each and the *Bicester Advertiser* commented that the amount of business 'augurs well for the prosperity of the undertaking'. A Grand Ball and supper celebrated the opening:

Attendance was numerous and respectable and the eatables and liquors, which were first rate, were supplied by Mr Stutchfield of the Crown Inn. Bell's celebrated Quadrille band from Leamington under the leadership of Mr Bell discoursed excellent music and the dancing was kept up till an early hour of the morning.

Part of the new climate was due to a reduction in Litchfield's influence. In 1846, he lost control over the editorial policy of the *Northampton Herald*; the other proprietors refused to back his out-and-out opposition to the repeal of the Corn Laws.[13] In 1847, he suffered a minor stroke while on holiday in Germany.[14] He recovered but some of the old fire had gone. In 1850 he wrote to the *Mercury* admitting that he might have been too extreme in the past. The *Mercury* condescended to forgive him – 'So manly an avowal of error reflects infinite credit on the heart and does not discredit the hand of the author.'[15]

Colonel William Cartwright experienced no such setbacks. In 1846, he became Deputy Lord Lieutenant of the County and, in 1851, permanent Chairman of the Quarter Sessions. Although he had left the army in 1825, he was still eligible for promotion while on the Half-Pay List. By 1856, he was a general. But Cartwright did experience one tragedy. His son, Aubrey, was killed at the Battle of Inkerman (5 November 1854) in the early stages of the Crimean War.

On 1 August 1856, the Home Secretary appointed Cartwright as the first national Inspector of Constabulary, surely a 'centralist's' dream job. Cartwright inspected the Northamptonshire Constabulary in 1857 and found it 'inefficient', largely because there were not enough policemen. The force was duly enlarged and Cartwright then issued a Certificate of Efficiency. He remained Inspector of Constabulary until 1869 and also became a Governor of the Northampton Hospital to add to his many other responsibilities. Cartwright's interest in the Poor Law and the police led him to encourage Unions to appoint policemen as Assistant Relieving Officers. In his later years, Cartwright showed a more attractive side to his character. He urged better pay and conditions for ordinary constables and helped to found a police orphanage. He was a generous subscriber to the Police Mutual Assurance Society. He suggested the appointment of police surgeons and the creation of a CID. When he died on 5 June 1873, he was widely described as 'the policeman's friend'; it is another matter whether he was also 'the pauper's friend'.[16]

But there was another way to improve lower-class behaviour – through education. This seems more benign than the other approaches. The young could prepare themselves for better jobs and the educational process itself could help them to become rational and law-abiding adults. But was it so benign? To Cartwright – and perhaps to the young themselves – the role of schoolteachers might not appear so different to that of policemen or Workhouse masters. The common element was confinement; paupers should be confined to Workhouses, criminals to prisons and children to schools – where they could be properly supervised and not allowed to wander free, picking up bad habits and generally getting into mischief. Nor does the list of confinements end there. In the early-Victorian ideal, lunatics should be confined to asylums, the sick to hospitals and soldiers to barracks – even married women to the home. No doubt it was well intentioned but, either literally or metaphorically, the essence of the solution was 'lock 'em up'. One way or another, this calculation lay behind much of the 'institutional building' of the Victorian age.

Education was controversial; traditionalists like Litchfield feared it would do more harm than good. Might not education give the poor 'ideas above their station'? Might not literacy expose them to dangerous

---

13   Greenall, 'Parson as a Man of Affairs', p.131.

14   Ibid.

15   *Northampton Mercury*, 23 February 1850.

16   For more biographical information on Colonel Cartwright, see Cooper, Nicholas, *Aynho: A Northamptonshire Village* (Banbury: Leopard's Head Press, 1984) pp.217–28, 244–45, 249.

and subversive political doctrines? If so, then education would weaken rather than strengthen the vital principle of deference. There were even graver doubts about adult education. Those who worked long hours could only learn to read and write at Night Schools. The Methodists were active in this field. In 1867, forty-seven 'evening scholars' were attending classes at the Brackley Chapel School. Litchfield disliked all evening schools, Methodist ones in particular. In 1868 he told Norman that he objected to 'everything that brings people out of their homes at night'.[17] In other words, he was concerned about what adult scholars would get up to under the cover of darkness. One of his more bizarre ideas was to place the lower orders under a strict curfew, making it a criminal offence for them to be found out of doors after dark without specific permission from one of their betters – 'confinement' with a vengeance.

In the twentieth century, schools were to become one of the key elements in Brackley. Grammar School Masters and Winchester House School Masters were to become the real successors of the dominant clergy and gentry of earlier times. In the 1930s, it could be said with justice that 'the business of Brackley is education'.[18] A hundred years earlier, in 1833, an 'Abstract of Education Returns' published by the Northampton National Schools Society, showed that there were already ten schools of various kinds in Brackley. In all there were 488 pupils, although 184 of these were Sunday School pupils.[19]

In 1818, the National, or Anglican, School had opened with William Spatcher as Headmaster. The school had got off to a good start and was still important in 1833, but it declined thereafter. There were only seventy-eight pupils in 1838. Rev Sage hoped that 'the Boys' school would soon be placed on a better footing', but the decline continued. By 1840, the school roll had fallen to fifty and it closed shortly afterwards. William Spatcher had been Headmaster throughout.[20] *Whellan's Directory* of 1849 describes him as a 'Sheriff's Officer' (bailiff) and his wife Sarah as a milliner and dressmaker.

The decline of the National School is surprising, especially when we remember that the population was rising. There should have been more rather than fewer pupils. It may be that Sage was partly to blame. He never seems to have been particularly energetic and he may well have shared Litchfield's doubts about the wisdom of educating the lower orders.

Although the National School closed, the Anglican Sunday School continued and there was also an Anglican Infants School in a 'neat stone building in the centre of the Town … erected in 1840 at the cost of about £400 by the Earl and Countess of Ellesmere'.[21] Some older children probably attended this school, which was supported by subscription and the interest on a legacy of £200 from Mr Thomas Arnold. The Infants School was in the Market Square, next to Clarke's, the ironmongers. The building, later absorbed into Clarke's premises, had high 'label mould' windows and leaded windows; it remained a distinctive feature of the centre of Brackley until the early 1960s.

Despite the Sunday School and the Infants School, however, the loss of the National School had seriously reduced educational provision, especially for the lower classes. By 1860, there were significantly fewer

17   'First Report of the Royal Commission on the Employment of Children, Young Persons and Women in Agriculture', Parliamentary Papers, 1867–88, p.xvii. Report of Mr F.H. Norman, p.xxvi.

18   By Mr Hayman, Headmaster of Winchester House School.

19   Turner, JD, *The Education of the Poor in Brackley during the Nineteenth Century – The Church of England's Part*. Brackley and District History Society, Occasional Paper, n.d. p.5.

20   Ibid, p.3.

21   Pevsner, N, *The Buildings of England: Northamptonshire* (Harmondsworth: Penguin Books, 2nd edition, 1973) p.118.

school places available for poor children than there had been in the 1820s, even though the population had increased by nearly 30 per cent.

While it is tempting to blame Sage, other factors may have been at work. Some attributed the closure of the National School to disillusionment with the 'monitorial system'. But, as so often, the poor themselves were identified as the main culprits. A Report to the Northamptonshire School Society in 1838 noted that child workers could be almost as productive as adults were, yet their wages were much lower. Thus, masters had every incentive to employ children; and so long as children were allowed to work, parents were either unable or unwilling to do without their wages, however good the schooling available. The Report contemplated drastic solutions:

> Either the liberty of the subject must be interfered with by the introduction of a compulsory system as in Prussia, or something much more substantial than theory must be provided, by the creation of an enormous Fund that shall at once provide Education for the Child and remunerate the Parents for the loss of its labour.[22]

But these measures were not adopted. Between 1860 and 1867, scarcely half of the recruits to the Northamptonshire Militia could sign their own names. Norman's 1868 Report confirms the impression that things were as bad or worse than in the 1830s. Parental attitudes and priorities remained unchanged. No doubt, when asked whether they valued education, virtually all labourers would say that they did – but that meant little. Even when children were sent to school, attendance was poor – 'they come for a fortnight and stay away for a month on frivolous excuses'. Children also left school far too young – 'before they can possibly have acquired a sufficient education'.[23]

But the alleged indifference of the lower classes to education did not prevent the Methodists making a determined attempt in this field, much to the chagrin of Litchfield and Sage. As we noted earlier, the 1904 article in the *Methodist Recorder* was to claim that in the middle years of the nineteenth century, but for the Methodists, 'there would have been neither education or piety in the town'. Their Sunday School – originally held in the Chapel – began about 1830. Detailed rules were printed in 1834:

> The scholars shall attend with their hands and faces washed and their hair combed.

> They shall not go out without leave of the teacher, and not a word to be spoken but to the teacher, and no lessons to be learnt aloud.

> If any scholar be found guilty of lying, swearing, quarrelling, pilfering, buying anything on the Lord's Day, or otherwise misbehaving, it shall be reported to the Superintendent, who shall admonish, reprove, or expel, as the case may require.

> Any scholar being absent three successive Sundays without sufficient cause shall be dismissed.

22 Annual Report of the Northamptonshire Society, 1838, National Society Archives, Church House, Westminster.

23 Norman, *First Report*, 1867–68, p.xl.

Every scholar must make a bow or courtesy [curtsy] on coming into or going out of school and behave decently.[24]

Taking advantage of the closure of the National School, the Methodists erected a small Sunday School alongside their Chapel in 1840. This building was enlarged in 1860. On 8 February 1864, the Methodists opened a Day School; to begin with there were nineteen girls and thirty-one boys but, by April, numbers had increased to ninety. The Master was John Browton assisted by Mrs Clark as Sewing Mistress. Browton was a strict disciplinarian. He had problems with dirty and unkempt pupils, especially with 'rough fighting boys who used abusive language and even brought knives to school'. Browton found that the children entering the school were 'quite ignorant although their ages are considerably above the average according to the Standards in which they are obliged to pass'. Home influence worked against education; when the children left school in the afternoon, they were left to run the streets and few parents even bothered to ask their children what they had been doing in the day.[25]

On 2 December 1867, the Methodist School was visited by Matthew Arnold, the most famous of the Victorian School Inspectors. Matthew Arnold was the son of Dr Arnold of Rugby and himself an important scholar and poet. But Matthew Arnold was not impressed either by Brackley or by the Methodist School. The people were poor and apathetic about education:

Still, if it is worthwhile to have a Day School here, it should be a better one than this. The failure in the examination is decidedly high; 30½ per cent of the examinees fail. The report last year was unfavourable. The discipline was fair. The School Room floor greatly needs repair. The Night School had done fairly. Looking to the warning given last year & to this Report, My Lords have ordered the Grant to be reduced by one fourth under Article 52a.[26]

Browton suspected that the inspectors were biased against Chapel Schools and, in 1871, noted that they had gone out of their way to criticise Methodist Schools at both Brackley and Silverstone – where the Master was the formidable John Denny.[27] Clearly not everything was right, but at least the Methodists were trying.

The tendency to decline, visible in the closure of the National School, extended to the education of the better off. In 1833, St James's Parish contained two day schools, with twenty-eight children of both sexes, one day and boarding school with twenty-seven female students and one boarding school for boys with ninety-nine pupils. In all of these, instruction was at the expense of the parents. In St Peter's Parish, Magdalen College School had ten scholarship boys and twenty-five fee-paying male pupils. There were also three private establishments but we are told nothing about the fees charged at these schools. Some were probably 'dame schools', little more than childminding facilities, where fees would have been no more than a few pence per week.[28]

24   *Methodist Recorder*, 4 February 1904.

25   NRO, Diary of Brackley Wesleyan Day School, p.30.

26   Ibid, p.96.

27   Howarth, J, 'The Liberal Revival in Northamptonshire, 1880–95', *The Historical Journal*, Vol. XII, No. 1, 1969, p.91.

28   Turner, *The Education of the Poor*, p.6.

Yet at least one of the private schools – the one with ninety-nine male boarders – was a place of greater standing. This was Brackley House Academy; in the twentieth century its buildings were to be used as the offices of the Brackley Rural District Council. Appropriately, the Academy was directly opposite its main rival, Magdalen College School. The proprietor and Headmaster of the Academy was a Mr Lee and most of his pupils were drawn from farmers' families. Some lived quite a long way from Brackley. In an elaborate advertisement, Lee announced, 'Young Gentlemen are Boarded, Kindly Treated and Carefully instructed in the English, French, Latin and Greek Languages, Writing, Arithmetic, Book-keeping, Geometry, Mensuration, Practical Surveying, Algebra, History and Geography'. Parents wishing to provide their sons with 'most of the departments of useful and polite literature, without incurring the usual extra Charges', would find the Academy 'peculiarly eligible', 'Washing and Books being the only extras'. Fees were 23 guineas per annum, but did not include 'Dancing, Drawing or Music'.[29]

Some letters from pupils to their parents have survived.[30] The tone of letters from the Matthews boys of Sanpit Farm, Stow-on-the-Wold, Gloucestershire, is extremely formal. They are so full of praise for Mr Lee and his school that we are bound to wonder if they were really composed by the boys. On 7 December 1830, John Matthews wrote to his parents:

> After having been deprived of your society for some time, which you will readily perceive has been devoted to the acquisition of those branches of learning considered requisite to my future designation in life, it is very natural for me to be anticipating the day of my return home, which I am requested to say is fixed for Friday, 17th Instant.

John wrote again on 6 June 1831, 'The half year is drawing towards its close; hence, the time is approaching when I shall consider myself accountable for the opportunity you have so kindly afforded me, for acquiring a liberal education'. John's brother, William, wrote on 5 June 1832:

> I am this morning deputed to present Mr and Mrs Lee's compliments, and to say that the day fixed for our breaking up is Friday the fifteenth instant; to which period, I can assure you, I look forward with delight: for although I meet here with cheerful and good society among my Schoolfellows, yet I cannot but say there is something delightful even in the thoughts of home.

A third brother, B Matthews, wrote on 2 June 1834, 'I am endeavouring to write this letter in such a manner as to produce a specimen of my writing, with which I hope you will be pleased, and that on examination, you will consider as generally improved'. The youngest of the Matthews boys was clearly regarded as a promising pupil and Lee deplored his father's decision to remove him. Lee wrote to Mr Matthews on 14 August 1835:

> I cannot but regret his absence, not from a selfish motive, but on his account. A Boy like himself is not to be found every day & perhaps we could have done more for him than you are aware of; his improvement since under my roof, it must be acknowledged, has been very great.

---

29   Advertisement in the author's possession.

30   Letters in the author's possession.

Although flourishing in the 1830s, the Academy closed in the 1860s when the lease expired. The educational 'gap' created by the closure of Lee's school should have given Magdalen College School a great opportunity. It was the obvious 'middle-class' school for the Brackley area and its endowed free places should have provided an important vehicle of social mobility for able boys from ordinary backgrounds. But there were few signs of life. Eric Forrester's classic *A History of Magdalen College School (Brackley)* speaks of a 'slump' between the death of Thomas Banister in 1821 and the reorganisation of 1860.[31] Banister's successor was a Mr Walker, about whom little is known.

In 1827, Thomas Hawkins Jr replaced Walker. Hawkins supplemented his salary by working as a land surveyor and may have neglected his teaching. Forrester notes that, in Hawkins's time the school was often described as 'Magdalen College Free School'. He believes that the omission of 'Grammar School' is significant and implies that Classics were no longer taught.[32] Academic standards seem to have been low. President Bulley of Magdalen College Oxford later recalled that in Hawkins's day, 'the School contained a few poor boys, superintended by an ignorant master'.[33]

In February 1856, Magdalen College decided to sack Hawkins, but he died before his notice expired. The school was then closed and remained shut for several years. This provoked increasing discontent among the normally quiescent middle classes. The discontent was led by Robert Weston Jr, son of Robert Weston, who had been Clerk to the Guardians at the time of the Workhouse Scandal, and who had now succeeded to his father's posts.

Robert Weston Jr may have been deferential to the Cartwrights but he showed a different side to his character in his dealings with Magdalen College. On 18 March 1856, Weston wrote to inform the President of Magdalen that the people of Brackley thought that the Mastership should be filled by 'a person of more Education and higher Attainments than hitherto it has been'. The ideal Master would be a clergyman who 'could also do duty in the College Chapel and together form a more respectable foundation for the benefit of the Town'.[34] Bulley replied that the whole matter had been referred to a College Committee.

At first, the signs were encouraging. In July 1856, Magdalen College resolved that the Brackley School should be 'made a middle-class school of the first order'.[35] The new Master was to have a salary of £100 per annum, exhibitions to the value of £50 were to be established and an architect was to be sent to report on the fabric. Nothing happened.

By the beginning of 1858, Weston was becoming angry. On 6 February, he wrote to Bulley, threatening to call 'a General Meeting of the Inhabitants of the Town to take the matter into their consideration'. He still hoped for an amicable solution but warned that, unless Magdalen acted soon, he would take the college to Court.[36] Bulley did not care for Weston's tone. He replied that the college had more than fulfilled its obligations by promising £500 towards the restoration of the Chapel and £600 for repairs to the school

---

31 Forrester, EG, *A History of Magdalen College School, Brackley, Northamptonshire, 1548–1949* (Buckingham: E.N. Hillier & Sons Ltd, 1950), Chapter Four, 'Slump and the "Reorganisation" of 1860 (*c.* 1821–64)', pp.45–72.

32 Ibid., p.45.

33 Ibid., p.54.

34 Ibid., p.50.

35 Ibid., p.54.

36 Ibid., p.51.

buildings. Bulley claimed that the real blame for the prolonged closure lay with local landowners who had failed to respond to Magdalen's stipulation that they should make an equivalent contribution. Even if successful, 'coercive measures' would produce less than the college had promised of its own free will. For good measure, Bulley suggested that, rather than stirring up hostility against Magdalen College, Weston would make better use of his time if he used his influence as a land agent to secure the co-operation of the local gentry.[37]

Although Magdalen had indeed been dilatory, Bulley had a point. Things were certainly not made any easier by the fact that even those landowners who were prepared to contribute were divided among themselves. Some, like Earl Spencer, saw the reopening of the school as the most urgent priority while others, such as the Earl of Ellesmere, wanted to concentrate on the restoration of the Chapel.

In June 1858, Weston issued a pamphlet exposing what he considered to be the college's empty promises. He then carried out his threat to hold a public meeting. According to the *Brackley Miscellany and Advertiser*, the meeting, held on 11 June, decided to give priority to the reopening of the school. But another meeting, held on 20 July, became bogged down over the future of the Chapel. A motion, proposed by Mr Stratton of Turweston, and seconded by Rev Sage, urged Magdalen College to 'allow the Chapel to be made a Chapel of Ease to the Parish of St Peter, reserving themselves the right of sittings for the Grammar School on Sundays, and of using the Chapel for the weekly services of the same'. But Stratton's motion was opposed by Lord Henley, who proposed that:

> … the College Chapel be not made a Chapel of Ease, but continue as a Private Chapel under Magdalen College, Oxford, who shall be respectfully requested to nominate a Chaplain to perform Sunday Duty or duties therein, subject to the approval of the Vicar and the concurrence of the Vicar.

The meeting was equally divided between the two motions.[38] No doubt, the question of the status of the Chapel needed to be resolved but, while the landowners bickered about the difference between 'Chapels of Ease' and 'Private Chapels', two of Brackley's most important assets were rotting away.

Eventually, Magdalen decided to keep the Chapel, providing most of the money needed for repairs. It also undertook work at the school, which finally reopened in January 1860, at a total cost of £1,261 17s 11d. The new Master was the Rev FB Falkner of St John's College, Cambridge. Falkner proved energetic; Latin was reinstated and a high standard was achieved in mathematics. A number of able boys were recruited, some of whom went on to university. Falkner's most significant recruit was Isaac Wodhams, the son of a local blacksmith, who later became Master himself and a major figure in late-Victorian Brackley.

Even so, Falkner still had to struggle against 'class feeling', 'grossly ignorant boys, 'vicious boys' and 'irregularity of attendance'.[39] In 1864, Falkner resigned to become Headmaster of the Grammar School at Ashby Magna, Leicestershire. Although the school stayed open, there was a long delay before a successor was appointed. During the interregnum, discipline declined and, according to Wodhams's later account, 'the boys were in the habit of playing in the streets'. When the new Master, Rev Thomas Russell arrived,

37   Ibid.

38   Ibid., p.52.

39   Ibid., p.62.

he found it hard to pull things together. Numbers stagnated and Forrester describes the period between 1864 and 1882 as one of 'partial relapse'. In view of the school's later pre-eminence in history, it is striking that an Examiners' Report describes the quality of history teaching as 'meagre and unsatisfactory'.[40]

Perhaps the best comment on the state of Brackley in the 1860s is to be found in a report, dated 1865, almost at the end of our early-Victorian period. The author is Rev Hugh William Smith. Smith was Sage's Curate, Vicar of Biddlesden, Chaplain to the Workhouse and Master of the Brackley Academy in succession to Lee.[41] In Sage's declining years, Smith was probably the most active figure in the Church. He certainly possessed greater social awareness than the elderly Vicar and had sufficient ability to describe and analyse Brackley's problems. Unfortunately, he lacked the vision to see any way forward.

Smith believed that the main reason for Brackley's rapid expansion in the first half of the century and the source of many of its ills had been the arrival of immigrants from the surrounding villages. In effect they had come to Brackley as 'refugees', having been driven from their places of birth by the squires' determination to create 'closed parishes'.

Like other refugees, their living conditions were poor. Smith speaks of a town of insanitary, jerry-built cottages, thrown up to accommodate the new arrivals. Many of the new inhabitants could not find regular work and relations between them and Brackley's more long-standing residents were tense. The newcomers were seen as the dregs of society, 'the feeble, the diseased, the idle, the dissolute and the profligate'. Their very presence was seen as a threat to public health and resulted in an intolerable burden on the Poor Rates. In turn, the immigrants resented their hostile reception, 'They feel themselves mere parvenus, outcasts on the face of the land, with no social sympathies, regards or affections for those around them'.

The construction of the railway at Helmdon and the cleansing of some ponds at Evenley had recently offered temporary alleviation of the problem of unemployment, but no more than that. Levels of unemployment appeared to fluctuate in an entirely unpredictable fashion; changes in the state of the weather offered the only possible explanation. In the surrounding 'closed parishes', the favoured few who remained formed the core of the workforce who were kept in employment even when the weather was bad. In good weather masters recruited more labourers from the pool of unemployed in Brackley, but dismissed them as soon as the weather got worse.

Smith's attitude to charity was a good deal more generous than that of his fellow clergyman, Thomas Mozley. His report includes a 'Copy of a Table of Benefactions in St Peter's Church in Brackley'. In all, Smith identified fourteen benefactions. Smith believed that the real problem was that the income from these benefactions was not directed to those who were in the greatest need. In many instances, it was reserved to those who had been born and bred in Brackley; the really poor newcomers were excluded from benefit. This was the case with the Feoffee Charity, the richest and most important. Insofar as Smith had any solution to the problem of poverty in the town, it was merely that new arrivals should no longer be discriminated against. While such a change might have helped individual families, it is hard to imagine that it would have gone very far to solve what was obviously a very serious problem.

Smith himself seems to have been connected with the establishment of a number of new charities. He was particularly proud of the Clothing Society, 'open to *all* inhabitants'. The new charities also contained an element of self-help. Members were encouraged to save a little week by week. Then, with interest, the help

40   Forrester, p.72.

41   Smith's report is printed in Turner, *Education of the Poor*, pp.12–16. Original in NRO, Brackley Parish Papers, 42, P/259.

of discounts for bulk purchases and some donations from the better off, they would receive goods worth more than their original contributions. Thus, in 1864, the members of the Clothing Society had subscribed £220 but received clothes to the value of £290. Other charities such as the Blanket Society and the Ladies Confinement Society did valuable work. Soup kitchen charities had generally been unsuccessful.

Smith's report is addressed to Sage. Although the tone is polite, there are hints of criticism. There is no suggestion that Sage had helped to found any charitable societies himself. The best that could be said was that the Blanket Charity had been established with his 'concurrence'. On his own there was not much that Smith could do. He was not Vicar and he was not rich. According to *Crockford's Clerical Dictionary*, the living of Biddlesden was worth £75 per annum.[42] The Workhouse Chaplaincy produced an additional £60. Smith may have made a little from his school but Sage was not the man to pay his curates generously. It would hardly have added up to a fortune.

Smith's report makes depressing reading. All in all, it is hard to escape the conclusion that the Church was more unpopular in Brackley than at any time since the 1630s. There were even signs of middle-class discontent. In the 1630s the next step had been revolution. Would the same happen again?

Of course, England as whole in the mid-1860s was a very different place to the England of 1642. However much the Methodists may have alarmed Mozley, they were really much more docile than the old Puritans. Jabez Bunting, John Wesley's successor as leader of the movement, is alleged to have told Methodists that they should hate democracy as they hated sin. Yet we should remember that there were probably more avowed republicans in the middle of Queen Victoria's reign than there are now. One Brackley man, at least, contemplated drastic changes and came close to concluding that the only way to achieve them was through violence.

---

42   *Crockford's Clerical Dictionary 1885*, p.1102. St John's College, Cambridge, BA 1835; MA 1838; Deacon 1838; Priest 1839 by
      Bishop of Lincoln; Vicar of Biddlesden, Diocese of Oxford, 1854; Patron G. Morgan Esq.

At *Brackley House Academy*

NORTHAMPTONSHIRE,

Conducted by

W Lee

Young Gentlemen

ARE BOARDED, KINDLY TREATED & CAREFULLY INSTRUCTED

In the English, French, Latin, & Greek Languages, Writing, Arithmetic, Book-keeping, Geometry, Mensuration, Practical Surveying, Algebra, History, & Geography.

Terms,

TWENTY THREE GUINEAS PER ANNUM. NO ENTRANCE REQUIRED.

Parents desirous of embracing most departments of useful & polite Literature for their Children, without incurring the usual extra Charges, would find this School peculiarly eligible, Washing and Books being the only extras.

Dancing, Drawing, & Music on the customary Terms.

A Quarters Notice is expected previous to the Removal of a Pupil.

RESPECTABLE REFERENCES.

A Coach from London passes the door every other day.

Brackley House Academy.

Brackley House Academy (later). (NRO)

Brackley Dame School. (NRO)

Mrs Baysley, Brackley lacemaker. (NRO)

A Constable in Northamptonshire Police Force.

Brackley Bottom Station, LNWR. (NRO)

WESTBURY,

Midway between Buckingham and Brackley.

32 Acres of Capital

GRASS

KEEPING,

Till Michaelmas Next,

On the farm of Mr. John Pipkin, at Westbury, who is leaving,

TO BE SOLD BY AUCTION, BY MESSRS.

JONAS & THOS. PAXTON

At the Reindeer Inn, Westbury,

On MONDAY, the 2nd day of MAY, 1859, at Four o'clock.

CATALOGUE.

		A	R	P
Lot 1.	The Bite of the Water Meadow and Close, till Michaelmas next, at per acre	10	0	0
Lot 2.	Ditto of the two Cherry Tree Meadows, till ditto	7	0	0
Lot 3.	Ditto of Great Close, till ditto	8	2	0
Lot 4.	Ditto of Little Banhill, till ditto	7	0	0
		32	2	0

The above Keeping is on good sound land, and may be viewed on application to Mr. Pipkin. Credit will be allowed on the customary conditions.

E. Smith and Son, Printers and Booksellers, Bicester.

Westbury grass-keeping.

Chapter Five

AWAKE

After long years of troubled slumber, Brackley finally 'woke up' in 1866. The man responsible was Thomas Judge.[1] If 1848 was the 'Year of Revolutions' in Continental Europe, the nearest Brackley came to a 'Year of Revolution' was in 1866–67. For some, especially for Judge, it was a time of great excitement; for others, the experience of Brackley 'awake' must have been even more terrible than Brackley in the grip of its protracted nightmare. The situation was tailormade for an agitator. The 'Cartwright programme' of 'strict discipline and no charity', running now for the best part of half a century, had failed. There were divisions and resentments at all levels. The upper classes were divided over the principles and details of educational policy. The small middle class was becoming resentful towards the two traditionally dominant elements – Magdalen College, Oxford, and the Egerton family. Its members deplored Magdalen's apparent reluctance to honour its obligations and promises, especially at a time when the ending of 'Beneficial Leases' was bringing rising rent rolls to the college. They also contrasted the enormous wealth of the Bridgewater Trustees with the Egertons' continued absence and indifference.

The lower orders, faced with acute problems of seasonal unemployment, were divided between the townspeople and 'comers-in'. The Church, in the person of Rev Sage, seemed more interested in defending its own privileges and financial interests than in serving the spiritual or physical welfare of the people of Brackley. The Church was probably more unpopular than at any time since the days of Sybthorpe in the 1630s. The Methodists and Congregationalists were making most of the running. From an Anglican perspective, the demolition of St James's Church (1836) had come at a particularly unfortunate time; the arrival of the railway, only fourteen years later, 'skewed' the development of Brackley towards the Bottom End, far away from St Peter's Church. The Congregationalists in the Banbury Road and the Methodists in Hill Street were far better placed.

There were three causes, all Radical ones, which woke Brackley from its sleep. Judge had a hand in all. They were the abolition of Church Rates, Parliamentary Reform and Trade Unionism. In 1866 Judge was only 24 years old but he was already emerging as a formidable character. From the mid-1860s

---

1   For more about Judge, see Phillips, P, *Thomas Judge: The Demon Grocer of Brackley* (Buckingham: Phillips Print, 2000).

until his death in 1910, he was probably the most effective local opponent the Brackley Establishment has ever encountered.

He came from a family of fairly prosperous butchers and grocers, with sufficient money to send the boy away to a private school at Weston, near Bath.[2] Yet the Judges had a grievance; their claim to a piece of land in the Open Fields of Brackley had been rejected at the time of Enclosure.[3] Perhaps this grievance lay behind Thomas Judge's lifelong Radicalism. Judge was already making his mark in the early 1860s, speaking at anniversary celebrations at both the Methodist and Congregational Chapels. In 1865, he became Vice President of the Brackley Temperance Society, a cause closely linked with Nonconformity.

The issue that first brought Judge into prominence was that of Church Rates. Sage had tried to raise money for the restoration of St Peter's in the 1840s, though the scheme was modest. There were some who liked Sage, notably the Parish Clerk, Nathaniel Blencowe, who was to die within a few days of his Master. Nathaniel's death in 1867 brought to an end an extraordinary period of 111 years during which the Parish Clerkship was held by successive generations of the same family: Nathaniel Blencowe 1756–91, John Blencowe 1791–1835 and Nathaniel Blencowe 1835–67. But hereditary offices and the kind of Vicar who approved of them were becoming anachronistic.

At Vestry Meetings, Sage still demanded the raising of Church Rates, a tax payable by all ratepayers – whether Churchgoers or not – to maintain the fabric of St Peter's and to keep the graveyard in good order. Not surprisingly, Nonconformists objected to Church Rates and, as they were entitled to attend Vestry Meetings, they could make trouble.

Judge and his supporters made their first attempt to stop the Church Rates being levied at the Vestry Meeting of 1864, but they were unsuccessful. Two years later, however, they achieved a major breakthrough; at the Vestry of 1866, they secured a majority for the motion that 'Consideration of the Churchwardens' Accounts be adjourned to this day twelve months'.[4] Thus, it appeared that no Church Rates would be collected in Brackley that year.

It might have been better if the Church authorities had accepted defeat. Church Rates had long since ceased to be raised in Banbury and many believed – correctly, as it turned out – that Parliament would soon intervene to abolish the tax. But the Churchwardens ignored the Vestry's decision and attempted to raise a rate regardless. Judge refused to pay his assessment of 2s 2d. He could well afford to pay; it was the principle he objected to. The Churchwardens duly issued a summons – Judge was required to appear in Court at Middleton Cheney. According to the *Bicester Herald*:

The defendant, not a particularly cool customer, was enraged at this course, and at once determined to give the greatest publicity to the proceedings, so posted outside his door the following sensational placard: – 'Fast to-day, rob tomorrow, robbery or no robbery, church-rate or no church-rate. To be tried at Middleton on Monday. Why not face it at Brackley?'[5]

---

2   Phillips, *Thomas Judge*, p.12.

3   Lowerson, J.R., 'Enclosure and Farm Holding in Brackley, 1829–1851', *Northamptonshire Past and Present*, Vol. VI, No. 1 (1978) p.40.

4   *Banbury Guardian*, 6 April 1866.

5   *Bicester Herald*, 6 April 1866.

Judge was hinting that the case was to be heard at Middleton, rather than Brackley, because the authorities were frightened of angry scenes, perhaps even violence. By the time of the hearing, Judge had secured the services of a competent London lawyer, Mr Bennet of Sergeant's Inn, a leading light in the Liberation Society. In Court, Bennet argued that the Churchwardens had acted illegally in trying to levy a Church Rate in defiance of the Vestry. Hence, Judge had been entirely justified when he refused to pay. The Chairman of the Bench, the redoubtable Litchfield, disliked Judge and everything he stood for. Perhaps Litchfield had 'mellowed' a little since his 'furious' days in the 1830s, but these things are relative. He had recently delivered a sermon in which he described the typical Dissenter as 'a weak-minded person incapable of reading and comprehending the scriptures'.

No doubt, Litchfield would have liked to uphold Church Rates in Brackley and to punish and humiliate Judge. But Judge was right in law and so it was Litchfield who was humiliated. He had no option but to agree with Bennet and to find for Judge. His only comfort was to refuse to award costs to the defendant. News of the outcome of the case soon reached Brackley. Judge put up a poster outside his shop bearing the legend:

> Won in a canter!!! No more church-rates at Brackley. T. Judge beat the church-wardens today. Of course those who have paid the rate will have their money returned. Else let them go to law and get it. What says the Law now?[6]

Judge's optimism was a little premature, but at least the Churchwardens resigned. It had been a notable victory.

Tensions in Brackley reflected trends in the country as a whole. The issue of Electoral Reform, dormant for many years, was back on the agenda. In May 1866 a new Reform Bill, introduced by Russell's Liberal Government was defeated by an alliance of Tories and right-wing Liberals. The government's defeat coincided almost exactly with Judge's victory in Court. Russell resigned and, in June, a Tory minority government headed by Lord Derby took office.

The Liberal measure had not been far reaching and Tories – who announced that they did not even intend to hold a session of Parliament until February of the following year – were expected to be even less sympathetic. Pro-Reform sentiment exploded and the government attempted to ban a meeting in Hyde Park called by the Reform League. Despite the ban, the meeting went ahead and considerable damage was done to the railings.

Thomas Judge was determined that Brackley, once so sleepy, should play its part in articulating the demand for Reform 'out of doors'. In Brackley's case it was to be literally out of doors. Judge was the moving spirit behind a 'Reform Demonstration' held in the Market Square outside the Town Hall on Monday, 17 December 1866.

Judge's ideas on Reform went far beyond those of the Liberal leadership. He was becoming interested in the plight of the poorly paid agricultural workers and was convinced that this downtrodden section of society needed to secure the vote if it was to obtain a living wage.

Even at the distance of almost 150 years, the Reform Demonstration seems extraordinary – somewhere between 2,000 and 3,000 people gathering in the middle of Brackley on a cold winter's night just before Christmas to hear no less than ten speeches in favour of a Radical cause! Every effort was made to create a theatrical effect. There were bands, and 'upwards of 100 torch lights and Chinese lanterns'. Then the crowd converged on a wagon in front of the Town Hall. According to the *Banbury Advertiser* of

---

6   *Bicester Herald*, 6 April 1866.

20 December, the wagon had been brought from several miles away – 'for it was said that none of the townsmen durst lend such a vehicle'.

The torches were extinguished and Judge, who acted as Chairman, began to speak. He declared that the size of the crowd proved that 'the people of Brackley and its neighbourhood were not content with the existing state of things, nor were they satisfied with ten shillings on a Saturday night for a whole week's labour – (cheers)'. He went on to endorse John Stuart Mill's description of the Tory Party as the 'stupid party' and to deride claims that the working man would do anything for a pint of beer:

> They must have an alteration, and an alteration they would have – an alteration that would give every man a vote who was twenty-one years of age, of sound mind, untainted with crime, and resident in any fixed district – an alteration which would give every voter the protection of the Ballot – (cheers) and then they would no longer have starvation with ten shillings a week in a land of plenty; for if every man had a vote he could then take care of himself, as they who now have the suffrage are able to protect their own interests.[7]

Other local Radicals, including Mr Bunton of Banbury and Mr Biss and Mr Small of Buckingham, took the same line. There were longer speeches from Mr Langley and from Mr George Mantell. Langley appreciated the symbolism of the torchlight procession. He confessed that he had never seen anything like it and asserted that whereas he had previously found Brackley 'fast asleep' it had now 'woken up'. The torches had surely 'thrown a flood of light' on politics of a town recently 'shrouded in mental political darkness'. Mantell, who had come in place of the arch-Radical Charles Bradlaugh, spoke on behalf of the Reform League. Like Langley, Mantell had been to Brackley before and provided interesting anecdotal evidence about the conduct of recent elections. Tories who objected to the extension of the franchise claimed that, if working men were given the vote, they would simply sell their suffrage to the highest bidder:

> But what do they now? They buy them, and sell them and coerce and intimidate them, and the working man would stand no such nonsense. How often had they stood in that very square and seen the mockery of an election, when men were brought to tender their votes upon compulsion, when they were as deaf as posts and dumb as tom-tits. He defied them to make it any worse than that. (hear, hear).

Mantell proceeded to attack the 'State Church', 'which is not the Church of the people', to denounce the game laws – both important issues in Brackley. He then went on to describe landownership itself as 'unparalleled robbery' and Parliament as 'a gigantic trades union of the owners of land and aristocracy of wealth who have got all the loaves and fishes on their own table, and yet grudge to the working class the veriest crumble'. Mantell was in full flight when the reporter from the *Banbury Advertiser* realised that he would miss the last train if he stayed any longer:

> Here the hour of nine pealed forth from the clock of the town hall, warning the reporter that the inexorable laws of the London and North Western required him to make the best way he could to the station, where the ringing cheers of the multitude were plainly audible.[8]

7   *Banbury Advertiser*, 20 December 1866.

8   Ibid.

He noted, however, that there were speeches from Messrs Thomas, Wrighton and Langton still to come.

Other local newspapers gave the event less extensive coverage. Correspondents writing to the *Bicester Herald* found the very idea of farm labourers voting so outrageous as to be positively comic; one commented that while the Reform Meeting had 'provided very little instruction', 'that sad deficiency was, in the view of some, amply compensated by the great amusement which it afforded'. But Judge was delighted with Reform Meeting and supplied the *Banbury Advertiser* with a copy of a letter of congratulation from John Bright:

> The greatest sufferer from class government in this country is the Agricultural labourer, and he will have no change so long as the Legislature is controlled by a class. I suppose that the towns will ultimately deliver him, but in some districts he may perhaps do something for himself, and may help on the movement which is intended to emancipate him.[9]

The tone of Bright's letter is a trifle condescending. Very much the urban Radical himself, Bright does not expect much from the countryside. The agricultural labourer is assigned only a minor role in his own liberation and even that is doubtful: 'he may perhaps do something for himself'. In the last resort, he would owe everything to the urban Radicals because 'the towns will ultimately deliver him'. Perhaps the urban Radicals and the Tory parsons and squires thought much the same about farm labourers. But Judge saw no slight and did everything to publicise Bright's letter. Much was made of it at another torchlight demonstration, this time held at Buckingham, on 31 January 1867.

The events of the winter of 1866–67 point to significant differences between Banbury, Brackley and Buckingham. The Radicals already controlled Banbury and were strongly committed to Reform. Brackley was still dominated by a conservative, not to say reactionary, clerical and landowning Establishment – hence the problem with the wagon. Buckingham's economy was more highly developed than Brackley's but less so than Banbury's. Its political position was also somewhere between the two. Some members of the Buckingham elite were sympathetic to Reform, although they did not go so far as their counterparts in Banbury. In Buckingham it was not necessary to hold the meeting out of doors; the Mayor had made the Town Hall available. The local MP, Sir Harry Verney, loaned flags and banners and, although not present in person, sent a cautiously sympathetic message.

Accounts of the Brackley Reform Meeting stress that, in general, 'order and propriety prevailed', but there was a less respectable side story. After the meeting ended, many of those who had attended went on to the public houses and quite a few got drunk. A favourite destination was The Locomotive at the bottom of Bridge Street. Here there were several fights, although they do not seem to have been connected with politics.

One involved John Anstee of Astwick and John Bull of Charlton who quarrelled over a girl, Betsy Grove, a pillow lace maker of Cross Lane, Brackley. There was another fight inside The Locomotive involving William Hawkins and William Crow. The cause is not clear; perhaps they were just drunk. The public house was crowded and there were about 200 people outside. The landlord, Stephen Hawkins said he would not allow the sale of any more beer, but many just helped themselves. It took Inspector Botterill and PC Barwell till the early hours of the morning to restore order.

The fact that the Reform Meeting had been followed by disturbances was a gift to Judge's enemies. It gave them the chance to highlight the links between Radical politics and violent behaviour. Above

9   Ibid.

71

all, Litchfield saw an opportunity to avenge his humiliation in the Church Rates case. When Litchfield took his place as Chairman of the Petty Sessions held at Middleton Cheney on 31 December 1866, the defendants must have known that he was unlikely to be merciful or understanding. A heavy fine was imposed on Stephen Hawkins, landlord of The Locomotive, for keeping a disorderly house – even though Hawkins had actually tried to stop the drinking.

But it was the political question that interested Litchfield. He argued that those who sought the vote hardly strengthened their case by getting drunk, 'The best way of convincing the world that they are deserving of a vote for a member of Parliament is to show by their conduct that they are worthy of it'. The implication was that men who got drunk and involved in fights were *not* worthy of the vote. Litchfield conveniently ignored the fact that most of those who had attended the demonstration had returned home quietly. Indeed, only a minority of those who went to public houses had actually had too much to drink. Several of the defendants claimed that they had stayed out unusually late just to listen to the band playing its way out of town. Litchfield seized his opportunity when he learnt that it was one of the bands at the Reform Demonstration. According to the *Banbury Advertiser*:

> Mr Litchfield added that he believed there was a heavy responsibility attaching to those who brought bands of music into a town and held political meetings at night; for while the police were engaged in quelling disturbances at one end of the town, thieves might be committing a robbery in the other. The defendants must be punished partly for their folly in going to such a meeting at all, but chiefly for not returning home as soon as it was over.[10]

For Litchfield, the events following the Reform Demonstration proved what he had long believed: it was folly to allow the lower orders out after dark. His remarks suggest that he did not care whether the accused had been drunk or involved in fights. If the newspaper account is accurate, he wanted to punish the defendants because they had attended a political meeting and then stayed out late. Here, he was on dangerous ground. He was trying to punish people for offences completely unknown to English law. Even Litchfield should have known that magistrates cannot simply 'invent' the law to suit their own prejudices.

Outraged Radicals seized on Litchfield's speech. The *Bicester Herald* of 25 January 1867 contained a letter from a correspondent who signed himself 'Rusticus' – ironically the same nom de plume that Litchfield himself had used in his letters to the *Northampton Mercury* over forty years earlier. The writer was appalled by what he described as Litchfield's 'inexcusable exhibition' which had revealed his 'unfitness for office', as well as 'political bias, illiberality and a want of magisterial decency'. He had jeered at the defendants as examples of 'those who would reform the nation' and punished them for attending a political meeting:

> I have yet to learn that it is an offence for working men to attend public meetings. To the contrary, I say working men have an undoubted right to do so and that if the conviction was as the Rev Litchfield has, by his observations, put it, the sooner he is removed from the commission of peace the better, and that the working men of England should arouse themselves and bring the conduct of the Rev Litchfield before the House of Commons.

10   *Banbury Advertiser*, 20 December 1866.

It is tempting to suppose that the author was Thomas Judge, yet this seems unlikely. Judge usually used his own name in letters to newspapers and claimed to despise those who cloaked their identities under a nom de plume.

In the spring of 1867, however, another, more parochial, issue returned. Despite Judge's victory over Church Rates in 1866, Sage and his supporters made a final attempt at the Vestry held on 8 April 1867. Church supporters made an uncharacteristic gesture of conciliation. In the past, Vestry Meetings in Brackley – as in most other places – had been chaired by the Vicar, or, on occasion, by his Curate. Now it was agreed, however, that Mr Fairthorne should take the Chair.

Fairthorne was a solicitor and a Congregationalist. He was also a Liberal, although more gentlemanly in style than the raucous Tommy Judge. Fairthorne was probably seen as a fairly neutral figure, even though it is unlikely that he approved of Church Rates. Following his earlier tactics, Judge immediately proposed an adjournment for twelve months. But Judge's motion was defeated and another, proposed by Thomas Hawkins, a prominent builder and churchgoer, to the effect that a Church Rate should be raised, was carried by a large majority.

When it suited him, Judge was all in favour of democracy, but, when the vote went against him, he was rather less keen. Despite the majority in favour of the Church Rate, the Vestry was soon in chaos. The *Bicester Herald* of 12 April 1867 reported:

> But somehow the business would not go on. The more everybody talked and bawled, and hooted and stamped and shouted and hissed, and insulted one another, the farther from the desired haven the meeting seemed to be. The Chairman who had certainly acted most impartially at length declared that he could not sit there and be insulted in such a manner, for he had endeavoured to do his duty, and he should, therefore, on account of the riotous state of the meeting, adjourn it. He then left the room and a number of others with him. We understand that a few persons stayed behind, and went through the form of passing the accounts and making a rate of 2d. in the pound.

Although the newspaper does not name those who had caused the mayhem, the fact that Judge later emerged as a master in the art of disrupting meetings suggests that he was probably responsible. The chaos served his purpose. With no Chairman and probably no quorum, any rate was likely to be held illegal – and this time the Churchwardens decided not to contest the matter. There were to be no more Church Rates in Brackley, and Parliament abolished them throughout the country the following year.

The chaotic Vestry of April 1867 gives some indication of what a divided society Brackley was becoming. In the event, the new Conservative Government proved surprisingly flexible over the Parliamentary Reform. By accepting radical amendments to his initial proposals, the Tory Prime Minister Benjamin Disraeli ended up by passing a Bill which actually went further than the Liberal one he had rejected as too Radical in 1866.

But while the Reform Act of 1867 was a step in the right direction, its main effect was to give the vote to urban working-class householders. Agricultural labourers in rural constituencies remained unenfranchised. In his letter to Judge, John Bright had said that agricultural labourers might do something for themselves, but without the vote, what could they do? For some the answer was not more political agitation, but direct action.

Judge had already raised the question of agricultural workers and their wages at the Reform Demonstration. Their plight had recently been worsened by an outbreak of cattle plague. The issue of the *Bicester Herald* containing an account of Judge's victory at Middleton Cheney also reports that beasts belonging to Mr Nichols of Halse had been affected. As a result, the 'Brackley Plague Committee' had ordered that all cattle which had come into contact with Nichols's stock should be slaughtered without delay and that his barns should be taken down and burned.

From May to August 1867, the correspondence columns of the *Bicester Herald* are dominated by a series of angry letters between Judge and a Mr FW Bignell of Loughton, Stony Stratford, on the subject of the agricultural worker. Bignell, a friend and supporter of Litchfield, maintained that wage levels must ultimately reflect the supply and demand for labour – nothing could alter that. Unions and strikes would only harm the labourers themselves. The old traditions of mutual consideration were now threatened, but farm workers should remember that while there might be labour shortages in the summer – the basis of demands for higher pay – in winter supply exceeded demand. In the past, there had been an implicit understanding that, if labourers did not demand excessive wages in summer, the masters would not throw them out of work in winter. If the old understanding was broken, labourers could expect no such consideration. If they formed Unions, so too would the farmers. Then labourers would face lockouts, dismissals and enforced reduction of wages at a time when they were most vulnerable.

On several occasions, Bignell accused Judge and his friends of encouraging both Unions and strikes and of 'leading misguided and ill-informed men to the utmost limits prescribed by the law'. Of course, what Bignell really meant was that Judge had urged them to go beyond the law.

The background to the debate between Judge and Bignell was a strike of farm workers at Evenley and Croughton, closely linked with similar action at Gawcott. Bignell believed that Judge was behind the strikes. He traced their origins to the excitement and disorder associated with the Reform Demonstration which, after all, had been organised by Judge.

If the aftermath of the demonstration had been violent, so too was the strike. The strikers were prepared to use extreme methods, including the intimidation and wounding of 'blacklegs'. Judge's shop on the east side of the Market Square, just below the Town Hall, was the effective headquarters of the strike. Judge helped the strikers to prepare and publish posters urging local farm workers to rebel against 'their paltry pittance of wages' and to continue to demand the vote. Men like Bignell and Litchfield were convinced that, whatever his protestations to the contrary, Judge was not only responsible for the strike but also for the accompanying violence.

In his letters to the *Bicester Herald*, Judge acknowledges that he approves of Unions because he believes that they offer a means of achieving real and lasting improvements in pay and conditions – not merely the temporary and self-defeating ones described by Bignell. In a letter of 13 June, however, Judge claims he is not usually in favour of strikes but still insists that they are justified on occasion – and the Evenley strike is one such case. But Judge flatly denies that he had encouraged actual violence; had he not used his restraining influence, things might have been much worse:

> My own conversation publicly and privately has been moderating rather than stimulating to the doings of the working men, and I believe that of my friends has been the same. Mr Bignell and friends may thank a kind providence for this, for had it been otherwise very serious consequences might have arisen. The only thanks we get is defamation.

For all his Radicalism, Judge was no Socialist. He believed in the free market, as indeed did his heroes like Bright. He insisted that he would blame no man for getting work done at any price, however low, provided that it was at the fair market price and no oppression was used. Judge seemed to be saying that farmers were seeking to 'rig' the market; so long as they did so it was legitimate for the labourers to do the same. Above all, Judge wanted to liberate the farm labourer.

It is striking that in the early 1860s, local newspapers, particularly the *Banbury Advertiser*, devoted much space to the American Civil War. Judge's outlook may well have been influenced by what was happening in the United States; he probably saw distinct similarities between the southern slaves and the farm workers of South Northamptonshire and between the great Plantation Houses and the fine country seats of the local squires.

Judge was emphatic that the labourers were oppressed. Paltry tricks and tyrannies were constantly used against them, 'to rob them of all spirit, and frighten them into submission, that they may be compelled to work for too low pay'. He was not specific about the nature of those tricks, but he probably had in mind such things as 'blacklisting', threats of eviction from tied cottages, and unscrupulous use of drink. When one of the Croughton strikers, John Cripps, withdrew his support for the Union and addressed a letter to the newspaper, Judge immediately identified the letter as composed by his master, the strikers' bête noire, John Lord of Astwick. Lord was obviously a tough customer and in Judge's account, at the time of the previous General Election in 1865, he had come into the grocer's shop and threatened to withdraw his custom unless Judge agreed to vote for the Conservatives.

Some of the Evenley strikers who were accused of violence were brought before the Petty Sessions. Judge appeared as a character witness, describing the strikers as 'honest, upright straightforward men'. Such testimony did not impress the magistrates who were clearly appalled at Judge's behaviour and demeanour. When the cases ended, Judge was called back and given a thorough dressing down by Litchfield. The Rector of Farthinghoe ridiculed his claims to be the labourer's friend, 'I think the men who stand here today have great reason to feel that but for your encouragement they would not have been here at all'.

It seems that Judge paid some of the fines from his own pocket. But by then the strike had been settled, with the masters agreeing to increase wages by 1 shilling a week – about 10 per cent. Judge was in an exultant mood when writing to the *Bicester Herald* on 3 July:

> What are the twenty or thirty pounds of fines in comparison with the independence of mind that has arisen, and the hundreds of pounds of hard cash that the labourers have received and are receiving as increases of wages.

Like the good teetotaller he was, Judge maintained that drink was more likely to lead to violence than political agitation, however extreme. Yet, although Judge made a show of deprecating violence, his attitude seems ambiguous. To say the least of it, the atmosphere in Brackley was highly charged. There must have been some who recalled the tragedy of William Hirons. As they contemplated monsters like Howe and irascible old parsons like Litchfield and Sage, many must have concluded that a measure of force was justified to secure a decent wage and a just society.

An unhappy period in Brackley's history seemed to be coming to an end; the obvious question was whether it would end in an explosion? It was coming to an end in one sense at least; by 1867 it became clear Rev Sage was dying. Even if the unpopular Vicar was safe in what remained of his life, would he be safe in death? There was only one grave in Brackley Churchyard surrounded by iron railings; it was Sage's. Those who erected the railings must have thought that desecration was a real possibility.

If the idea of 'Revolutionary Brackley' seems a contradiction in terms, we should remember the Reform Demonstration of 17 December 1866. It is interesting to discover that the events in Brackley were being followed by someone further to the Left than Thomas Judge, a real Socialist, the apostle of world revolution – Karl Marx himself. Marx was sufficiently impressed to mention the strikes at Evenley, Croughton and Gawcott in *Das Kapital*, where he describes the Brackley area as 'one of the most downtrodden agricultural districts in England' and stresses the importance of the strikes as marking a renewal of 'the movement of the English agricultural proletariat, entirely crushed since the suppression of its violent manifestations in 1830 and especially since the introduction of the new Poor Laws'.[11]

Inspired by the success of the strikes, the farm workers soon formed a branch of Joseph Arch's National Agricultural Labourers' Union. In 1873 there were ninety members in Brackley. The Union song indicates a high level of militancy:

> Then up, be doing, brave hearted men, Stand shoulder to shoulder again and again. Then ask for your rights and you'll have them when
> Each man has joined the Union.
>
> We won't be idle, we won't stand still, We're willing to work, to plough and till; But if we don't get a rise, we'll strike, we will
> For all have joined the Union.[12]

On occasion – though not often – we may indulge in historical 'might have beens'. Could there have been a 'Brackley Commune' about 1870, reproducing in miniature some of the horrors of the one in Paris? If this is too fanciful – and it probably is – then we can hardly disagree with Mr Langley that Brackley had indeed woken up. But what would be its waking state? Would it be the Radical and potentially revolutionary consciousness of Thomas Judge?

There was no way that the old-style Toryism represented by Sage and Litchfield could make a comeback. The slightly more modern version, tinged with Benthamism, and represented by Colonel Cartwright was scarcely better placed. But of all possible candidates to provide an alternative consciousness, the Church of England, in its enfeebled state after forty years of Sage, must have seemed the least likely. How could such a discredited organisation provide the leadership to soothe class tensions, to bring energy and purpose to a community almost at the end of its tether? It would surely take a miracle. If proof is needed that God is an Anglican gentleman we need look no further; the miracle happened and was performed by the new Vicar, Rev Francis Thicknesse.

---

11   Karl Marx, *Das Kapital* (London: Everyman, 1962) Vol. 1, Part III, p.255.

12   Hodgkins, R., *Over the Hills to Glory: Radicalism in Banburyshire* (Southend-on-Sea: Clifton Press, 1978) p.64.

Florrie Blackwell. (NRO)

An old soldier.

Brackley Gasworks.

Old Banbury Road corner, 1877. (NRO)

Cycling club outside the Crown Inn.

Middle-class housing, Banbury Road.

Chapter Six

THE THICKNESSE REVOLUTION

Brackley's 'saviour', Francis Henry Thicknesse – known to his family and friends as Frank – was inducted as Vicar on 18 March 1868. He retained the living until 1879 and became the dominant figure in a revolution that transformed both Church and town, much to the advantage of both.

Of course, he could not do everything on his own; others, like the Earl of Ellesmere and, perhaps even more, the Earl's uncle, Algernon Egerton, played major roles. As always, what happened in Brackley must be related to broader social, intellectual and economic trends. Yet, when every allowance has been made, Francis Thicknesse's contribution remains outstanding. Despite the claims of Robert Sybthorpe and Thomas Bowles, he is my candidate for the title of 'the greatest Vicar of Brackley'.

The name Thicknesse will be familiar to readers of my *Yesterday's Brackley*. In the eighteenth century, Rev John Thicknesse was Rector of Farthinghoe. His daughter, Joyce, married Richard Grey, Rector of Hinton-in-the-Hedges and protégé of Bishop Crewe of Steane. Joyce Thicknesse's mother was a member of a junior branch of the Egerton family. In 1868, the Bridgewater Trustees – representing the Egerton family – were still Patrons of the living of Brackley. So, was Francis Thicknesse's appointment just a straightforward example of 'family patronage'? Not quite; Francis Thicknesse was not really a Thicknesse at all.

He had been born in 1828 as Francis Henry Coldwell, the second son of Rev William Coldwell, Prebend of Litchfield and Rector of Stafford. Mr Coldwell had a large family to provide for, but Francis was an able boy. When he entered Brasenose College, Oxford, in 1847, he was awarded the Mordaunt Scholarship and a Hulmean Exhibition. He took his BA in 1850 and proceeded to MA in 1856. He was ordained Deacon in 1853 and Priest in 1854.

In 1855, he was presented to the living of Deane, Lancashire. There he met Miss Anne Thicknesse of Beech Hill, sole surviving child of Ralph Thicknesse, formerly MP for Wigan. Anne's only brother had been drowned in a boating accident on Lake Windermere in 1853. Ralph Thicknesse died on 22 August 1854 and Anne inherited his entire estate. This extremely rich young woman soon developed a passion for Francis Coldwell, a strikingly handsome, if somewhat impecunious, young clergyman.

At first, he was unaware of her feelings. Victorian ladies were not supposed to make the opening moves in a courtship. Canon Danter once told me how Miss Thicknesse overcame the problem. Rev Coldwell found that his bank statements were healthier than anticipated; an unknown person was paying large sums into his account. Eventually, Coldwell discovered the identity of his benefactor and the two were married in July 1855. On 29 March 1859, Coldwell assumed the name and arms of Thicknesse. Until recently these arms could be seen over the entrance to the now sadly demolished Egerton House.

Although Thicknesse remained Vicar of Deane until he moved to Brackley, he was soon given additional responsibilities. He was Rural Dean of Bolton-le-Moore from 1857 to 1868 and an Honorary Canon of Manchester Cathedral from 1863 to 1875.[1] It follows that Thicknesse had experience of the industrial north-west. Here was a man who knew the slums of Manchester and Wigan at first hand and who was well acquainted with the latest ideas on how to improve conditions in major industrial towns. But why should a man like Thicknesse agree to become the Vicar of a small market town? The living was relatively poor – the income less than £300 a year – but he did not really need the money. Perhaps he was concerned about the health of his wife and growing family of five sons and one daughter. He may have been persuaded that Brackley would be a real challenge; in view of what we have seen earlier, 'challenge' seems an understatement. The most likely reason, however, is that he agreed to become Vicar of Brackley because his friend, Algernon Egerton, asked him to take the job.

During his time in Lancashire, Thicknesse had encountered several members of the Egerton family. The Earldom of Ellesmere had been revived in 1846. It had now passed to the 3rd Earl, Francis Charles Granville Egerton, who had succeeded his father in 1862; he was then only 15. The 2nd Earl had been a chronic invalid and the strongest influence upon the boy was his uncle, Algernon Fulke Egerton (1825–91).

During the 2nd Earl's illness and the 3rd Earl's minority, Algernon Egerton was the effective head of the family and the dominant figure in the Bridgewater Trust. Thicknesse (then Coldwell) and Algernon Egerton may have met at Oxford. They went up about the same time although they were at different colleges. Algernon was an able and serious man; he was elected as a Fellow of All Souls College in 1851 and took his doctorate in Civil Law in 1857. He was Tory MP for South Lancashire from 1859 to 1868 and for South East Lancashire from 1868 to 1880. From 1882 to 1885, he represented Wigan, the seat once held by Mrs Thicknesse's father. Thicknesse and Algernon Egerton certainly worked together in Lancashire. When speaking at the opening of the new Church School on 24 May 1871, Egerton said that he had known Thicknesse for many years. While still at Deane, 'their Vicar was engaged, as he had been since he came to Brackley, in the good works with which his name was connected'.

In March 1868 the 3rd Earl was still a minor and would not attain his majority until the next month – so there can be little doubt that it was Algernon Egerton who was chiefly responsible for bringing Thicknesse to Brackley. In any case, the young Earl had things other than ecclesiastical patronage on his mind. He had recently become engaged to Katherine Louisa Phipps, the 18-year-old daughter of the 2nd Marquess of Normanby. They were to marry at St James's Piccadilly on 9 December 1868.

Algernon Egerton probably had a personal reason for urging Thicknesse to become Vicar of Brackley. It was clear that the Earl did not share the industrial interests of his indirect ancestor, the 5th Duke of Bridgewater; indeed, it looks as if he was not even encouraged to do so. *The Complete Peerage* describes the 3rd Earl as 'a keen sportsman and an enthusiastic Volunteer; a successful breeder of Shire Horses and pigs; a member of the Jockey Club from 1879, but not particularly successful on the Turf'. He bought a horse appropriately named 'None the Wiser', hitherto a frequent winner, for 9,000 guineas; the wretched

---

1   For details of Thicknesse's career, see Longden, H Isham, *Northamptonshire and Rutland Clergy from 1500* (Northampton: Archer Goodman, 1938–52) Vol. XIII, 1942, pp.185–87.

animal never won again. Such a man had neither the inclination, nor perhaps the ability, to direct the great commercial interests of the Egerton family; Algernon Egerton believed he possessed the necessary qualities.

The Egertons' ancestral home, Worsley Old Hall – the building in which the Bridgewater Canal had been planned and its construction supervised – was now on the outskirts of Manchester and, by the 1860s, the house was surrounded by the slag-heaps of the Egerton coal mines. A man with the Earl's rural tastes was unlikely to want to live in an industrial region, though he was doubtless willing enough to enjoy the income such industry produced. More than most people in Victorian England, the Earl could live as he liked. In 1883 the Bridgewater estates were reckoned to produce £71,000 a year and in 1887 the Trustees sold the Bridgewater Canal to the Manchester Ship Canal Company for the huge sum of £1,700,000.[2]

Algernon Egerton was fond of his nephew but, not surprisingly, seems to have been reluctant to give up his position as effective head of the family when the Earl came of age. It could have occurred to Algernon that, if he wanted to retain his old role, the best thing to do would be to persuade his young nephew to live far away from Lancashire. There is no evidence that such a plan existed and, in any event, the Earl and his future bride intended to take extended foreign tours before settling down. Yet the appointment of Francis Thicknesse may have been the first part of a benign 'plot' conceived by Algernon Egerton to 'exile' his nephew to Brackley. If the Earl sought his uncle's advice on where to live, Algernon would have had a ready answer. There was a little town in Northamptonshire where the 'most noble family' had extensive property – although they had neglected it for centuries. The town, which until recently had had serious social problems, was now being transformed by a truly wonderful Vicar – who happened to be an old friend. Would it not be a splendid opportunity for a young nobleman to work alongside such a hero?

Algernon Egerton probably suspected that Thicknesse would soon be coming up with all kinds of worthy schemes, schemes that would have the merit of occupying the Earl's attention fairly harmlessly. In order to facilitate matters, Algernon would use his influence with the Bridgewater Trustees to make sure that adequate funds were available. However grand Thicknesse's projects, they would not make a serious dent in what were often described as 'the Bridgewater Millions'. Thus, we may suspect that Thicknesse was being put in place to act as a 'minder' for a nice but perhaps not terribly bright young man whose uncle wanted him out of the way. One rather unflattering way of looking at 'the Brackley miracle' of the 1870s is to see it as 'the Earl of Ellesmere's toy', provided by his uncle and his uncle's friend to prevent him from poking his nose into affairs which Algernon Egerton wanted to keep to himself.

Yet if there was an element of cynicism in Algernon Egerton, there was massive idealism in Francis Thicknesse. His social and political philosophy is best described as 'Tory paternalism'. This differed markedly from the incipient Benthamism of Colonel Cartwright, the 'furious' or ultra-Toryism of Litchfield in his prime or the do-nothing attitude of Charles Sage. In some ways, Thicknesse's objectives were the same as theirs. He too wanted to make the poor deferential to their betters. He too wanted to strengthen the Anglican Church and generally 'do down' the Nonconformists. He certainly had no time for the quasi-revolutionary Radicalism espoused by Thomas Judge. The difference was in the means.

Thicknesse believed that the Church and the traditional rulers could survive and even strengthen their position, but only if they showed themselves to be energetic and hardworking, striving ceaselessly to help the poor, giving them better housing, better education, better medical care and generally more security. Whereas, in their different ways, Cartwright, Litchfield and Sage wanted to beat the poor into submission, Thicknesse included an element of bribe.

2   GEC, *The Complete Peerage* (Gloucester: Alan Sutton, 1982) Vol. 5, p.56, Note a.

Some may have feared that such a philosophy would simply breathe new life into Mozley's 'foul dragon of charity'. Yet this 'new style charity' was unlike the indiscriminate charity of the Old Poor Law; it was carefully directed and had many strings attached. It was not really backward looking and actually depended heavily on modern technology. It was unashamedly elitist. Perhaps its ultimate purpose was to prove to the people of Brackley that the word 'aristocracy' had regained its original Greek meaning – and that is 'the rule of the best'. But how was this philosophy to be translated into practice? The pattern is significant. It looks as if Thicknesse always took the first steps, then gained Algernon Egerton's approval, and finally the Earl of Ellesmere was allowed to take the public credit. Although not quite complete by the time Thicknesse left Brackley, the bulk of the 'master plan' had been implemented by 1879. Put simply, it had two main elements: 'below ground' (in a sense unseen) and 'above ground' and highly visible.

The below ground aspect reflected Thicknesse's preoccupation with public health. His first initiative concerned burials. He believed that the crowded graveyard around the Church constituted a health hazard and persuaded the Bridgewater Trustees to donate some land to be used for new graves. In December 1869 they gave 'three rods and twenty-four perches, called the Churchyard Close and lying on the South side of the Church and Churchyard of St Peter's Brackley aforesaid and bounded on the East by a road from Turweston to the Old Town'.[3] Thicknesse later proceeded to a further tightening of policy on burials. He wrote to Dr PA Holland, Home Office Inspector of Burials, on 16 August 1876:

> I beg leave to empower you to report that no more burials shall be permitted in graves which are not free from water in St James's Mortuary Ground or in the old part of St Peter's Churchyard on the North Side of the Church without the express sanction of the Medical Officer of Health.[4]

Thicknesse's public health campaign extended far beyond the graveyards. To modern eyes it seems strange that the Vicar should have played such a crucial role in issues such as drainage and water supply. Here we must refer to the system of local government. The most striking feature is the lack of any real democratic element. There were to be no County Councils until the Local Government Act of 1888. Some County matters like highways were controlled by the magistrates – chosen by the Lord Lieutenant – and meetings at the Quarter Sessions. The Town Council had been stripped of most of its limited powers in the 1830s and had never been much more than a self-perpetuating oligarchy. The only forum in which ordinary householders could express their opinions was at the Parish Vestry, chaired, ex officio, by the Vicar.

Traditionally, the Vestry dealt both with Church and general parish matters. As we have seen, however, in Sage's time, the Vestry had been dominated by disputes over Church Rates, but Church Rates were abolished by Parliament in the summer of 1868, shortly after Thicknesse arrived in Brackley. The new Vicar was not sorry about abolition. Even if it did produce a crisis in Church finances, he had enough private means to make good any temporary deficiency. He appreciated that abolition would deprive the Nonconformists of their most effective complaint and remove a major cause of the Church of England's unpopularity in the town as a whole. Above all, it meant that the Vestry could concentrate upon more important matters. Although the idea of a Parish Vestry as a prime instrument of public health reform may seem bizarre, with Thicknesse in charge, that is what it became.

3   NRO, Brackley Parish Records, Churchwardens' Minute Book 1844–69, 42P/60.

4   Ibid.

For many years, Brackley had been notorious for evil-smelling drains, and some of the inhabitants were just as bad. Back in the eighteenth century, Mary Leapor had written in her poem *Artemisia: A Dialogue*:

This Br---ly is the worst of airs,
Where standing wells, and putrid drains,
And sweating nymphs, and sprawling swains,
On either side, before, behind,
Provide a stench for every wind.[5]

There is no reason to suppose that things had improved in the meantime. In 1864 the people of Brackley wrote to the Home Secretary to complain about the state of the town's drainage. Recently, there had been a number of deaths from enteric fever. Dr Acland of Oxford had been consulted and had pointed to the danger of allowing water supplies to be contaminated with sewage. The stench from the Turweston Brook was overwhelming, fish were dying in large numbers, cattle could not drink from the stream and even passengers on the London & North Western Railway complained of the horrible smell as they approached Brackley. For the time being, however, nothing was done and the toll from enteric fever continued to mount.[6]

On 26 October 1868, a Vestry Meeting agreed to form a Committee, chaired by Thicknesse, 'to act as Agents of the Vestry Sewage Authority and also to create a Drainage District for the Parishes of St Peter and St James in accordance with the provisions of the Sanitary Act, 1866'. The Vestry also resolved to accept Algernon Egerton's offer to send an inspector 'to report on the best manner and probable cost of carrying out the drainage'. On 27 January 1869, Thicknesse chaired a meeting in the Town Hall to consider the plans drawn up by Mr Barnes of Manchester. To allay any fears among the ratepayers, the Vicar read a letter from Algernon Egerton promising that the Bridgewater Trustees would contribute £500 towards the project. The newly married Earl of Ellesmere was present in person and said a few words in favour of the project. The proposal for a drainage scheme received overwhelming support, despite protests from Thomas Judge and Mr Fairthorne that the project should have been considered by separate meetings of the two Brackley parishes. Judge proposed the formation of a Board of Health, pointing out that, at thirty per thousand, the premature death rate in Brackley was considerably higher than in neighbouring Banbury.[7]

In the event, Brackley did not acquire a Board of Health, even though the idea had the backing of both Judge and Thicknesse. Yet the project agreed in 1868 went ahead and thus Brackley gained a sanitation scheme far in advance of other towns in the area (Buckingham's came twenty-five years later), but there were teething problems. Initially, the joints of the sewage pipes were not properly sealed and this resulted in further contamination of some of the wells. In 1871 there was another outbreak of fever and there were eleven deaths in one row of cottages alone.[8] Thus, Thicknesse was drawn to the next logical step – a system of piped water. It might have been wiser to do things the other way around, but at least Thicknesse grasped the golden rule of Victorian public health. If water supplies and sewage got mixed up there would

5   Quoted in Greene, R., *Mary Leapor* (Oxford: Clarendon Press, 1994) p.18.

6   NRO, Churchwardens' Minute Book, 1844–69, 42P/60.

7   Ibid.

8   NRO Churchwardens' Minute Book, 1869–73, 42P/61.

be disease. If they could be kept apart, there would be fewer epidemics and the health of the community would be greatly improved.

On 30 June 1876, the Vicar chaired a meeting 'to consider the means of obtaining a Water Supply for the town'. He secured a majority for a motion that 'the Water supply of Brackley is inefficient and contaminated in many parts of the town and that a better system of supplying the Town is necessary'. He also carried a further motion calling on the Sanitary Authority 'to take steps to provide a good supply of wholesome water upon such a plan as shall place it within reach of all the inhabitants of the town'.[9]

It looked as if Thicknesse had triumphed again, but, with a distressing lack of clerical solidarity, Rev HW Smith successfully called for a poll of all householders. During Sage's declining years, Smith had been the Church's main representative in Brackley. His report to Sage suggests that he saw himself as the friend of the poor. But now he had been totally 'upstaged' by Thicknesse and there was probably an element of pique in his opposition to the Water Scheme. Despite obtaining ninety-one votes – including those of the influential Mr Stratton of Turweston, the Earl of Ellesmere's local agent, Mr Russel, the iron monger John Clarke and the builder Samuel Alcock (a devotee of all things 'modern') – the proposal was defeated. Opponents included the elderly Doctor Collier, Mr Bannerman of East Hill, the miller Thomas Course and a host of poorer householders, including my ancestor Harry Spittals. Curiously, the Radical, Thomas Judge, voted with the minority.[10]

Undaunted, Thicknesse drew up a petition to the Local Government Board urging that the scheme be adopted despite the adverse vote. The petition stresses that enteric fever is still a problem – with more than twelve cases currently in the town. Work on the drainage scheme had shown that the soil was extremely porous, hence the problem of seepage into the wells. Even if the arterial system of drainage was perfect – 'which is much to be doubted' – many years would elapse before the wells would yield pure water. The present condition of the well water was extremely dangerous, a statement confirmed by 'the analysis of eminent Chemists which accompany this memorial'.[11] Sadly the Water Scheme was delayed for a few years, although it was finally installed in the 1880s, still well ahead of many other places.

Although Thicknesse's achievements 'below ground' were crucial to the long-term improvement of public health, the changes 'above ground' were more obvious and spectacular. They included alterations to arrangements for worship in the Church and a massive building programme. When Thicknesse arrived, St Peter's was still filled with high pews. Most of these were either rented or leased to individual parishioners. In all, no fewer than 450 of the 662 seats in the Church were 'reserved' and the income from the rented pews formed a significant part of total Church revenue.[12] Thicknesse was determined to change the entire system. Here he was opposed by some of his parishioners. Men like the farmer, Isaac Bartlett, argued that it would be particularly foolish to give up pew rents at a time when Church finances were still suffering as a result of the abolition of Church Rates. Bartlett, a pew owner himself, declared, 'The Church would not have been repaired if we had not bought the pews'[13] – a reference to the modest restoration carried out by Sage in the 1840s.

9   Churchwardens' Minute Book, 1873–83, 42P/62.

10   Ibid.

11   Ibid.

12   Churchwardens' Minute Book, 1844–69, 42P/60.

13   Ibid.

Thicknesse proposed to deal with the financial problem by introducing a weekly offertory. This was a controversial step, much disapproved of by old-fashioned Churchgoers and clergy alike. Rev Jack Linnell, author of *Old Oak* and Thicknesse's junior by fifteen years, insisted, 'It was a pity that a man couldn't go to church without a money bag being thrust under his nose'.[14] But Thicknesse believed that the evil of pew rents far outweighed any disadvantages of collections. Thus, he wrote an open letter to the people of Brackley, dated 'Monday before Easter 1873', asking them to give a fair trial to a system of 'regular voluntary contributions'. He pointed out that the plan, already accepted by a majority of the Parish, had the approval of the Churchwardens and had been recommended by the Bishop. Thicknesse claimed that rented or private pews left insufficient places for the poor who were thus effectively excluded from Church services. If all seats were free, however, he could:

> … welcome as Brethren all who may be persuaded to Worship with us, whether they be those whose families once belonging to the Faith of their Forefathers have for want of accommodation in their Parish Church wandered to other Communions; or those who too poor to pay for a seat have unhappily absented themselves from all Public Worship whatever.

The letter ends with an impassioned plea:

> I invite *all* in Christ's name, as I have never been able to do before, to come to their own Parish Church when it is reopened and renovated and to prove by their constant presence there, that they value and love this Home and Refuge both of Rich and Poor from the cares and sorrows which are common to us all and indeed to prepare themselves by the Worship of the Church on Earth for meeting as 'one in Christ'.[15]

Thus, Brackley Church acquired new low pews and free seats. But Thicknesse introduced many other changes.

His first objective was to bring greater decorum to the services. On 10 October 1870, it was resolved that 'the Churchwardens make use of their authority to prevent any young persons or others from behaving in an irreverent or unbecoming way either before or during the time of Divine Service'.[16] In November 1872, shortened services were introduced. Opinions were mixed. Mr W Blencowe heartily approved of the new services. He had not been brought up as a Churchman and came with open eyes and prepared to criticise. He could see no reason why under the old Service Book there should be three Lord's Prayers and two Creeds. Dr Hoctor, however, 'did not see the necessity for this smaller book. It was most desirable not to interfere with the old established custom of the Church by introducing anything new.'[17]

But refusal to contemplate anything new had been one of the things that had brought the Church to a low ebb under Sage, and Mr Blencowe's comments indicate that Thicknesse's congregation was beginning to include some who had not previously considered themselves as Anglicans. This was clearly a central objective of the 'free seats' policy. Indeed, what Thicknesse wanted to do was to seize the initiative for the Church of England and generally 'marginalise' the Nonconformists. Although, in some ways, Francis

14   Jack Linnell, *Old Oak*, p.xx.

15   NRO, Brackley Parish Papers, 42P/249.

16   Churchwardens' Minute Book 1869–73, 42P/62.

17   Ibid.

Thicknesse was a modern-minded and progressive man, his thinking did not run to ecumenism. In his own way, he was as much of an Anglican exclusivist as Sage or even Sybthorpe.

Thicknesse looked upon the Church of England as the natural as well as the national Church. In determining religious allegiance, the onus of proof was upon those who declined to be Anglicans. He had no sympathy for those who said that they liked going to Chapel or that religion should be a matter of individual conscience. The only possible justification for going to Chapel was when the Church was clearly failing in its duty. Thus, while it might have been forgivable to be a Methodist in Sage's time, it was unforgivable now. Once the Church put its house in order, the 'excuse' was gone and all those who had 'wandered to other Communions' should repair contrite to the Parish Church with all possible speed. To continue as a Dissenter in the Brackley of the 1870s seemed inexplicably perverse. Although Thicknesse was never quite as offensive to the Nonconformists as Litchfield had been, any words of praise tended to be grudging and his day-to-day dealings with Wesleyan and Congregational ministers were far from friendly. Throughout his time in Brackley, he tried to prevent Nonconformist ministers holding any form of service over the graves of Dissenters who, in many instances, continued to be buried in the Churchyard.

A desire to rout the Dissenters was a factor – although by no means the only one – in Thicknesse's building programme. He was more closely associated with some projects than others, but he had a hand in all and the list helps us to appreciate the full grandeur of his 'vision' for Brackley. It may not be too extreme to see the project as a kind of 'Anglican Counter-Reformation', the sort of thing Sybthorpe might have attempted if he had had the money and Charles I's Personal Rule had lasted. All of the buildings had a practical purpose: to educate the young (the Church School); to provide proper places for worship (the restoration of the College Chapel and the restoration or replacement of the Parish Church); a proper residence for the Earl of Ellesmere (the Manor House); appropriate accommodation for his Stewards and officials (houses in the High Street), cottages for his servants (the Manor Road); smarter shops (the Banbury Road corner); a new Vicarage; and a place to heal the sick (the Cottage Hospital). Yet at least some of these buildings – the Vicarage, the Manor House and, above all, the Church School – were far grander than they needed to be. They were designed to impress, to evoke awe and wonder in the eye of the beholder. They certainly helped to restore a sense of pride in the community, a feeling in dangerously short supply in recent years.

One project was already under discussion when Thicknesse came to Brackley: the restoration of the College Chapel. But little progress had been made, not least because of Sage's obstructive attitude. Thicknesse was anxious to improve relations with Magdalen. When still Vicar designate, he went with Algernon Egerton to see President Bulley. After lengthy discussions and several visits, the college agreed to lease the Chapel to the Vicar for a period of forty years at a nominal rent. But Magdalen specifically excluded any idea of 'ceding in perpetuity a Chapel which has been in their possession almost from the time of the Founder'.

In every other respect Thicknesse got what he wanted. The college agreed to grant £200 towards a new floor for the Chapel. It also promised to contribute £15 a year towards the salary of a second Curate and even agreed to allow Thicknesse to take the iron gates from the front of the Chapel to use at his planned new Vicarage. Together, Francis Thicknesse and Algernon Egerton must have been a formidable negotiating team.

Now that matters were settled with Magdalen, Thicknesse threw himself into fundraising activities, cajoling subscriptions from parishioners and neighbouring gentry and contributing generously himself. The restoration work, by the Oxford architect Charles Buckeridge (1832–73) – who also restored

St Lawrence's Church, Radstone – commenced in April 1869.[18] The Clerk of Works, Mr Nurse, ensured that good progress was made, so much so that Alfred Green's *History of Brackley*, published in the summer of the same year, could declare:

> The present Restoration consists of a thorough renewal of the internal walls, and stone work, rebuilding of the arches, sedilia, etc. – reglazing the windows, an entirely new floor of encaustic tiles, new choir stalls of oak, massive oaken altar table, stone and marble reredos, complete warming apparatus, furniture and fixing for Divine Service, etc. which are being carried out by a subscription raised by the Rev Canon Thicknesse, Vicar of Brackley.[19]

The choice of Buckeridge may owe something both to Magdalen and to Algernon Egerton. Buckeridge had designed a gateway to the college stables and been responsible for additions to the building that was later the Library. Buckeridge may also have been linked to Algernon Egerton. Egerton was a friend of Montagu Burrows, like himself a Fellow of All Souls, and Buckeridge had designed Burrows's house at 9 Norham Gardens (1862–63), described by Andrew Saint as 'the most uncompromisingly Gothic House in the whole of North Oxford'.[20]

While Buckeridge was engaged in restoration work at Brackley, he was also designing a new church at Avon Dassett, Warwickshire. Some of the interior pillars and arches resemble those in the College Chapel.[21] But why did Thicknesse give such high priority to the College Chapel? As we have seen, one of the most serious problems facing the Church was the inconvenient position of St Peter's. The restored Chapel would be used for Parish services as well as by the school. In effect, the Chapel would allow Thicknesse to establish an Anglican presence in the centre of Brackley, an area that had become largely 'Nonconformist territory'.

The first service in the restored Chapel was held at 3 p.m. on Advent Sunday 1869. In an account of the service sent to the President of Magdalen, Thicknesse made a number of characteristic points. The poor had 'taken most kindly to their free chairs in good situations'. The choir, from St Peter's, had been 'surpliced' for the first time and 'it was edifying to see two or three middle-aged men, who a few months ago were great lights at the Wesleyan Chapel, looking very proud of their Surplice'.

Perhaps inevitably, Thicknesse's energy was combined with a tendency to high-handedness. He infringed the letter of the agreement with Magdalen College by interfering with arrangements for weekday school services. This may have been the reason why the college rejected his request for its own choir to sing at the formal reopening on Shrove Tuesday (1 March) 1870. Although President Bulley attended, he was dismayed to discover that his part in the ceremony was restricted to reading the second lesson.

Bishop Magee of Peterborough performed the reopening but the sermon was preached by Thicknesse himself. The sermon, on the text 'The Poor have the Gospel preached to them', must have been vintage

---

18   For an assessment of Buckeridge as an architect, see Saint, A., 'Charles Buckeridge and his Family', *Oxoniensia*, Vol. XXXVIII (1973), pp.357–73.

19   Green, Alfred, *Outlines of the History of Brackley from the Best Authors* (Brackley: Green, 1869). (Copy in NRO, Brackley Parish Records. 42P/300.)

20   Saint, op. cit., p.360.

21   Ibid., p.369 and Plate xxviii, A and B.

Thicknesse and made a great impression on Lady Louisa Knightley, wife of Sir Rainald Knightley, the local MP. She wrote in her diary:

> As he spoke of close parishes and village schools, of bad cottages and the alarming state of affairs, warning us, the prosperous ones of the earth, to fight against these evils lest our national greatness and virtue should crumble to decay, one felt nerved and encouraged to do one's very best.[22]

After lunch, where Lady Knightley sat between Thicknesse and the Duke of Grafton, the party moved to the Parish Church where Magee consecrated the new burial ground. At least in Lady Knightley's opinion, Magee's address compared poorly with Thicknesse's sermon in the morning. She was disappointed by 'its lack of serious thought, reminding me of Lord Salisbury's excellent "speaking machine"'. Thereafter things only got worse and the drive home to Fawsley over rolling stones, in pouring rain, was hardly pleasant'.[23] Clearly, Thicknesse's sermon had been the high point of Lady Louisa's day.

Despite his efforts to restore the College Chapel, Thicknesse played virtually no role in the development of Magdalen College School. Perhaps this was because he was no longer *persona grata* with the President and Fellows, but there could have been other reasons. Thicknesse really wanted to take over the College Chapel completely for parochial use; the more successful the school, the less likely this was to happen. Furthermore, although the College Chapel had the advantage of a central position, it was smaller than St Peter's and could not possibly accommodate the large congregations, including the penitent ex-Nonconformists Thicknesse hoped to attract. Thus, he wanted to go further than the 1869 restoration and to create a big church in the middle of Brackley. Thicknesse told the Vestry of 19 November 1872, 'I regret there is not one central church'.[24] Fortunately the scheme came to nothing. If it had, St Peter's Church would have been demolished, like St James's a generation earlier, and the character of the College Chapel would have been totally destroyed.

At the same time Thicknesse was campaigning so energetically for the restoration of the College Chapel he was also involved in the building of a new Vicarage, again with Charles Buckeridge as architect. In part, the need for a new Vicarage sprang from Thicknesse's preoccupation with drains and sanitary matters. The eighteenth-century Vicarage shown in prints of the Church in the 1840s had become run down and its drains were in a dreadful condition. Thicknesse insisted that only complete demolition and a fresh start would do.

It was to be an expensive project; according to *The Builder* of 20 June 1868, tenders ranged between £2,896 and £3,240, and Thicknesse may have contributed part of the costs. The Vicarage did not look at all like any of Buckeridge's other buildings. Normally, he was an out-and-out supporter of Gothic architecture and believed that the style was ideally suited for secular as well as ecclesiastical buildings. As early as November 1856, Buckeridge had read a paper to the Oxford Architectural Society entitled *The Universal Applicability of Gothic Architecture*. His enthusiasm was so great that he wanted to make 'every piece of furniture breathe the same Gothic spirit'.[25] But the new Vicarage was in no sense 'Gothic'.

22   Cartwright, Julia (ed.), *The Journals of Lady Knightley of Fawsley* (London: Murray, 1915) p.188.

23   Ibid.

24   Churchwardens' Minute Book 1869–73, 42P/61.

25   Saint, op. cit., p.358.

Saint comments that 'despite a certain coarseness it shows very early study of the kind of half-timbered and tall-chimneyed forms that were to dominate domestic architecture for the next fifty years'.[26] In other words, the Vicarage was 'Tudorbethan' rather than 'Gothic'.

Saint ascribes this development to 'signs of restlessness with domestic Gothic' visible in the works of other good architects at the end of the 1860s. But one wonders if Thicknesse himself did not have some influence on the design. There may have been some friction between the Vicar and Buckeridge because of an 'ideological problem' with Gothic architecture, which carried a hint of association with the pre-Reformation Church, that is, with Catholicism. Thicknesse may have introduced a surpliced choir, but, apart from that, he was completely untouched by the Oxford or Ritualist movements. After all, he had arrived at Brasenose when the university was still reeling from the shock of Newman's 'defection' to Rome in 1845.

Thicknesse was really a 'Broad' rather than a 'High' Churchman. Now he may have feared that the slightest hint of 'Romish tendencies' would antagonise those Nonconformists he was so anxious to win back to the Church of England. Significantly these were precisely the arguments used against Ritualism by AC Tait, Archbishop of Canterbury during Thicknesse's time at Brackley.[27] Yet Buckeridge was a militant Tractarian and Ritualist; his four best-known buildings were for religious orders – Ascot Priory, Holy Trinity Convent Oxford (now St Antony's College), St John's Hospital Cowley and Llanthony, Capel-y-Ffin (designed for the notorious Father Ignatius) high in the hills of Breconshire. It is highly unlikely that Thicknesse approved of these 'monastic' associations. In any case, a man of his tastes probably regarded the Middle Ages as too backward, simply too dirty and insanitary, for Gothic buildings to be a suitable model for the nineteenth century.

Although Brackley Vicarage was attributed to Buckeridge, he had a large practice and delegated much work to others. A good deal of the design may not have been his at all and the 'real' architect was probably Charles Bather of St Mary East, Shrewsbury. The 'black and white' style would have reflected Bather's preferences – and indeed Thicknesse's own. The Vicarage was ready for occupation by the summer of 1870, although there were still a few 'teething' problems to be sorted out. No doubt aware of Thicknesse's preoccupations, Bather wrote on 18 August 1870 that he had examined the ditch below the Vicarage and had directed 'Grove' to employ a labourer to clean it out. He had also examined the sink and WC in and adjoining the butler's pantry; everything was in proper working order, 'clean and free from bad smells'.

He could reply with confidence to Thicknesse's question about the old drains. He had given particular instructions that all were to be taken up and believed that this had now been done:

Nothing is required to complete the system of drainage at the Vicarage but the trap in the street and this will not be required and cannot be applied until the junction is made with the new sewer ... The rain water from the tank smells rather strong in the cistern at the top of the house. I have directed Goodliffe to close it in and to put a pipe therefrom to the roof and in addition to fill all the inlet pipes from the roof with charcoal and to place two charcoal trays under the inlets into the Tank and to clean out the Tank before the next rain. This will tend much to sweeten and purify the rain water.[28]

26   Ibid., p.362.

27   See Archibald Campbell Tait, *The Church of the Future: A Diocesan Charge* (London: 1880) p.21.

28   NRO, Brackley Parish Papers, 42P/192.

But it was not just a matter of drains. Thicknesse wanted his Vicarage to be as impressive as possible. In the difficult days ahead, it would be an advantage for the Vicar to be seen as a man of substance as well as a faithful pastor. Thicknesse may have used some of his wife's wealth as a contribution to the cost of the Vicarage but most of the money came from the Earl of Ellesmere, via Algernon Egerton.

Bather was an employee of the Bridgewater Trust and did not practise independently. The choice of the 'black and white' was important to the future townscape of Brackley; the same feature appears in the Church School, at the Manor House and in houses at the corner of the Banbury Road. Of course, half-timbered buildings are not really appropriate to an area like South Northamptonshire, which has abundant supplies of good building stone available locally. In fact, such buildings are characteristic of the traditional architecture of Shropshire and Cheshire. Perhaps the best way of describing the most important buildings of the 1870s and 1880s is 'Brackley Shropshire' or 'Brackley Cheshire'; they may not be quite right for the area but they are certainly impressive.

It is worth considering the ideological implications of Tudor or Elizabethan buildings. Unlike Gothic structures, they were firmly Protestant and nationalist, evoking the days of 'Good Queen Bess' and the Spanish Armada. Perhaps they also carried overtones of 'Merrie England' – of a united and happy time in the past. There had certainly been no hint of 'Merrie England' in the architecture of the Workhouse. They were also subtle propaganda for the Egerton family. Their regional associations recalled the Egertons' origins in Cheshire and the style the days when the first Earl of Ellesmere had been rising to greatness.

At the Church Schools, designed by Bather on his own, the Elizabethan theme reaches its climax. A huge building in stone and half-timber, surmounted by a high tower, was erected on what is arguably the best site in Brackley, at the brow of the hill of the High Street. In some ways the buildings even eclipsed those of Magdalen College School and the College Chapel on the other side of the road. Both literally and metaphorically, they totally overshadowed the humble little brick Chapel School in Hill Street.

The Church School was intended for ordinary children. The message was overpowering. If you went to Church your children would be educated in what must have seemed like a palace; if you went to Chapel they would have to make do with little more than a hovel. In the soaring tower of the Church School we find Anglican triumphalism carried to the edge of megalomania; no other building in Brackley sums up so well Thicknesse's determination to cultivate the poor, to restore the ascendency of the Church and to crush the Dissenters under his feet. Robert Sybthorpe must have been cheering from the grave. But what would Bather and Thicknesse have come up with if the 'Central Church' had ever become a reality? I suspect that nothing less than a 'Tudor cathedral' would have done.

The story of the establishment of the Church School has been well covered in Jack Turner's pamphlet, *The Education of the Poor in Brackley in the 19th century – the Church of England's part*, so it need not be told again in detail. There are a number of points, however, that are worth stressing. As with the Water Scheme, Thicknesse was fortunate in that events were already moving in his direction. In 1868, Francis Jeune, Magee's predecessor as Bishop of Peterborough, declared that it was a public scandal that there was no Church School whatsoever in Brackley.[29]

In her account of the lunch party on Shrove Tuesday 1870, Lady Knightley noted that she had had an interesting discussion about the Education Bill with Thicknesse and the Duke of Grafton.[30] The Education

29   Turner, p.8.

30   *Journal of Lady Knightley of Fawsley*, p.188.

Bill was to become Forster's Education Act of 1870. For the first time, attendance at elementary schools was to be made compulsory, although education was still not completely free. In areas where there were insufficient school places – and Brackley was such a place – School Boards were to be set up to remedy the deficiency. Board Schools would provide general Christian teaching but would not promote the doctrines of any particular Church. Understandably Churchmen were alarmed by this provision. There was, however, a period of grace before the School Boards came into operation. In the meantime, it was up to the various churches to set up their own schools, which would be eligible for some state funding.

Clearly the Church of England would have to move fast if the rising generation was to receive a distinctly Anglican education. With Thicknesse as Vicar of Brackley, things moved very fast indeed. The Bridgewater Trustees gave the site and £500 towards the building. The Earl of Ellesmere made an additional personal gift of £700. Together, these contributions represented a significant proportion of the total cost, estimated at 'between two and three thousand pounds'.[31]

The new Church Schools (there were separate schools for boys and girls) were opened with some ceremony on 24 May 1871. Once more, Magee performed the official opening, but the main speeches were given by Algernon Egerton and by Thicknesse. The Earl and Countess of Ellesmere were in America. On the face of it Egerton was quite generous to the Methodists. He admitted that, for many years, Brackley had been 'in a stagnant state' and readily acknowledged that the only good work in the educational field had been done by the Methodists. But, although the language was guarded, it is hard not to detect a note of 'crowing'. Egerton 'would not say that the time of the Wesleyans was gone by' but it is clear that is precisely what he did mean. He said that he hoped that the Wesleyan School would continue but proceeded to cast doubt on its likely chances of survival. He then went on to discuss the question of School Boards and Board Schools; they might be necessary in large towns but, in country districts, it was far better that 'schools should be denominational and belong to the Church of the nation'.[32]

As with his sermon on Shrove Tuesday 1870, Thicknesse's address had a strong social dimension. He was pleased with the way Brackley had responded to him. There might be wealthier communities in the Diocese of Peterborough, 'but none more willing, none that showed a more single-minded attachment to the Church'. Thicknesse focused on Christ's injunction to 'Feed My Lambs' – the text was in letters of gold over the entrance and the school was sometimes referred to by that name. The Church should follow this divine command out of love for the Lord and for 'the little ones of his Flock'. The benefits to society would be incalculable:

> … and when the labouring classes know that their children are being taught by the kindness and good will of their employers [a reference to the subscriptions] must that not touch them and form a link of friendship and union which no rate, or law, or compulsion can affect?

Thicknesse acknowledged that the principle of compelling parents to send their children to school was a difficult one, but what concerned him most was the likely difference between Church Schools and Board Schools. He had no doubt of the superiority of Church Schools and urged his audience to even greater efforts to fund the building of a teacher's house:

31   Turner, p.9.

32   *Banbury Guardian*, 27 May 1871.

Let them pledge themselves to this completion of the work. He would not run into debt. He had not done so in other designs in the parish. But let them supply the means to give real completeness and efficiency both by present donations and annual subscriptions to this great cause, and so might they hope to be the means of pouring ever fresh life blood into the heart of their beloved parish – nay, as far as it lay in their power, into the heart also of their beloved country and of their beloved Church.[33]

The opening of the Church Schools must be regarded as Thicknesse's finest hour. A suggestion from the Methodist School Committee for the formation of a joint School Board was brushed aside.[34] The next major step was to 'capture' the Earl of Ellesmere for Brackley and turn him into a resident grandee – with all of the advantages to local employment and social deference that the presence of such a wealthy and well-meaning man would bring. The trouble was that no existing house was big enough or sufficiently impressive. Although the Egerton family had been Lords of the Manor of Brackley since 1600, they did not acquire the Manor House (still called the Tithe House on the *Town Map* of 1760)[35] until 26 June 1733. Then, Scrope Egerton, 1st Duke of Bridgewater, entered into an agreement with William Crofts to buy – among other things – 'all that Capital Messuage or Tenement with the Appurtenances in Brackley in the County of Northampton wherein Philip Lord Wenman theretofore lived, sometime William Lisles'.[36]

For nearly a century and a half, the attractive but modest early-seventeenth-century house was let to a succession of tenants, often mere farmers. The nineteenth century had increasing expectations of comfort and convenience and, by the 1860s, the facilities at the Manor House fell far short of what was considered appropriate for a 'gentleman's residence', let alone for the house of one of the richest noblemen in England.

Fate intervened at the end of the 1860s with a fire that gutted the old house. Here was a splendid opportunity to rebuild on an appropriate scale and with all modern conveniences. The new Manor House, like the Vicarage in a generally 'Tudorbethan' style, was built between 1875 and 1878.[37] Unlike the original house, fronting onto the High Street, some of the most important apartments were now almost halfway between the High Street and Back Lane. The Earl of Ellesmere rather fancied his talents as an amateur architect and he was credited with the design. No doubt Algernon Egerton and Francis Thicknesse did nothing to dampen his enthusiasm, although, in more technical matters, Charles Bather probably assisted the Earl.

In an article entitled 'Brackley 50 Years Ago', published in the *Brackley Advertiser* of 11 April 1947, Luther Brailsford noted that craftsmen from elsewhere carried out most of the decorative work. Yet 'the skill of a Brackley workman is in evidence by the large wrought iron gates to the Manor made by John Mobbs, a local blacksmith'. Brailsford also referred to an old oak door from the previous house which had been reused, repeating the legend, probably false, that 'it was through this doorway King John passed when he was on his way to Runnymede to sign Magna Carta in 1215'.

The large Victorian house was certainly a symbol of the Egertons' commitment to Brackley; it was a tangible proof that, 300 years after they had acquired the benefits of the Lordship, they were finally taking

33 Ibid.

34 NRO, Diary of Brackley Wesleyan Day School, 11 May 1871.

35 Clarke, *Yesterday's Brackley*, p.59.

36 Ibid., p.125.

37 Pevsner, *Northamptonshire*, p.120.

on its responsibilities. Most of the Manor House (now Winchester House School) is built in soft Cheshire sandstone, which, even in the Brackley air erodes quickly. The choice of Cheshire sandstone may have been natural to a man from the north-west but it still seems perverse. Much better building stone was readily available within a few miles of Brackley – at Helmdon for example. As it was, the cost of bringing thousands of tons of stone from Cheshire must have added significantly to the total bill, but a plutocrat like the Earl of Ellesmere did not have to bother with such trifles.

But if the Manor was something of an extravagance, it was also 'socially committed'. Ever since the late sixteenth century, the fashion had been for new 'seats' to be located in open country and surrounded by parkland and high walls. If one of the Dukes of Bridgewater had decided to move to Brackley in the eighteenth century, he would surely have evicted a few of the Halse farmers and erected a splendid Classical house there, perhaps as a rival to Stowe. But the 3rd Earl of Ellesmere had no such ambitions. He wanted to live in the centre of Brackley, among 'his people', in the middle of 'his' town and attended by 'his' faithful Vicar.

At the same time, Bridgewater Trustees were busily acquiring more land and house properties in the town – partly for charitable purposes and partly for redevelopment to provide appropriate housing for officials, workers and even visiting gentry. The acquisitions included:

1874   Purchase of Royal Oak public house from Richard Carter (£410)
1875   Purchase of Medical Hall from Henry Webb (£520)
1876   Purchase of cottages on corner of High Street and Pebble Lane from Feoffee Charity (£300)
        Site later used for Agent's House.
1876   Purchase of land in Bridge Street from Frederick Butterfield (£300). Later shops and offices.
1882   Lease of land in Banbury Road from Magdalen College.
        Purchase of Bell Close from Magdalen College.
        Purchase of land on the West side of High Street from the Feoffee Charity (later site of
        Red House).[38]

The 'Thicknesse Programme' was virtually complete when the Earl and his family were installed in splendour in the new Manor House. But the Vicar was not to enjoy the fruits of his labours for long and Francis Thicknesse left Brackley only one year after the completion of the Manor House. In 1879, Thicknesse was 51, but 51 is young for a clergyman and he still had a long career ahead of him. On 15 July 1888, he was consecrated as Bishop of Leicester, the only Vicar of Brackley to become a Bishop. He died, aged 93, on 2 November 1921 and is buried in Peterborough Cathedral. His son, grandson and great-grandson were to follow him into the Church.[39]

There can be no doubt of the importance of Francis Thicknesse to the history of Brackley. When he became Archdeacon of Northampton, the Churchwardens and Sidesmen presented him with an address which described Thicknesse as having 'laboured unceasingly for those entrusted to your charge both for their temporal and eternal welfare, and against many discouragements which would have daunted a less resolute man'. They spoke no more than the truth. Thicknesse even gained the admiration of Sage's

38   NRO, Ellesmere Papers, X 9637, Vol. 16.

39   Longden, op. cit.

most bitter adversary, Thomas Judge. The two collaborated in persuading the Earl of Ellesmere to widen Pebble Lane and to re-site the outlets of St Rumbold's Well and the Golden Spring.

A letter to Judge, dated 27 March 1875, reveals quite a lot about Thicknesse and his priorities:

Pray accept my sincere thanks for all your kind expressions which I value extremely because I know they come from an honest and true conviction – and that you are far above saying what you do not really believe and think. At the same time you give me credit for far too much. I know many men who would be far better Vicars of Brackley or Archdeacons of Northampton than I shall ever make. But GOD helping me I will continue to do my best for the temporal and spiritual welfare of this place, and I shall ever value as most dear to me any cooperation to those ends which may be rendered by those who will be actuated by the single purpose of promoting God's glory and the people's good.[40]

In 1920, shortly before his death, Francis Thicknesse paid a final visit to Brackley. He was present at the dedication of a new stained-glass window in the Lady Chapel of St Peter's Church. My father had already been a member of the Church choir. He was to sing in it until shortly before his death in 1998 – eighty years in all. Through him, I feel I have a link with Brackley's greatest Vicar.

40   Letter shown to me by Mrs Patricia Phillips.

College Chapel, south side.

Magdalen College School, High Street front. The school flourished under Isaac Wodhams.

College Chapel, High Street front.

The Old Tithe House before rebuilding.

The Earl of Ellesmere. (NRO)

The Old Vicarage, later Egerton House School. (NRO)

The Manor House. (NRO)

The Manor House.

The church choir at the Vicarage.

The Ellesmere family at Brackley Pageant. (NRO)

'Feed My Lambs' – The Church School, part of the Thicknesse Revolution.

Chapter Seven

VOTES FOR KISSES?

There are various ways of looking at Thicknesse's departure from Brackley. Perhaps he thought he had achieved most of his objectives and was ready to face new challenges. Yet it is surprising that he left so soon; after all, the idea of a resident Lord of the Manor working in harmony with an energetic and charismatic Vicar had been central to the 'Thicknesse revolution'. The reality of the partnership may not have lived up to the expectation. While Thicknesse had used the name and prestige of the Egertons during his early years in Brackley, with the Earl away it had been the Vicar who had been the real 'uncrowned king'. Now, with the Lord of the Manor in residence, the Earl of Ellesmere's wealth and status, regardless of his personal qualities, inevitably gave him more influence than a mere clergyman – however forceful. From the Earl's point of view, it would have been one thing to admire Thicknesse from afar, but another to have almost daily contact. He probably found the Vicar's energy and enthusiasm a trifle wearisome.

Although the Earl had a genuine concern for the poor, his first priorities were sporting and literary. In his study at the Manor House, he was to write a number of novels, including *Sir Hector's Watch* (1887) and *Mrs John Foster* (1897). To put it politely, they scarcely rank as great literature. To the earnest Thicknesse, novel writing, good or bad, would have seemed a frivolous waste of God's precious time.

The Earl may have suspected that Thicknesse's real loyalty was to Algernon Egerton rather than to himself and even wondered about Uncle Algernon's motives in encouraging the move to Brackley. Thicknesse and Algernon Egerton probably continued to treat the Earl like a boy. No doubt, he still admired them, but, rising 30 and with a family of his own, he could be forgiven for wanting to assert himself a little. This would be easier if the overpowering Thicknesse moved on.

While Algernon Egerton had been responsible for Thicknesse's appointment, the Earl would choose the next Vicar. In many ways, the choice represented the culmination of everything that had happened since 1868. Although Thicknesse had been associated with the Egertons, the blood of 'the most noble family' did not run through his veins. His successor was a member of that family. For the first and only time, Lord of the Manor and Vicar had the same surname. The new incumbent was Rev Brooke de Malpas Egerton, the Earl's second cousin.

Apart from the family link, the two men were virtually the same age. Both were fundamentally decent and well meaning, although the Vicar was probably more intelligent. He could also be relied upon to maintain Thicknesse's traditions, but, mercifully, not with quite the same manic energy. Like Thicknesse, Egerton had been at Brasenose College and had served as Thicknesse's Curate in Brackley in the early 1870s. He had been a popular figure and most people were glad to welcome him back after a few years as Rector of Uplyme, Devonshire. Egerton was a genuinely devout, even saintly man. Despite his aristocratic lineage, he was more gentle and humble than his predecessor, although he could be fierce enough when the interests of the Church were threatened. He actually tried to identify himself to some extent with ordinary parishioners.

Perhaps more than anything else, the characters of three successive Vicars sum up the very different moods of Victorian Brackley. Sage, the reactionary despiser of the poor, typifies the attitudes of the early period. Thicknesse, caring, dynamic, but with a touch of arrogance, reflects the spirit of the middle period. Egerton, still more caring but less self-confident and elitist, echoes the lower profile adopted by the local Establishment in late-Victorian Brackley.

Despite its massive achievements, the Thicknesse Revolution soon came under threat. There had been straws in the wind even in Thicknesse's last years – witness the failure of the Water Scheme. The grandiose idea of a Central Church was abandoned and the new Cottage Hospital constructed on more modest lines than the Church School. It is tempting to explain this in personal terms. Thicknesse had become so useful to the Diocesan authorities that, in 1875, he had been appointed Archdeacon of Northampton – while remaining Vicar of Brackley. Inevitably, he was away a good deal and his influence declined a little. The Cottage Hospital Committee actually complained of his increasing tendency to 'cut' meetings.

But there was more to it than that. The forces that shaped late-Victorian Brackley were essentially economic and, from the end of the 1870s, most of the indicators were adverse. Thicknesse's paternalistic vision was based upon an expectation of deference in return for care and protection. Care and protection do not come cheap, and, what price deference if care and protection are withdrawn? Of course, Brackley was better placed than many communities in that the Earl of Ellesmere remained as wealthy as ever. But not even the Egertons could do everything on their own. The full Thicknesse programme was based upon the presumption of a number of socially responsible and wealthy landowners and clergy working alongside the Earl of Ellesmere. Now there were signs, which grew ever clearer over the next twenty years, that the 'supporting cast' could not perform as Thicknesse had intended. Not even the Bridgewater millions could alter the fact that Brackley was a small market town in a farming district and hence, in the last resort, its success depended on the prosperity of agriculture.

Thicknesse was typically mid-Victorian in his assumption of agricultural prosperity. In 1855, when the Crimean War was at its peak, wheat had sold for 74 shillings a quarter. Thereafter, prices drifted down, reaching 50 shillings by 1877. On the whole, however, improved farming techniques and generally good harvests enabled tenants and landlords to cope with the lower prices. From 1879, however, agricultural depression began to bite. The depression proved remarkably prolonged; apart from a brief respite in the early twentieth century and during World War I, it was to continue until the 1930s. The collapse of agricultural prosperity was the underlying reason for the decline in Brackley's population, by some 20 per cent, between 1891 and 1931.

The depression had its origins in the adoption of Free Trade policies symbolised by the repeal of the Corn Laws in 1846. For many years, however, there was no world surplus of grain and high transport costs meant that imports could barely compete with home-produced food. Yet the opening of the

American Mid-West did create a surplus. Above all, the construction of an American railway network and improvements in marine technology, especially the introduction of the triple-expansion engine, brought a dramatic reduction in freight rates. By 1881, the cost of bringing a bushel of grain from New York to Liverpool was only a tenth of what it had been in 1874.[1]

The year of Thicknesse's departure, 1879, was crucial both for Brackley and for the nation. Apart from 1852, it was the wettest year of the nineteenth century. There was so little sun and so much rain that ears of corn rotted on the stalk and never ripened. Tennyson, the Poet Laureate, had 1879 in mind when he wrote:

> The cuckoo of a joyless June
> Is calling through the dark.[2]

At other times, as during the Revolutionary and Napoleonic Wars, bad weather and poor harvests were welcomed by farmers because they brought high prices. Now, despite reduced home production, ever increasing supplies of cheap imports meant that prices continued to fall.

The weather showed no improvement in the early 1880s. On 4 July 1880, Lady Knightley noted that there had been 'incessant torrents of rain and extraordinarily low temperatures'. Little hope remained of a good harvest, 'so sorely needed by the farmers after four bad seasons'. It was not just grain that was affected. Sheep were dying from rot and fluke; five or six of the Knightleys' tenants had already given up their farms while others were demanding rent reductions.[3]

Although cattle-rearing Northamptonshire may not have been quite so badly hit as old corn areas like the Maldon area of Essex, Brackley had special problems of its own. There were epidemics of cattle plague in 1877, 1881 and 1882, resulting in the closure of markets for months at a time. The profits of the main local bank, Gilletts of Banbury, which had a branch in Brackley, fell by two-thirds between 1878 and 1884 and remained low thereafter.[4]

Many of the gentry families had been living beyond their means, even in the good years of the 1850s and '60s, spending large sums to preserve their political influence. If their estates were already mortgaged in 1879, how would they fare when the going got really rough? In the 1860s, Benjamin Disraeli could still assert, 'It is difficult, if not impossible, to ruin a family well rooted in the land'; twenty years later, the impossible was about to happen.

The position of the Oxford colleges was not dissimilar to that of the gentry. Magdalen still owned several farms in Brackley and Evenley. Merton had land at Radstone and Water Stratford, New College at Radclive, Worcester at Whitfield and All Souls at Lois Weedon and Padbury. The agricultural depression came as a particularly unpleasant surprise to the Fellows of these colleges because they had expected revenues to rise in the 1880s. Traditionally, college land had been let on Beneficial Leases, an arrangement which produced relatively modest income. In the 1860s and '70s, however, colleges phased out Beneficial Leases and raised rents to commercial levels. With this prospect in view, they planned new buildings and more Fellowships.

---

1   20 cents per bushel in 1874, 2 cents per bushel in 1881. Stone, Norman, *Europe Transformed, 1879–1919* (London: Fontana, 1983), p.23.

2   Quoted in Young, GM, *Victorian England: Portrait of an Age* (London: Oxford University Press, 1973), p.145.

3   Cartwright, Julia (ed.), *The Journals of Lady Knightley of Fawsley*, p.336.

4   Taylor, Audrey M, *Gilletts: Bankers at Banbury and Oxford* (Oxford, Clarendon Press, 1964) p.157.

In the prosperous years of the 1860s and early '70s, most tenants were prepared to accept the new terms, but it was a different matter when nature turned hostile and prices continued to fall. College farms, notoriously run down and poorly repaired, were in no position to compete with cheap imports. Tenants complained that they could not pay and colleges were forced to grant remissions, thus more than wiping out the anticipated gains. Unless they were lucky enough to own a lot of urban land – All Souls was fortunate in this respect – colleges would be forced into drastic retrenchment.

Nor would the gentry and the colleges be the only victims. The Church too was still dependent upon agriculture. As tithe and glebe revenues collapsed, a career in the Church became less attractive than in the past. Compared to the financial rewards of other professions, clerical incomes reached their all-time high about 1870, but fell sharply thereafter. By the beginning of the twentieth century, they were down by an average of 30 per cent. But as clerical incomes fell, those of doctors, lawyers, civil servants and headmasters rose – with inevitable effects upon status and influence. Those who entered the Church now were making a conscious decision to eschew a well-paid career. On the credit side, this might mean that the new clergy would be more committed Christians than some of their predecessors, but would this be sufficient to balance the Church's likely failure to recruit the really able and ambitious? However unfairly, some twentieth-century Vicars of Brackley were to be regarded as slightly ridiculous figures. Some people may go to Church because they admire the Vicar's piety but – on the whole – power, ability, wealth and force of character bring larger congregations than piety.

The effects of the agricultural depression caused several spectacular bankruptcies in Banbury – the capital of the local economy. In the first half of 1881, two long-established Banbury law firms, Messrs Pain & Hawtin, and BW Aplin, collapsed with total liabilities of nearly £100,000. Within the next three months, there were at least sixteen more failures in the Banbury area.[5] It is true that the weather improved in 1883 and Mr Stratton of Turweston told a local agricultural society that farmers 'had a better season in every way'.[6] But the improvement was short-lived and gradually the realisation dawned that it was not bad weather but cheap imports that were the real problem; at a time when Free Trade was almost an article of faith, nothing could be done about that.

As she looked out at the rain in the summer of 1880, Lady Knightley wondered about 'the likely consequences for rents and elections'; she suspected they would not be favourable to her kind.[7] But even the perceptive Louisa Knightley could not have guessed that she was witnessing the beginning of the end of the regime of squires, parsons and colleges – sometimes at each other's throats, more lately working in harmony – that had dominated South Northamptonshire since Tudor times. The economic maelstrom facing the gentry encouraged those who resented their political pre-eminence.

Despite their importance in national life, the Reform Bills of 1832 and 1867, even the introduction of the Secret Ballot of 1872, had made remarkably little difference to rural politics. After 1867, there were quite different electorates in Borough and County constituencies. In towns, householders had the vote; in the countryside, they did not. Thus, the towns became 'democratic' while the countryside remained under the political control of the gentry and aristocracy. In South Northamptonshire, they were overwhelmingly Tory. It is true that some aristocrats, like Earl Spencer, were Liberals, but the Spencers were reluctant

5   Taylor, op. cit., p.168.

6   Taylor, op. cit., p.172.

7   As Note 3.

to break ranks with their fellow landowners. At the General Election of 1880, Earl Spencer refused to promote a Liberal candidate and the two Conservatives, Sir Rainald Knightley and FW Cartwright, were returned unopposed. It was the last of the old-style elections.

Even in 1880, some Radicals had deplored Spencer's inaction. In a speech to the Daventry Liberal Club, EF Ashworth Briggs urged his audience to forget deference to aristocrats, even Liberal ones:

> They found out long ago that if they trusted to county families they should be leaning on a broken reed. (Cheers). Family arrangements, private agreements, the necessity of avoiding a breach between families who were privately connected would, no doubt, account for their not having a Liberal candidate in South Northamptonshire for the last 13 years … He said that the people had too long been led by the nose by the aristocracy, and dazzled by hereditary titles.[8]

For all his brave words, however, Briggs must have known that, unless the Spencers intervened, the Liberal cause was a non-starter under the existing franchise. But there were already some significant changes. FW Cartwright died on 2 February 1881. His successor, although a Tory, was not of the landed gentry. Knightley's new colleague was Pickering Phipps, Managing Director of the Northampton brewers, P. Phipps & Co. The Phipps family was wealthy and, for many years, the local euphemism for a heavy drinker was to describe him as a man who 'puts all his money into Phipps's bank'. Even in the Conservative Party, it looked as if the agricultural depression meant that the landowners would be elbowed aside by commercial men.

The real political transformation came with the Reform Act of 1884 whose central provision was the extension of the householder franchise to rural constituencies. In other words, many working men, even farm labourers, would have the vote. Only twenty years earlier, many in the Brackley area had found the very idea wonderfully comic. Now, at long last things seemed to be going the way Thomas Judge had wanted in the last days of Sage.

We hear relatively little of Judge during the Thicknesse years; perhaps his influence was simply overwhelmed by the power and dynamism of the Vicar. But Judge was about to re-emerge and become a formidable figure in the 'democratic' Brackley that came into being after 1884. Judge calculated that, once enfranchised, farm labourers and others would 'rebel' against the Knightleys, Cartwrights and their kind. The Old Tory MPs would be replaced by a new breed of Liberal members and Judge had a clear idea of that these 'new men' should do.

No friend to the Church of England, Judge's hero was Henry Du Pré Labouchère, elected as MP for Northampton in 1880 with the support of the powerful Nonconformist elements in the town. Judge subscribed wholeheartedly to Labouchère's programme, known as 'the three Fs': Free Church (disestablish the Church of England), free land (distribute aristocratic and gentry estates to farm labourers to create a new English peasantry), and Free Schools (nondenominational education) in a 'free state' (not entirely clear but possibly a republic). The implementation of even part of his programme would ruin a local Establishment already weakened by agricultural depression.

'Tommy' Judge was a difficult customer by anybody's standards – aggressive, tough, eloquent and fearless. William Ryland Dent Adkins's *Our County* (1893) calls him 'the *enfant terrible* of Northamptonshire politics'. From

---

8   Quoted in Howarth, Janet, 'Politics and Society in late Victorian Northamptonshire'. *Northamptonshire Past and Present*, Vol. 4, No. 5 (1970–71) p.270.

his remote home on the edge of the county, he relished the role of a prophet crying in the Tory wilderness. He may have lacked prophetic wisdom but he had a double measure of prophetic zeal. He was 'a Radical of Radicals', who seemed like 'a messenger of Satan' to the sedate and solemn Tories of the Brackley area:

> For there is nothing retiring in Mr Judge's temperament, and he does not mince his language in describing his opponents, as well as their opinions. Endowed with a sturdy frame that does not know fatigue and gifted with a fluency of speech beyond any of his rivals, he has long been a redoubtable figure at Liberal demonstrations in the extreme south of Northamptonshire.[9]

Judge had reason to be optimistic. In Northamptonshire as a whole, the 1884 Act tripled the electorate. His hopes rose still further in 1885 when more legislation abolished the traditional double-member constituencies in favour of the smaller single-member divisions familiar to us. Of course, under the new system, voters could no longer hedge their bets by voting for two candidates from rival parties.

Brackley, since 1832 part of the Northamptonshire (South) constituency, was included in the new Towcester Division. Although strange to modern voters, accustomed to regarding the constituency as a 'safe' Tory seat, in 1885, the Towcester Division was a promising Liberal 'prospect'. There was a Liberal tradition in the Nonconformist Chapels and, despite Mr Thicknesse, his surpliced choir and his school, the Nonconformists were by no means 'out' in Brackley.

There were Liberals too in towns like Towcester and Daventry and in villages such as Middleton Cheney and Silverstone. The biggest difference with present arrangements was that, in 1885, the Northamptonshire border still went as far as Banbury Bridge. Hence, the largely working-class Banbury suburb of Grimsbury was included in the Towcester Division.[10] As Barrie Trinder has shown, Liberal activism was a way of life in Banbury and nowhere more so than in Grimsbury. In other words, the first election under the new franchise might be a close call.

But who was to defend the Church and the squires? The choice was not inspired. Well in advance of the election date, 27 November 1885, the Tories announced that their candidate would be one of the sitting members, Sir Rainald Knightley of Fawsley. Pickering Phipps would stand for another Northamptonshire seat. Knightley was now 66 and had held one of the Northamptonshire (South) seats since 1852.[11] Ryland Adkins admits that Knightley always showed to friends and opponents alike 'that old world courtesy which is the rarest of survivals'. Representing 'the agricultural interest' more steadily than almost any other member, he had been 'an ideal county representative of the ancient type'. If these polite comments contain a hint that Knightley was a trifle anachronistic, Adkins's other observations have sharper barbs. Knightley had 'vindicated his title to intellectual distinction by serving in 1865 on the committee which settled the laws of whist', while his shrewd political judgement had been acquired 'during many silent years in Parliament'.[12]

9   Adkins, William Ryland Dent, *Our County* (London: Elliot Stock, 1893) p.28.

10   Pelling, Henry, *The Social Geography of British Elections, 1885–1910* (London, 1967) pp.120–21.

11   Rainald Knightley entered Parliament on the retirement of his father, Sir Charles, who had been Member for South Northamptonshire for eighteen years. Rainald was the twelfth member of the family to sit in Parliament. Gordon, Peter, 'Lady Knightley and the South Northamptonshire Election of 1885', *Northamptonshire Past and Present*, Vol. 6, No. 6 (1981–82) p.265.

12   Adkins, op. cit., p.20.

Knightley was on the Right of the Tory Party. He disliked Disraeli and consistently refused to take office in any government in which 'Dizzy' was involved.[13] In the forthcoming election, Knightley could give no answer to the repeated charge that he had always voted against proposals to extend the franchise. He had voted against the Liberals' Reform Bill in 1884, even against his own party's Bill in 1867. In his heart of hearts, Knightley probably thought that the great Reform Act of 1832 itself had been a mistake. In short, he seems more like a representative of early- rather than mid-Victorian England.

Both Rainald and Louisa Knightley blamed most of the ills facing society on the advance of 'democracy'. Lady Knightley commented sourly on the Liberal victory in the 1880 General Election, 'All this comes of Dizzy's Reform Act [1867], putting the power in the hands of an uneducated, unreasoning mob'.[14]

In the early days of the 1885 campaign, Knightley made no attempt to court the new electorate, hardly a recipe for victory. Although he was sure he disapproved of democracy, Knightley made scant attempt to discover what it was. He told a meeting in Brackley Town Hall on 7 August 1885:

I believe I know very well I am a Constitutional Conservative. You may call me an Old Tory if you like, and I will not refute the appellation, but I hope you will not call me a Tory Democrat – as I have not the vaguest conception of what that is supposed to be.[15]

Although a local man, Knightley had not been a 'good constituency MP'. We have noted his visit to Brackley with Lady Louisa on 1 March 1870 but there were few later ones – perhaps the rain put them off. On 15 August 1885, the Liberal/Radical *Northamptonshire Guardian* could assert without fear of contradiction:

His [Knightley's] intercourse with the Division has been so restricted – his visits, like angels' visits, have been so few and far between – that to the great bulk of his constituency his personality has been an enigma. He has been a sort of political Buddha, for whom a conventional worship has been encouraged by the Tories of 'the good old school', but whose existence has been veiled in the dim haze of distance.

Knightley tried to argue that, as a conscientious member, he had spent most of his time at Westminster and could hardly have been expected to be in two places at once (*Northampton Herald*, 15 August 1885). But he spoiled his case by a later admission that he had voted in only twenty-four of the 266 divisions in the 1884–85 session of Parliament. (*Northampton Mercury*, 26 September 1885). In short, Knightley displayed few of the skills necessary to give his party much of a chance in a democratic age.

Nominally, Knightley's opponent was the official Liberal candidate, the Irishman Sir Maurice Fitzgerald. Of course, Fitzgerald faced the charge of 'mere carpet bagging'. But while he had no previous connections with South Northamptonshire, Fitzgerald had some advantages. He was well connected and undoubtedly a gentleman – which might reassure waverers. He was the second son of the Duke of Leinster and had married a daughter of the Earl of Granard. He had extensive estates in County Wexford, where

13   By 1877, Knightley was almost 'the solitary unconverted member of the anti-Disraeli Tory clique'. Buckle, G.E. (ed.), *The Life of Benjamin Disraeli, Earl of Beaconsfield*, Vol. VI (London: 1929) p.164.

14   Cartwright, *The Journals of Lady Knightley of Fawsley*, p.338.

15   *Northampton Daily Chronicle*, 12 August 1885. Quoted in Gordon, 'Lady Knightley and the South Northamptonshire Election of 1885', op. cit., p.265.

he was an untypically good landlord. His views seemed moderate. He would not support Home Rule for Ireland and, if elected, his chief objectives would be to secure completely free elementary education and more allotments for the poor – worthy, no doubt, but far short of what Judge wanted.[16]

It is unlikely that Knightley was really frightened of Fitzgerald, yet he displayed little stomach for the fight. On the day of the Brackley meeting, Lady Knightley recorded in her diary, 'R. went groaning off for the first of his meetings at Brackley'.[17] It would be unfair to accuse Knightley of cowardice. No doubt, he knew that some of his audience would be hostile; that was politics. But Brackley was different. At Brackley, Knightley would encounter Tommy Judge. Judge was no respecter of persons and he was also an expert heckler with a knack of turning dull Tory meetings into undignified chaos.

Despite an unpromising start, Knightley was to emerge victorious, although by the narrowest of margins. If everything had depended upon Rainald Knightley, he would surely have lost. He probably owed his survival to three people – to Tommy Judge himself, to his wife, Lady Louisa Knightley and, as far as Brackley voters were concerned, to Brooke de Malpas Egerton. The inclusion of Judge may seem surprising. As Ryland Adkins noted, however, Judge's 'fervid enthusiasm' sometimes led him 'into ferocity of expression'. He went too far in the 1885 campaign and alienated voters by the things he said about the Tories. He was supposed to have asserted that he wished Sir Rainald safely installed, not at Westminster, but in Fawsley Churchyard.[18]

Yet Judge's most outrageous remarks were not about Knightley himself, but about Lady Louisa. There were times when the official candidates, Rainald Knightley and Sir Maurice Fitzgerald (dubbed 'the Knight of Kerry'), seem to fade into insignificance, leaving the stage to Judge and Lady Knightley. 'respectable Brackley' was to be both horrified and fascinated by the things Judge implied about Lady Louisa. Lady Knightley herself expressed outrage at his remarks, but one wonders if she really cared; she certainly gave as good as she got.

Of course, at this time, women could neither vote nor sit in Parliament, yet Lady Knightley was a remarkable woman. Ryland Adkins describes her as 'almost the only lady in the county who has gained influence and consideration by active political work' and notes that it was widely believed that her efforts had secured her husband's victories in 1885 and 1886.[19] Unlike most of the 'characters' discussed in this book, she defies all attempts to label her as early-, mid- or late-Victorian. She combines elements of all three ages in her complex personality. Her marriage to Rainald Knightley suggests identification with the early years, yet, as we have seen, she was very taken with the mid-Victorian Francis Thicknesse. In private, she agreed with her husband's strictures on democracy, but she came to realise that it would be political suicide to talk like that in public. She wanted to preserve as much of the old order as possible and thought that something could be saved from the wreck. If that required her to talk democracy then she was quite willing to do so.

She soon found that she had a natural talent for such things. Her *Journals* are full of expressions of cloying wifely devotion to 'Darling Rainald', yet there are hints that she found the whist expert too much of a fuddy-duddy. In Louisa Knightley, there is 'an emancipated woman' struggling to get out. In short,

16   Gordon, op. cit., p 267.

17   Ibid., p.266.

18   Adkins, op. cit., p.29.

19   Ibid., p.21.

she is a superb example of the resourcefulness and adaptability, perhaps the lack of scruple, which representatives of the old order could display in the face of adversity. Curiously, it was often the women who responded thus. Many of the gentlemen of late-Victorian and Edwardian Northamptonshire were pretty feeble creatures. Lady Knightley had no children of her own, but she collected a group of strong-minded girls about herself. They were High Tories in politics but keen on women's emancipation. One of her 'daughters', the slightly mannish Beatrice Cartwright, was still a force to be reckoned with in Brackley at the time of my birth in 1947.

Louisa Bowater had married Rainald Knightley in 1869 when he was 50 and she 27. As a girl she had moved on the fringes of Court circles. After her marriage, she regularly attended Parliamentary debates and her *Journals* contain accounts of conversations with politicians like Gladstone, Disraeli, Lord Salisbury and Sir Stafford Northcote.[20] Lady Knightley had more interest than her husband in social questions and, despite her reservations about Disraeli, welcomed the social reforms introduced by the Tories between 1874 and 1880. Before 1885, however, Lady Knightley's main interest was in voluntary organisations, especially those involving young women.

In the 1870s, she emerged as one of the leading figures in the Girls' Friendly Society (GFS) – 'for Church, Queen and Family' – and was largely responsible for gaining royal support for the movement.[21] Now Lady Knightley perceived that the techniques she had developed in the GFS could be transferred to politics. They could be used to give new voters a sense of participation and involvement – an illusion perhaps, but a plausible one – which could turn them into committed Tories.

At the end of July, Louisa Knightley decided to 'rescue' the Tory campaign. To begin with, she was very much the Victorian lady, insisting in her *Journal* that all she wanted was to 'support my own darling husband' because of her deep conviction that 'the cause he will support is the cause of religion, of liberty and prosperity for this country and *every* class of its inhabitants'.[22] But then she attended a meeting at the Assembly Room, Daventry, and found it 'very exciting'.[23] Louisa Knightley was 'hooked'.

Armed with specially prepared instructions from Conservative Central Office, she toured the constituency and, by 23 October, had arranged for the canvassing of every village. These activities brought her into closer touch with ordinary people and she was forced to admit that the new electors were generally more rational and better behaved than she had expected. She found at least 90 per cent of the men sitting by their firesides, often with children round their knees. She encountered few cases of drunkenness and everywhere was received with courtesy, even intelligence. Some were prepared to concede a point – 'that's right enough' – but others wanted to argue. At Daventry she met the Radical, Aubrey Hickman, 'He talked about Russia and Afghanistan and completely posed Mrs Willoughby and me about the Bankruptcy Act'. Direct experience of bad housing forced her to question her own position. At Towcester, she came across some Radical shoemakers who lived 'in some horrid little Courts' and admitted, 'I should be a Radical myself if I lived in such holes'.[24]

---

20   Gordon, 'Lady Knightley …', op. cit., p.265.

21   Harrison, B, 'For Church, Queen and Family: The Girls' Friendly Society 1874–1920', *Past and Present*, No. 61, November 1973, p.109.

22   Lady Knightley's *Journal*, 29 July 1885. Quoted in Gordon, 'Lady Knightley …', op. cit., p.268.

23   Ibid., p.269.

24   Ibid., p.270.

Lady Knightley could not do everything on her own. She saw the need to mobilise Conservative ladies and, even more, women who aspired to be Conservative ladies. She shamelessly exploited the social aspirations of lower middle, and even upper working-class women, the wives of shopkeepers and skilled craftsmen. The reward for unstinting door-to-door canvassing could be that vision of paradise, tea on the lawn at Fawsley next summer!

Soon Lady Knightley's ladies were enrolled into the Primrose League, with its titles and pseudo-Medieval ceremonies. In private, Lady Knightley felt only contemptuous amusement, 'it all sounds rubbish'. But it worked like magic and the flummery was worth it if it produced that election-winning force, 'an army of unpaid canvassers'. Yet, behind the cynicism there was a feminist angle. Nearly forty years before women received the vote, they were allowed to join the Primrose League on equal terms with men, and much of that was Lady Knightley's doing. The local branch of the League quickly established a 'Knightley Habitation' and, with a slightly wry face, Lady Louisa was installed as its 'Presiding Dame'.[25]

The methods employed by Lady Knightley and her ladies were controversial. The Liberal *Northampton Mercury* declared that the Primrose League should be renamed 'the Rural Intimidation Society' and waxed indignant about 'the phenomenal degree of pressure' used on the new electorate.[26] There was some justification for these complaints. When the Tory canvasser visited the cottage of a new voter, the voter's master or landlord often joined her. The obvious question was would refusal to vote Tory mean the sack? One of the loudest critics was Moses Manfield, the Northampton shoe manufacturer, who piously urged Lady Knightley 'to examine her conscience' about such tactics. Louisa Knightley had the measure of that old hypocrite, however, 'he had better think of the paper shoes he supplied to the poor French soldiers in 1870–1 before he talks to me of *conscience*'.[27]

But Louisa Knightley herself was not always accompanied by an employer, or even by another lady. While 'official' Liberal complaints centred on possible intimidation, other questions were forming in more prudish or prurient minds. Lady Knightley was doing something new and shocking. Here was a high-born lady, middle-aged it was true, but still obviously energetic and – perhaps significantly – married to a much older husband, deliberately seeking out the company of rough labourers to solicit their vote. No doubt there were occasions when the labourer's wife was not at home. To a straight-laced age, the scenario had definite sexual overtones. It would be surprising if in less polite male society – in the tap room or at the work place perhaps – some crude oaf did not wonder aloud just what Lady Knightley would be willing to do to get his vote?

Of course, there was the old story about the Duchess of Devonshire and the Westminster Election of 1784. It was claimed that, when campaigning for Charles James Fox, the Duchess had offered 'kisses for votes'. Was Lady Knightley up to the same tricks? However intriguing the speculation, few can have imagined that anyone would dare to raise the idea in public. But the unmentionable was mentioned at a Conservative meeting at Silverstone on 19 October 1885. There was only one man who could have done it – Tommy Judge.

Judge and others had already reduced the meeting to a shambles when Rainald Knightley unwisely mentioned the valiant support he had received from Lady Louisa. At this, Judge stood up. Mr Loder, the

25   Robb, J.H., *The Primrose League, 1883–1906* (London: 1968), p.56.

26   *Northampton Mercury*, 5 December 1885.

27   Lady Knightley's *Journal*, 27 October 1885.

harassed Chairman, thinking that the Brackley grocer was about to attack Lady Knightley, warned him that it would not be in accordance with good taste to mention a lady who was not present. Tommy Judge cared nothing for good taste but he had no intention of attacking Lady Knightley, at least for the moment. He began, 'There is a story of the Duchess of Devonshire …'.

Loder could not see where Judge's remarks were leading. With lamentable ignorance of history, he supposed that Judge had introduced an entirely irrelevant issue. No doubt, he thought here was an opportunity for some fun at the grocer's expense. He asked, 'Whatever has the Duchess of Devonshire to do with this meeting?' Equally ignorant Tories joined in the laughter. Judge ploughed on, 'It is said that the Duchess of Devonshire …' Still the penny had not dropped and Loder tried to continue the joke, observing, 'Sir Rainald has not had the pleasure of knowing the Duchess of Devonshire …' But then Judge enlightened them about what he was driving at:

> Taking advantage of a temporary lull in the storm, Mr Judge shouted the remainder of his sentence, 'That she gave a butcher a kiss for a vote'. 'Now', continued Mr Judge, 'I should like to ask Sir Rainald this question – How many butchers had Lady Knightley kissed, or how many does she intend to kiss'?' (Immense uproar.)[28]

All hell broke loose. The Chairman asked the audience whether they would allow Judge to go on 'after this gross insult'. There was a roar of 'No!' and the cry went up, 'Chuck him out, Old Weigh Sugar, Butterine!'

Tories moved towards Judge with the intention of ejecting him, probably none too gently. Fights broke out as Judge's supporters, some of them armed with clubs, surrounded their hero to protect him. Above the din, Rainald Knightley, normally calm and refined, screamed in fury at Judge, 'No man in Northamptonshire has yet been such a gross black-guard as to insult my wife!'

Judge had gone too far and his crude remarks undoubtedly brought about a wave of sympathy for Knightley. Tory supporters turned out in force for the remaining meetings and were always reminded of Judge's disgraceful behaviour. At Paulerspury shortly before Polling Day, Loder, again in the Chair:

> … first thanked the meeting for the hearty reception accorded to Sir Rainald and himself, and then alluded in strong terms to the insult offered to Lady Knightley at Silverstone and called for three hearty cheers for that lady, which were readily given.[29]

Although the tide was turning the Tory way, would it be enough? The political struggle between Tory and Liberal was still largely a matter of Church versus Chapel, so the outcome would depend substantially on the religious affiliations of the new voters. Here the achievements and personality of Brooke de Malpas Egerton would be crucial, at least in Brackley. Although Egerton was not so great a man as Thicknesse, he was in the same league. We should remember that, whereas Thicknesse's achievements in the early 1870s had been at a time when the gentry were still riding high and enjoying something of an Indian Summer, Egerton had to work in a more difficult climate.

28   *Northampton Herald*, 24 October 1885.

29   Ibid., 21 November 1885.

In the event, he was to play his poorer hand with consummate skill. Thicknesse had tried to turn the people of Brackley into Churchgoers through his grandiose projects and the sheer power of his personality. Egerton set out to give them a feeling of belonging, a feeling that St Peter's was *their* Church and they were involved in its running. The Vicar might be the cousin of the Earl of Ellesmere but he was also the friend of the poorest of his parishioners. What Egerton was trying to do for the Church was something similar to what Lady Knightley was trying to do for the Tory Party.

The best way to approach Egerton's programme is through the pages of the *Brackley Parish Magazine*, launched in January 1883. It is a measure of Egerton's success that, well into the 1950s, when Brackley people spoke of 'the *Magazine*', they meant the *Parish Magazine*. The *Magazine* had two sections. The larger part consisted of a collection of sermons, missionary news and uplifting short stories under the title of 'The Banner of Faith', printed in London for the Church Extension Association; the second, locally produced and more important section contained accounts of the previous month's parish activities, details of forthcoming events, a record of baptisms, marriages and burials and a letter from the Vicar. The letter always began, 'My dear friends' and was signed, 'Your faithful friend and Pastor'.

In the first number, Egerton hoped that 'our little publication' would prove useful in 'creating still greater love for the Church and for Church work, and of drawing us all more closely in the unity of Faith and in the bond of Peace'. The *Magazine* was treasured in cottage homes and some took the trouble to have it bound. Others sent copies to friends and relations who had left Brackley. During the 'years of migration', from the 1890s to the 1930s, the *Magazine* helped to preserve the 'Brackley identity' of many forced by economic circumstances to live and work elsewhere. It was one of the most powerful instruments in maintaining the cult of 'Dear old Brackley'.

Like Lady Knightley's, Egerton's scheme depended on voluntary work by women. On 3 January 1883, a meeting was held in the Girls' School Room, where 'several ladies' offered their services as 'District Visitors'. Initially most of the District Visitors were middle class or even grander, but soon they expanded to include the wives of traders and skilled artisans. For these women, especially, appointment as a District Visitor conferred a certain status and authority.

The ostensible purpose of the scheme was to help with the distribution of the *Magazine*. But when delivering the eagerly awaited booklet – and, thanks to the Church Schools, literacy rates were rising – the District Visitor could bring the conversation round to more regular attendance at Church, sending a child to Sunday School or even volunteering a promising boy for the choir. She could even act as a kind of social worker, bringing the Vicar's attention to cases of real hardship among the 'deserving poor'. In other words, she formed a vital link in the essential work of 'intelligence gathering', just like Lady Knightley's Tory canvassers. The *Magazine* of April 1883 helpfully provides us with a table of districts and their visitors:

District	Visitor
Bandilands & Old Town	Mrs Egerton
Taylor's Lane	Mrs & Miss Stace
Church Lane	Lady Bannerman
Cross Lane & Norris's Cottages	Mrs Scott
Almshouses and Martin's Yard	Mrs Boughton
Pebble Lane	Miss Smith
Malthouse Yard & Wootton's Yard	The Misses Blencowe

Boot Yard, Blackwell's Yard and Part of High Street	Mrs Bayley
Chapel Lane	Mrs Luffman
Buckingham Road & The Croft	Miss Weston
Hatwell's Cottages & New Road	Miss Butterfield
Banbury Road	Mrs Gilchrist
Backway	Miss Harris
Hall's Lane	Mrs & Miss Chapman
Bridge Street (East Side)	Mrs I Wodhams
Bridge Street (West Side)	Mrs Mallins & Miss Leonard
Sewell's Yard	Mrs GH Clarke
Wrighton's Yard	Miss Bartlett

The list is important social document and shows that, under Egerton's direction, the Church was reaching out into the Yards, containing the worst housing in the town, the sort of hovels Smith had described in 1865. Many of the people in the Yards were too poor, perhaps too badly dressed, to relish coming to Church. Egerton was prepared to take the Church to them by holding evening services in the Yards themselves. The list also shows that 'clergy wives' were allocated the most difficult assignments. The Curate's wife, Mrs Luffman, was allocated Chapel Lane, taking the war into enemy territory with a vengeance. Most remarkable of all is the allocation of Bandilands, which probably had the most wretched cottages in Brackley. Here the District Visitor was Alice Egerton, the Vicar's lady herself.

Nor were the men forgotten. Here the central device was the choir. Not only was singing enjoyable but, of course, the choir sang in the chancel, traditionally the part of the Church that specially 'belonged' to the Vicar. By entering the choir, choristers became in a sense 'the Vicar's men'; indeed, as they donned their white surplices, some may have fancied that they were 'almost' clergymen, 'almost' gentlemen. 'Almost' gentlemen knew that they would advance their claims still further if they made it clear that, come Election Day, they would vote Tory. The identity was pushed home further with Choir Suppers, held in the Vicarage itself.

Of course, the *Magazine* was used to publicise the achievements of the Church School, the 'flagship' of the Thicknesse Revolution. It was also used to give advanced publicity to festivities like St Peter's Feast, now revived by Egerton. Perhaps Egerton was trying to revive something of the old 'community spirit', under threat since the attack launched by the 'strict discipline' party at the end of the eighteenth century. But it was not really the old world restored; the replacement of beer by tea meant that 'community' was managed and respectable; it was, at best, a pseudo-*gemeinschaft*.

The essence of the Egerton programme was to recruit the people of Brackley as junior partners to support a religious and social Establishment whose financial underpinnings were becoming increasingly shaky. But there was one further strand to the strategy. The vision could be made even more alluring if, for a few – perhaps even only for one man – ability and loyal service to the Establishment could be shown to culminate in full membership of that Establishment, not as a junior but as an equal partner. In other words, it might be necessary to incorporate a dash of social mobility into the conservative order.

There was one figure in the Brackley of the 1880s, like Egerton a clergyman, who exemplified the possibility of social advancement through the Church. His name was Isaac Wodhams. We have already encountered Wodhams, the son of a blacksmith, as one of the able boys at Magdalen College School in the 'false dawn' of improvement during the Mastership of Rev FB Falkner. By 1866, Wodhams was undertaking some teaching for the school and became an Assistant Master in 1870. He left in 1872 to become an undergraduate at Cambridge, taking his BA in 1876. The same year he was ordained and became one of Thicknesse's Curates, although he moved away again in 1879 to take a curacy at St Sepulchre's, Northampton, once Robert Sybthorpe's Church. He was appointed Master of Magdalen College School on 5 August 1882. He was to prove a brilliant Master but, for our purposes, his work was less important than the man himself. Here was living proof that hard work and devotion to the Church could transform one's social status. The blacksmith's son was treated as an equal by the aristocratic Mr Egerton. Of course, not every boy in Brackley could be an Isaac Wodhams, but that such a thing was possible at all must have been a powerful argument for voting Tory in 1885.

The story of Magdalen College School and of Isaac Wodhams has been told by Eric Forrester, so it is unnecessary to give more than a bare outline here.[30] As we have seen, relations between Magdalen College and Francis Thicknesse had not been entirely cordial. Indeed, the school seems to have been little affected by the drive and energy which marked the Thicknesse Revolution. In 1882, there were only sixteen day boys and one boarder on the school roll. The Master, Rev John William Boyd (1879–82), 'had the misfortune to lose his only son from typhoid fever which he attributed to the insanitary state of the house'.[31] Wodhams, appointed on 5 August 1882, brought about changes to the school equivalent to Thicknesse's work in the town at large. By the time Wodhams left in 1899, numbers had risen to eighty – divided almost equally between boarders and day boys. Academic standards rose as pupils were entered for Oxford Local Delegacy Examinations, there were new buildings, improvements to the Chapel and a much-expanded Library. Above all, Wodhams's own example of social mobility through education suggested that others could do the same.

Although Egerton did not have the same resources as Thicknesse, he had to do something spectacular in 1885. He could not afford a new Church as Thicknesse had wanted – and in any case Egerton was more of an architectural traditionalist – so he chose the right moment to launch a plan to restore St Peter's. The work would help to create jobs at a time when many local men, including some who would shortly be voting for the first time, were facing the prospect of unemployment and hence the dreaded Workhouse. In the January 1885 edition of the *Magazine*, the Vicar noted that the recent severe weather had 'caused considerable increase in the number of sick people and, alas! so many working men have been thrown out of employment that there has been much need of temporary assistance'. Much help had been given already but 'the Clergy will be glad to be informed of any urgent cases that will need special attention'.

From the time of the Choir Supper in January, the calendar of Church events was unusually full that year. In May, the Vicar was able to report that the number of Easter communicants, the key test of Anglican identity, was rising steadily: 147 in 1882, 177 in 1883, 190 in 1884 and 210 in 1885. But it was the restoration project that dominated the pages of the *Magazine*. The donations were coming in: £300 from the Earl of Ellesmere, 100 guineas from the brewer Alfred Hopcraft, £50 from Mrs Bayley, £30 from Mrs Mallins, £25 from Mr TB Cartwright, £25 from Mr William Blencowe, £25 from Dr Hare, £25 from Mr GA Campbell and many smaller donations. Even Tommy Judge gave 2 guineas. The foundation stone for the extended chancel was laid on 17 July 1885 and, by the time of the election, the fund stood at £1,453 17s 9d.

30 Forrester, Eric G, *A History of Magdalen College School, Brackley, Northamptonshire, 1548–1949*, Chapter VI, 'The Rev Isaac Wodhams (1882–1899), The Second Founder and Father of the School', pp.97–165.

31 Magdalen Report of 1895 (President's Lodgings). Quoted in Forrester, op. cit., p.95.

The restoration project becomes all the more significant when we remember that the Church was a major issue in the election. Judge campaigned openly for Disestablishment and even the more moderate Fitzgerald hinted at it. The policy doubtless appealed to Nonconformists but it horrified Anglicans. Egerton wrote a lengthy 'Pastoral' for the crucial November edition of the *Magazine*, entitled 'The National Church and the Liberation Society'. It is a blatant piece of Tory propaganda, though the Vicar pretended it was not:

> Now, if the coming election simply concerned us with reference to the probable balance of power in either of the great Parties in the State, I should not say one word upon the subject here, for the Parish Clergyman ought not to be a political partisan; he is not the Minister of one section only of his Parishioners – it is his high privilege and duty to exercise his sacred calling amongst all those committed to his care, quite irrespective of what their political views may be.

But this was no ordinary election. The existence of the Church as the 'Church of the nation' was threatened and 'when very many candidates for seats in Parliament have already pledged themselves, if elected, to advocate Disestablishment of the Church, then, I think, the time for silence has gone by'. True, for the moment, the precise details of the Disestablishment scheme remained unclear but there can be little doubt about where it was all leading. Churches and Cathedrals would be taken over by the state and used for secular purposes. The running of churches would be removed from the control of the clergy and Churchwardens and entrusted to elected boards likely to include non-Churchmen. There would be no guarantee that the Vicar of a parish would even be a member:

> But can we live without our Churches? Can we bow to the vote of a Parochial Board – and see our churches used for secular purposes, our congregations scattered, God's Altar desecrated, our teaching scattered to the four winds? No, we could not submit to this dishonour without protest. Are Churchmen, nay more, are religious Nonconformists prepared to see the Ancient Parish churches of England dealt with in this way? Are they prepared to see buildings which have been solemnly set apart for the worship of God – buildings in which the voice of prayer and praise has risen up from one generation to another to the throne of God, buildings hallowed by all the memories and associations of the past, hallowed as enshrining the dust of the holy dead, – hallowed above all by the spiritual presence of the Lord himself, in the midst of His faithful worshippers; – are they prepared to see these buildings turned to secular uses – let to the highest bidder, or sold as useless encumbrances? I do not believe it for one moment.

If any readers were uncertain about what Egerton was getting at, his meaning became crystal clear in the last paragraph. Here, his sights were on the new voters – 'Remember this, also, that if the Church is disestablished and disendowed, the loss will fall heavily upon the poor'. Although some people may have been daunted by Egerton's complicated sentences, they must have realised that what he really meant was 'vote Tory'.

And then it was Election Day. By this time, one has the feeling that the gentlemanly official candidates were almost irrelevant. The real battle was between the raucous Radicalism of Tommy Judge and the 'populist' Tory Anglicanism of Lady Knightley, Brooke de Malpas Egerton and Isaac Wodhams. The electorate voted and 83.9 per cent of that electorate went to the polls. Knightley received 4,074 votes and

Fitzgerald 4,012 – a Tory majority of sixty-two.[32] The December edition of the *Magazine*, which reported good progress on the restoration project, also contains the Vicar's reflection on the election result:

> Sir Rainald Knightley, who has already represented the County as one of its members for 33 years, has again been returned to Parliament. The Parish Magazine is not political [actually it was highly political] so we will only say here, that very many churchmen in the Division will feel thankful that they have in their representative one who has pledged himself to resist to the very utmost any measure for Disestablishment and Disendowment of the Church.

On the face of it, the old order had triumphed but, as Egerton admitted, the result had been very close, indeed, in order to win the old order had had to change.

Benjamin Disraeli once defined democracy as 'the exclusion of gentlemen from politics'. In the Brackley area, it might not quite come to that but, after 1885, things would never be the same again. Perhaps the biggest change was in Lady Knightley herself. On the day of the election, the Knightleys went to the Polling Station at Badby. Sir Rainald voted for himself, but 'I waited outside and felt, for the first time personally, the utter anomaly of my not having a vote, while John Bull has!'[33]

32 Gordon, 'Lady Knightley …', op. cit., p.273.

33 Lady Knightley's *Journal*, 27 November 1885.

Banbury Road corner: note the black and white architecture.

St Peter's Church, south door.

Clockwise from above: Isaac Wodhams; The
Plough Inn: note the gateway, now demolished;
St Peter's interior, July 1886.

Chapter Eight

A NEW COURSE?

The neck-and-neck result at the polls in November 1885 indicated an uncertain future. Brackley's experience in the 1880s seems to substantiate Norman Stone's suggestion that these were the most confusing years of the nineteenth century, not just in Britain but throughout Europe. Yet, beneath the confusion, one central fact emerges: a decisive shift was taking place from forms of government based on landed oligarchies to those founded on wide electorates and mass political participation.[1] In local terms, everything depended on the answers to three crucial questions:

1 Would the agricultural depression continue and complete the economic ruin of the gentry and the Anglican clergy dominant since Tudor times?

2 If their economic decline continued, could these groups still maintain their social and political power by adapting themselves to 'democracy'? Lady Knightley's brilliant populism suggested that they still had a chance – but it would be touch and go.

3 If they failed, could Nonconformist, Liberal and Radical groups, representing an alternative tradition – often hidden but never entirely absent since the seventeenth century – assume leadership by winning the loyalty of the newly enfranchised agricultural labourers and transforming the entire character of the area? Here the representative figure was Tommy Judge, but the Radicals and the Nonconformists had their own problems and their victory was by no means assured.

Answers of a sort began to emerge over the next few years. The agricultural depression, already eroding the position of the local gentry, showed no sign of lifting. If the weather was too wet in the late 1870s it was too dry in the 1890s:

1 Stone, Norman, *Europe Transformed, 1878–1919* (London: Fontana, 1983) p.74.

Character of Summers and Harvests in Northants 1875–1893.

1875	Very wet, except harvest.
1876	Fine commencement, showery end.
1877	Wet & cold. 2 floods. V. bad crops.
1878	Showery. Crops inferior.
1879	Late, cold, wet. V. bad crops.
1880	Fine commencement. V. wet end.
1881	Fine start, wet middle, fine end.
1882	Fine first fortnight. V. wet after.
1883	Showery all through.
1884	Very dry & hot, Fair crops.
1885	Fair season. Beans v. bad & late.
1886	Fair. 10 days showery in harvest.
1887	Very dry summer. Excellent crops.
1888	Wet, cold July. Late season.
1889	Wet July. Fine & dry harvest.
1890	Fair season.
1891	Fine start, wet end.
1892	V. fair season. Frost not felt here.
1893	Very fair and dry.

The 'Report on the Agriculture of Bedfordshire, Huntingdonshire and Northamptonshire' produced by R Hunter Pringle in 1895 makes depressing reading. The heavy clay soil meant that ploughing was expensive and there was much 'three horse land' around Brackley. By 1895, the years of neglect had taken their toll:

> There can be no doubt it was the failure to keep these lands in workable order, and the heavy losses suffered by those who occupied them that reduced the thin-skinned clays of these counties to a condition very little better than that of the Maldon Union of Essex. All over the north of Bedford, the west of Huntingdon, and the east and south of Northampton, wide tracts of miserable grass land are seen at the present day; strong clay is well suited to the growth of wheat and beans, but now represents little value either to the landlord or tenant and gives no employment to the labourer.

The bad weather did more than kill sheep and consume capital. The pastures themselves were deteriorating, with the better varieties of grass dying out to be replaced by coarse herbage. The landowners were partly to blame. They had been slow to accept the inevitability of lower rents; only after 1888 did they grant substantial reductions, from 12s to as little as 6s 8½d per acre by 1893. But the fall in wages had been more modest: 29s 10d per week in 1888 to 27s 8d in 1893. Pringle believed that if wages had fallen in the same proportion as rent, much of the abandoned land would still be under cultivation. Pringle's sympathies were with the tenants:

Between the time when a farmer's affairs show signs of complication and the day of final collapse, several years may elapse. He fights and struggles amid his difficulties, he disposes of his stock to pay his debts and his labourers; he gets into arrears with his rent; he signs bills and promissory notes; he seeks the assistance of dealers and money lenders; and all the while letting down the condition of the land he farms. There has either been a melting away of the working capital represented by livestock, accompanied by increasing indebtedness to tradesmen, dependence on dealers, and an all-round deterioration of farming, ultimately resulting in bankruptcy or abandonment, or the private banking account and investments are being drawn upon to meet liabilities.

Until 1890 farmers of the best grazing land managed tolerably well with good seasons in 1882 and 1888, but the value of fat stock had fallen recently while the costs of stores had risen. Now the fat-stock trade was little more than a gamble with everything depending on 'the quantity of foreign meat afloat and about to arrive'. Once every village along the River Ouse or the Nene had had its own mill but, as Lord Wantage observed:

It is an industry which has been knocked on the head; a little miller is knocked out of time by a bigger miller, but at present the bigger miller is knocked out of time by the still bigger American miller. It is an industry which has gone.

Village shopkeepers would soon face the same fate.

Much the same story is found in another work, published in 1902. *Rural England* by Henry Rider Haggard, better known as the author of *King Solomon's Mines*, devoted a chapter to Northamptonshire. Haggard interviewed several landowners and tenants in the Brackley area, including Sir Charles Knightley, Rainald Knightley's successor at Fawsley. Sir Charles insisted that 'the agricultural industry of these parts had gone down very much of late years, the rents having fallen from 30 to 35 per cent'. As a result, many 'big houses' had been given up. A county once as famous for its squires as for its spires, now had 'few gentry and practically no society'.[2] Knightley claimed that 'were it not for the hunting there would be nobody in the district', although by 'nobody' he clearly meant 'no ladies or gentlemen'.

Sir Hereward Wake was equally gloomy, insisting that landowners could no longer live on their rents; hence, a landed agricultural estate was little more than 'a beautiful toy for a rich man'.[3]

The depression also affected tenant farmers. Whereas graziers once expected to make £5 profit on each bullock, £3 was now nearer the mark. If more than a couple of bullocks died before sale, the profit disappeared completely. In some instances, new tenants, more skilled in cutting costs, came in from Devonshire, bringing with them the Devon breed of cattle.

Although tenants did not suffer quite as much as landowners, few could do more than make ends meet. Those who appeared to do well in life generally 'cut up badly when they died'.[4] Haggard was told that 'grazing is a thing of the past'. The transit of animals from abroad was improving and oxen arriving at Deptford after a long sea voyage were in no worse shape than animals brought to London from Northamptonshire in a railway cattle truck. A few optimists thought that cheap foreign store cattle might

2   Haggard, H Rider, *Rural England*, two volumes (London: 1902), Vol. 2, pp.125–26.

3   Ibid., p.137.

4   Ibid., p.129.

help but the majority believed that 'pleuro-pneumonia might come with them and that would be the last nail in our coffin'.[5]

The depression resulted in a massive shift from grain to animal farming. In 1868, there were 82,000 acres under plough in Northamptonshire but this fell to 58,000 in 1885 and to only 31,000 in 1895 – as Audrey Taylor remarks, '"Up horn, down corn" with a vengeance'.[6] Cattle grazing required little labour – on average only two men for 300 acres. Those who tended cattle were called 'shepherds'.[7] Although less labour was required than in the past, there was no corresponding reduction in wage bills. Most observers felt that labourers had done better than either landowners or tenants. Emigration to towns and the availability of other employment in rural areas reduced the supply of labour even more than the demand. Haggard was told that 'labourers must be very gently handled'. Farm workers might be better off than before but, inevitably, they compared their wages with those in other occupations, especially in railway service.

Things might have been different if farmers could have offered their workers 30s a week, but that was impossible with the low level of prices. Nor was it just a matter of money: 'Schoolmasters taught lads to look down on agriculture', so the 'lads' went off for the 'regular work, high wages, fixed holidays and cheap fares' they could get at the Wolverton works of the LNWR. The result was depopulation, with some parts of the county becoming 'as lonesome as the veldt'. Those who remained no longer respected their betters or even themselves:

> The farm labourer, looked down upon especially by the young women of his own class, consequently looks down upon himself. At the bottom of the social scale, without pride or hope for the future, he could no longer even be bothered to acquire the traditional arts of husbandry. Haggard was appalled: 'if unchecked it may mean the ruin of the race.'[8]

Although the economic tide was running against them, at least some of the gentry and their allies had no thought of giving up. Moreover, in Brackley, the problem was masked by the wealth (largely non-agricultural and hence more secure) of the Earl of Ellesmere and by the energy and dedication of Vicar Egerton.

On the national stage, the Tories were assisted by Gladstone's conversion to Irish Home Rule. The new policy split the Liberals and Gladstone's government was defeated in Parliament in June 1886. Another General Election was called only a few months after the previous one. In the Towcester Division, the Liberal candidate, Sir James Carmichael, did his best, but Rainald Knightley, standing for the last time, increased his majority to 316. In the country as a whole, the Tories obtained an overall majority of 118 seats – barring total disaster enough to enable for a full term of seven years. Thus, the Tory gentry and clergy were given a breathing space to prove their democratic credentials before the next election.

One of the most attractive representatives of the old order was Rev Brooke de Malpas Egerton. As we have seen, Egerton had responded to a deteriorating financial situation by creating a caring and slightly

5   Ibid., p.128.

6   The comparable figures for Oxfordshire were 64,000 acres in 1868, 48,000 in 1885 and 23,000 in 1895. Taylor, Audrey M., *Gilletts: Bankers at Banbury and Oxford* (Oxford: Clarendon Press, 1964) p.164.

7   Haggard, op. cit., p.126.

8   Ibid., p.140.

populist Anglicanism at least as attractive as the intimidating triumphalism of his predecessor. In 1886, Egerton was at the height of his powers. Readers of the *Magazine* were constantly reminded how much the Church had done for them. In the issue of January 1886, Egerton asserted:

> The death rate has again been low, much below the average rate a few years ago, and there has been no outbreak of fever or other epidemic, nor any other serious accident or disaster to interfere with the quiet order of our life.

But even Thicknesse's drains did not give Brackley total protection against disease and there was heavy mortality in February and March 1886: nineteen burials in those two months alone compared to thirty-one in the whole of 1885. There would be 'many sad hearts and homes in consequence'. The March burials reveal that only one of those who had died – Daniel King – had reached a good age; the rest were of infants, children or adults all far short of their 'allotted span'.[9]

BURIALS

'Blessed are the dead that die in the Lord'

4 March	Dorcas Jarvis	36 years
5 March	Alfred Arnold	45 years
6 March	George Edward Porter	8 months
8 March	Phyllis Faulkner	1 month
10 March	Mary Anne Turvey	30 years
11 March	William Hearn	3 months
12 March	Catherine Spittals	49 years [my great-grandmother]
13 March	John Knibbs	26 years
15 March	Daniel King	80 years
15 March	Florence Moore	18 days
18 March	Horace Faulkner	4 months
18 March	John Henry Garrett	34 years
22 March	Ernest Henry Fennimore	7 months

But there was much to do. It was vital to secure a forceful and effective Headmaster for the Church School. Mr Bamford left after eleven years and was replaced by Mr William Garrett. Garrett, who had been trained at Culham College, proved an excellent choice. A stern disciplinarian, he was to serve for many years. The choir was presented with a new set of surplices and cassocks. There was the Cottage Hospital, the Reading Room and Library, the Mutual Improvement Society and the Sunday Schools to organise.

In view of the issues raised at the previous election, Egerton set up a Brackley branch of the Church Defence Institution. A successful inaugural meeting was held in the Town Hall on 25 March 1886.

---

9   The heavy death rate was due to an epidemic of influenza, involving a virus similar to the one which caused the better-known outbreak at the end of World War I. In 1919 it was noted that relatively young people were the most vulnerable. Older people, who had experienced the 1886 epidemic, and thus had some immunity, were less likely to die.

There was the restoration project to press ahead. An impressive service was held on 14 May to mark the completion of the work:

> Now that we can see the true relative proportions of the nave and chancel, I feel sure that all will acknowledge the beauty and merit of the architect's design, and the admirable manner in which the work has been carried out. All our anxious thoughts and care have been amply repaid, for the chancel is very beautiful, quiet in tone, but rich and handsome. Stone and woodwork, tiles and window glass, floor and roof, pendants, and screen, and sanctuary hangings are all in harmony with each other, and combine to give an effect which is most striking, solemn and beautiful.

A spectacular Grand Bazaar was held on 20, 21 and 22 July to raise money to pay off the debt. The upper Town Hall, 'arranged under the skilful hand of Mr Bernasconi', was disguised as a ruined abbey, with the stalls placed inside the Gothic arches and windows. Appropriately, the Bazaar was opened by Lady Knightley, a woman who understood the advantages of Medieval ceremonial when defending the Tory Party and the Church of England. The Bazaar was a huge success, raising nearly £500 (at least £50,000 in modern money) for the restoration fund.

On a more practical note, it was gratifying to learn that the Church School, now in Mr Garrett's care, had found favour with the School Inspectors, Mr Currey and Mr Simpson. All three schools – Boys', Girls' and Infants' – were rated as 'good' under the headings of 'Religious Knowledge', 'General Reports' and 'Discipline and Tone'. At the Boys' School, 'Discipline and Tone' achieved 'very good'.

And so it goes on – the Harvest Festival in the autumn (marred by news of the death of Mrs Thicknesse) and then the winter programme of social and charitable activities, including the establishment of a drum and fife band. Although Egerton was less of a dynamo of energy than Francis Thicknesse, he packed a lot into one year. One doubts if Sage did as much in his entire time in Brackley.

Although ultimately Tory, Egerton's ideal was overtly non-political. For him, political debate was a divisive force in a society that should have been cohesive and harmonious. But politics would not go away and the Liberals still looked to the future with confidence. They had not done badly even in 1886 and, despite disarray in the national party, the Towcester seat appeared winnable.

Knightley's vote had actually fallen from 4,074 in 1885 to 4,003 in 1886. His victory could be attributed to Liberal abstentions indicated by a smaller turnout – at 79.8 per cent, the lowest in any election between 1885 and 1914. Those who abstained might be easier to recapture than those who switched directly to the Tories, but there were hardly any of those.

Some of the abstainers may have been Liberal 'Unionists'. Yet, although the Tories were later to call themselves the Conservative and Unionist Party, Liberal Unionism was never a strong force around Brackley. This was probably the result of the line taken by Earl Spencer. Many 'Whig grandees' elsewhere now left the Liberal Party, but Spencer remained loyal to Gladstone and supported Home Rule.[10] Thus local Liberals still had access to the financial support of an extremely wealthy family, an advantage now denied to many

---

10   Spencer served in every Liberal Cabinet between 1880 and 1895. When the 'Grand Old Man' finally retired in 1895, he wanted Spencer, rather than Lord Rosebery, to succeed him as leader of the Liberal Party. Ensor, RCK, *England: 1870–1914* (Oxford: Clarendon Press, 1936) p.215.

other Liberal organisations.[11] At a Liberal Meeting in Brackley in April 1887, Sir James Carmichael insisted that at a future contest 'victory was absolutely within their grasp'. The Liberals hoped to turn some of the promised 'democratic legislation' of the new Tory Government to their own advantage. Above all, they were poised to exploit any miscalculations on the part of their old enemies, the parsons.

One such opening came as early as 1887 when Rev Wodhams ordered boarders at Magdalen College School not to buy sweets from a shop run by Mrs Eliza Sealey – a few of Mrs Sealey's sweet packets contained a coin so the purchase involved an element of gambling. The Radical *Northampton Daily Reporter* took up the story and gave it a political slant with the headline 'Boycotting by the Primrose League'. Mrs Sealey claimed that she had been invited to join the Brackley Habitation of the League. She attended a few meetings but then refused to join. It was then that Wodhams banned her shop. Mrs Sealey took her complaint to 'the clergy of the parish' but received no help. 'It is not necessary to go to Ireland for boycotting and intimidation. Have we in England to live under a sort of Spanish Inquisition?' Although Wodhams was vindicated, Tory clergymen were prime targets of popular resentment.[12]

But the clergy were no longer virtually all Tories. A few, significantly recruited from the towns and from the middle classes, were Liberals. As yet, they were only a small minority in the Brackley area, but the Rector of Middleton Cheney, Rev IW Openshaw, a former Grammar School Master from Bristol, inducted in 1882, was a staunch Liberal. Thus, on occasion it was possible to cross the great divide and Openshaw became an ally of Thomas Judge. (Curiously, Judge and Openshaw were to die in the same week in February 1910.) Another prominent Liberal cleric was Rev J Blackburn-Kane, Vicar of Bicester; though an Irish Protestant, Blackburn-Kane was an ardent supporter of Home Rule.

Since 1832, the Brackley Corporation had no powers or meaningful function. For over half a century it had gone through the motions of co-opting new and unelected burgesses, aldermen and officials, but none had anything to do. Benjamin Pearson's *Local Gleanings* gives a list of these officials in 1881.

Officers of the Corporation[13]

Office	Name
Afferers	Mr W Hawkins
	Mr W H Nichols
Constables	Mr B Howard
	Mr J A Wootton
Thirdboroughs	Mr J Lathbury
	Mr J Everett
Inspectors of Raw Hides & Skins	Mr W Trotman

11   Spencer was Lord Lieutenant of Northamptonshire, three times Master of the Pytchley Hunt, Chairman of the Quarter Sessions in the 1870s and later first Chairman of the County Council. He owned nearly 17,000 acres in Northamptonshire. Janet Howarth describes him as 'by any standard the most eminent man in the county' in 'The Liberal Revival in Northamptonshire', *The Historical Journal*, Vol. XII, Part 1 (1969), p.81.

12   For the story of Mrs Sealey and her sweets, see Forrester, Eric G., *A History of Magdalen College School …*, pp.137–39.

13   Pearson, B.E., *Local Gleanings: No II, The Town Hall.*, op. cit., p.36.

	Mr E G Holdom
Examiner and sealer of leather	Mr W Hawkins (Taylor)
Ale Taster & Bread Weigher	Mr T Norris
Hayward of the Field	Mr W Austin
Bellman	Mr B Butcher
Clerks to the Market	Mr W Cave
	Mr E Bartlett
	Mr Willis
Fieldsmen	Mr J Richardson
	Mr J Walsh
Crier	Mr N Blencowe

The farce was finally brought to an end in 1884 when the old Corporation was abolished under the terms of Sir Charles Dilke's Municipal Corporations (Unreformed) Act.

One of the few remaining responsibilities of the Mayor had been to act in conjunction with the representatives of the Feoffee Charity to decide on the distribution of the income arising from the cottages and lands owned by the charity. Income had been risen appreciably since the 1820s:

	£	s	d
1820	131	10	4
1840	162	2	0
1850	187	14	3
1860	216	16	0
1870	246	11	0
1880	291	6	9

For many years, however, there had been no clear guidelines on how this income should be distributed. In 1886, however, the Charity Commissioners issued a new scheme that was sanctioned by the Board on 29 October. Net income was to be divided into three equal 'branches' – the 'Poor Branch', the 'Church Branch' and the 'Education Branch'. In 1889, most of the 'Poor Branch' grant was devoted to the Coal Club, although £10 was given to the Cottage Hospital. Under the heading of the 'Church Branch', money was to be devoted to 'the repair of the fabric and furniture of the Parish Church of Brackley'. Any unspent sums were to be invested, but if the fund thus created reached £500, any additional sums were to be transferred to the 'Poor Branch'. Arrangements for the 'Education Branch' were more complicated, and were divided into six sections:

1   Rewards to Children residing in the Parish who have been to some Elementary School for not less than one year.

2   Rewards to Children (to encourage their continuance at School), who are not less than eleven years of age, and who have been to some Elementary School for not less than five years, and are qualified by Examination to leave School.

3   Exhibitions, to enable Scholars who have been at School for not less than six years, to pass into higher grade Schools, or to take the situation of Pupil Teachers.

4   The maintenance of a School Library.

5   The provision of Lectures or Evening Classes.

6   A contribution to the general fund of any Public Elementary School in the Parish of Brackley, for the maintenance of such School.

The elementary schools qualifying were the Church Schools and the Methodist School, with the respective shares being determined by the size of their school rolls.

The reorganisation of the Feoffee Charity went hand in hand with the wider task of the reorganisation of local government. The *Parish Magazine* for October 1886 announced that news had just been received that 'Her Majesty has granted under letters patent, a Charter for the Incorporation of the Borough of Brackley'. For the first time, Brackley would have an elected Council endowed with some worthwhile powers. Voting took place on 1 March 1887 and the new Council was in place for the celebration of Queen Victoria's Golden Jubilee.

MAYOR
W Blencowe

ALDERMEN

JG Clarke	G Bannerman
JL Stratton	W Blencowe

COUNCILLORS

J Elliott	ES Chapman	E Bartlett
C Gardner	W Ellis	TK Curtis
R Hawkins	J Farmer	W Hawkins
RT Judge	AH Russel	T Judge

TOWN CLERK
A Weston

Although the election was not fought on party lines, the political associations of most of the councillors are clear. Tommy Judge, Tommy Curtis and Charlie Gardner (long a leading light in the Congregational Chapel) were Liberals but most of the others were Tories and Churchmen. The early mayors and aldermen were all in this category. but mayors and aldermen were chosen by the other councillors, not directly by the electorate; if they had been, things might have been different. There were eighteen candidates for the twelve seats at the first Town Council Election, but it was Tommy Judge who topped the poll with 275 votes compared to 238 for William Blencowe, the highest-placed Tory. The other new aldermen – Clarke, Stratton and Bannerman – obtained 204, 180 and 175 votes respectively. It is striking that the *Magazine* places Tommy Judge, who had secured the largest number of votes, last on the list of councillors and makes no reference to the actual poll. According to the *Banbury Advertiser*, some amusing election 'skits' were circulated, including 'The Brackley Steeplechase', 'Election Addresses' and 'Notes on Shakespeare', 'giving each candidate a nice little "rub"'. When the results were declared at midnight, Judge was carried shoulder high from the Hall. He claimed later that some of working men who had voted for him were counted as Tory supporters, but, in reality, they were 'as rank Radicals as himself, and desired change as ardently'.

On Monday, 18 April 1887, the new Mayor held a dinner at the Wheat Sheaf Inn for the members of the Council and other prominent citizens. Toasts were proposed to 'Our gracious Sovereign and Queen', 'The Prince and Princess of Wales and the rest of the royal family', 'Bishop and Clergy, and ministers of all denominations', 'The Army, Navy and Volunteers', 'The Mayor', 'The Aldermen', 'The Councillors', 'The Town Clerk', 'The Treasurer', 'Better success to agriculture', 'Lord Ellesmere and the Trustees of the Bridgewater estate', 'The Mayoress', 'Prosperity to the Town and Trade of Brackley' and 'The Ladies'. Several speakers, including the Vicar, hoped that the new Corporation would do more than the old one. Alderman Clarke declared that the old system of entrusting parish administration to a variety of bodies had proved expensive and unsatisfactory. The new arrangement would enable rates to be reduced by at least 7d in the pound; the rateable value of house property in Brackley had risen by 70 per cent since 1874. The mood in April 1887 was conciliatory. Even Judge, sometimes suspected of Republicanism, was moved to declare that the enormous extension and prosperity of the Empire had been 'very greatly due to the constitutional manner in which the Queen had exercised her Queenly functions'.

Yet older people might have had a sense of déjà vu, for 1887 was a year of dinners, and there had been a great dinner at the time of the Workhouse Scandal. Now the issue was 'pauper emigration'. It was proposed that an illegitimate 9-year-old girl, currently living in the Workhouse, should be sent to Canada. Some funds had already been raised by private subscription and the Guardians had to decide whether to find a further £12 from the rates. Some Guardians thought that £5 should be sufficient.

Even though the Board now contained at least two Radicals – Judge and Curtis – no one questioned the rightness of separating a young girl from her mother. Curtis opposed the £12 proposal and Judge supported it, but both on grounds of cost. Curtis was against anything that might encourage women with illegitimate children to enter the Workhouse, 'in order to get rid of their children at the expense of the rate payers'. But Judge argued that if the girl were sent to Canada, her mother could leave the Workhouse and get a job as a servant. If the girl remained in the Workhouse, she would cost £50 over five years; the £12 contribution to her fare represented a good deal. Clearly Brackley Radicalism did not extend to any solicitude for single mothers. The only hint of 'progressive' views came from an unexpected quarter. The Chairman, JL Stratton – who also supported the proposal – said that he had great sympathy for illegitimate children, 'as a great slur was cast upon them in England, which they would get rid of by going to another country'.

There were some signs of more generous attitudes. The Workhouse children were given an annual tea by Mrs Gilchrist and a blind boy named Shepherd was sent to a special school in Liverpool. Both Judge and Egerton tried to abolish the practice of making Workhouse children wear a distinctive uniform, but were thwarted by Bannerman. Following several deaths from typhoid fever, improvements were made to the drainage system, with Stratton insisting that if poor people were compelled to enter the Workhouse, the Guardians must ensure that the house was kept in a good sanitary condition. Stratton, the supposed reactionary, appears more liberal than either Judge or Curtis, both of whom opposed the drainage improvements. Yet there was growing dislike of aspects of the Workhouse system, particularly the treatment of the elderly. Judge was echoing a widespread sentiment when he deplored the fact that most of the poor people he had known had been forced to enter the Workhouse to end their days when they were too old to work.

The Tory *Northampton Herald* of 22 September 1911 gives valuable biographical details of the Mayors of Brackley from 1887 onwards. All had been Tories and, of the eight mayors to date, seven had been members of the 1887 Council. The first mayor was William Blencowe, Chairman and Manager of Messrs Blencowe & Co. Ltd who owned a brewery in the town. Coming from an old Brackley family, he was one of the promoters of the Brackley steeplechases, a regular follower of the Grafton and Bicester Hounds and a stalwart of the Brackley Agricultural Show.

Blencowe's successor, George Bannerman (1888–90) was a Baronet whose ancestors had been hereditary standard bearers to the Kings of Scotland in the Middle Ages – hence the name. Bannerman himself had had a colourful career, travelling in the Canadian West and then running a coffee plantation in Ceylon in the 1860s. He moved to Brackley in the 1870s when he bought East Hill House. He quickly became involved in the affairs of the Church and town, becoming a Churchwarden, Poor Law Guardian and Trustee of the Feoffee Charity.

Although Bannerman was popular, there are suggestions that he was not very energetic. At the AGM of the General Committee of the Cottage Hospital in 1882, he was proposed as Chairman in succession to JL Stratton. Stratton commented wryly, 'as the Committee had so little to do they could not do better than elect Sir George Bannerman, Bart. as chairman in place of himself'.[14] Bannerman died on 3 December 1901 and was succeeded by his son Alexander Bannerman, currently 'Commander of the Army Balloon School at Farnborough'.

But the man who dominated the Borough Council was John Locke Stratton, Squire of Turweston and Mayor of Brackley for an unprecedented seven years from 1890 till 1897. In some ways, Stratton belonged to an earlier age. Born on 2 January 1818, he was already 72 when he became mayor and had a lifetime of public service behind him. He served as a magistrate for fifty-nine years – from July 1844 until his death in September 1903. The *Northampton Herald* described Stratton as 'an ardent Conservative' and 'a devoted Churchman' and saw his career as 'an exemplification of how local affairs should be attended to and the interests of the community studied'. Stratton was deeply interested in highways, agriculture and education and was a good friend to Magdalen College School. Council meetings were often quite stormy; as Ryland Adkins observed:

---

14   Smith, Donald, *Brackley Cottage Hospital 1876–1996*, Brackley and District History Society, Occasional Paper, No. 2 (1996) p.28.

There are Mr Judge and Mr Curtis, neither of them shy nor silent; and Mr Bartlett has axes to grind and Mr [Rev] Ardenne grievances to ventilate, so that it is not all easy going even in Sleepy Hollow.[15]

But Stratton usually got his way.

The grant of a new Charter to Brackley was followed by a measure of greater importance. In 1888, the Salisbury Government established a new system of local government in which elected County Councils took over many of the administrative responsibilities of the Quarter Sessions. Elections for the first Northamptonshire County Council were held on 17 January 1889. The Brackley area did well in terms of representation. It was awarded two seats – one for the town and one for the rural hinterland, known as the Middleton Cheney Division. There were only 506 voters per seat compared to 1,061 voters per seat at Rothwell and Rushden. Although still unenfranchised in Parliamentary elections, women could vote in County Council elections. Brackley was unusual in that 1 in 4½ voters were women – compared to 1 in 26 at Duston.[16]

The area revealed its Tory and Radical sides sharply in the personalities of its councillors. Both main parties could draw consolation from the outcome. The successful candidate for Brackley was John Locke Stratton, while the Daventry Liberal, Ashworth Briggs, was returned for the Middleton Cheney Division. Sadly, Ashworth Briggs died as a result of injuries received when he fell from a moving train near Blisworth on 31 October 1890. The vacant seat was contested between the Tory, JH Blacklock of Overthorpe Hall and Thomas Judge.

Judge was returned by a narrow majority of eleven votes – as compared to Briggs's seventy-nine over A T C Cartwright in 1889. As a newcomer to the area, Blacklock did surprisingly well. The *Banbury Advertiser* attributed this to an excellent committee and hard work by the ladies of the Primrose League; in particular, it mentioned Miss Beatrice Cartwright. Yet Judge increased his lead to sixty-six at the next election.

For the next decade and more, Brackley was represented in the County Council by a very contrasting duo – Thomas Judge and John Locke Stratton. Although technically representing the Middleton Division, Judge often spoke on Brackley matters. It was largely because of their membership of the County Council that Stratton and Judge have chapters devoted to them in *Our County*. Adkins made much of the contrast between Judge, 'the Paladin of Brackley', and Stratton, 'the Complete Squire'. As a Liberal, Adkins probably preferred Judge to Stratton, but he was fair-minded enough to see the good, bad and indeed the funny sides of both men.

Adkins was distressed by Judge's loudness – *vox et praetera nihil* – but he also admired the Brackley grocer for rising above the habits and restrictions of his class:

As a rule, the tradesmen in small towns and villages take one of two courses: if a Conservative, the shopkeeper follows piously and modestly in the wake of the local gentry and takes with elaborate gratitude such crumbs of patronage as fall from the Ruling Councillor's table: if a Liberal he gives a timid half-crown to the local association and then when the election is safely passed thanks God that he has been able to vote straightly though quietly, and yet not lose the whole of his custom. Neither of these methods has commended itself to Mr Judge. He has proclaimed his opinions on many platforms. There is little

15   Adkins, WRD, *Our County*, p.121.

16   Gordon, Peter, 'A County Parliament: the first Northamptonshire County Council', *Northamptonshire Past and Present*, Vol. VII, No. 3 (1985–86), p.188.

done at Brackley Town Council or the Board of Guardians without his knowing the reason why. He has shown that it is possible to be aggressively independent and yet to lose nothing in consideration or material prosperity. He is much more of an example than alarming.[17]

At County Council Meetings, Judge sometimes made a fool of himself by sounding off about matters he did not understand – drawing a joke from Earl Spencer about the dangers of 'Judge made law'. With Stratton, there were well-justified complaints about his autocratic temper and pride of class. But Adkins thought that it was too much to expect that the elderly Squire of Turweston would discard all of the attitudes of his youth when squires had been supreme and no one thought of extending political rights to the lower orders. He also noted:

> But with the view of ancient squires, he has their gift of agreeable ways. He has done some graceful things to opponents on the County Council. His feelings may be quickly roused to dissent or indignation, but he is quicker still to reciprocate courtesies. He is free from undue primness. The luncheon interval at the quarterly Council meetings always finds him placidly smoking his pipe on the steps of the County Hall.[18]

Although disagreeing about most things, Stratton and Judge were united in their desire to serve Brackley. When it came to asking the County Council to contribute more to the upkeep of Brackley footpaths they were on the same side:

> Mr Judge thunders from one side of the room, Mr Stratton argues and appeals from the other; and a cynic who knew what poles asunder these orators are on every other subject might reflect with much amusement how the touch of nature involved in an attack on the county purse makes opponents kin.[19]

Given the close links between the Liberals and the Nonconformist Churches, it is not surprising that a Liberal revival should have been foreshadowed by renewed vigour in the Chapels. As we have seen, the Thicknesse Revolution, ably continued by Egerton, dealt a tremendous blow to the Congregationalists and Methodists. The homely Methodist Chapel was in a side street. Perhaps by accident – perhaps by design – the enormous bulk of Thicknesse's Church Schools made the Chapel invisible from the High Street.

The Methodists wanted to raise their profile in Brackley and dreamed of a more impressive Chapel, preferably on the High Street, to challenge the dominance of the Church of England. But, even if they raised enough money – and the Methodists were poor – they would find it hard to acquire an appropriate site. The land fronting the High Street was built up and thus the Methodists would have to buy and demolish existing property. Most of the houses on the High Street were occupied by tenants holding leases from either Magdalen College or from the Earl of Ellesmere (technically from the Bridgewater Trustees). Neither Magdalen nor the Earl would have contemplated a sale to the Methodists and so the only solution was to buy freehold property – something in short supply in the centre of Brackley.

17   Adkins, *Our County*, pp.29–30.

18   Ibid., p.122.

19   Ibid.

In 1891, however, the Methodists had a stroke of luck; the ideal site, fronting the High Street but adjoining the existing Chapel and school, was available. It was then occupied by six small cottages and two shops. Knowing that they were in a strong position, the vendors drove a hard bargain. The Methodists had to borrow money to pay the asking price of £500.[20] They must have known that a long time would elapse before they could complete their new Chapel. Yet the mere fact that the Methodists had managed to acquire the site of their present Chapel was a warning to the Church of England and its supporters that the Thicknesse Revolution, already challenged economically and politically, would eventually be challenged in stone.

Only a few months after the Methodists made their dramatic purchase, a General Election was called. In the contest of July 1892, the Liberals presented the electorate with something like a modern election manifesto, reflecting decisions taken at a recent Party Conference at Newcastle. The central commitment was to Irish Home Rule but there was much to appeal to lower-class and Nonconformist voters. A definite proposal for the Disestablishment of the Welsh and Scottish Churches pointed to eventual Disestablishment in England itself. This would please the Chapelgoers – as would the planned local veto on the sale of intoxicating liquors. Agricultural labourers would be drawn to the promised reform of the land laws, to the creation of district and parish councils, to powers for the acquisition of land for allotments, for Employers' Liability for Accidents and for shorter working hours.

Once the campaign began, it was obvious that it would not be like previous ones. The Church of England clergy were notably less partisan. Most of the local parsons did not give their flocks a clear lead as to how they wanted them to vote. Much of the change was due to the influence of the new Bishop of Peterborough.

The old Bishop, William Connor Magee, had been at Peterborough from 1868 till 1891. He then became Archbishop of York, but died almost at once. Magee had been an unabashed Tory; he was totally opposed to the largely Liberal Temperance lobby, declaring in public that he 'would rather see England free than England sober'. The new Bishop of Peterborough, Mandell Creighton, was an academic, one of the greatest historians of the Middle Ages. Creighton did not want his clergy to be involved in politics. As Adkins put it, the Bishop had 'too much knowledge of the past to meet the present in a vulgar or partisan spirit'.[21] Significantly, the *Brackley Parish Magazine*, so blatantly Tory in 1885, makes no mention of the election in 1892.

To begin with, Creighton did not 'go down well' in Northamptonshire. He irritated some with his pedantic insistence that he should be referred to as 'The Right Reverend Father in God, Mandell, *Petriburgensis Episcopus*'. But the biggest problem with Creighton was that he was a High Churchman. Adkins observed, 'Few would deny that he emphasises the points of identity between Anglican and Roman ceremonial in a way which, to Protestants, is of sinister importance.'[22] Despite Creighton's attempts to stay out of politics, suspicion of his 'Romish ways' helped the Liberals. Perhaps Creighton should have consulted Francis Thicknesse, whose views on architecture included an appreciation of the dangers of the association between the Middle Ages and 'Popery'.

20   *Methodist Recorder*, 4 February 1904.

21   Adkins, *Our County*, p.15.

22   Ibid., p.14.

When the election was called, Rainald Knightley announced his retirement; he was subsequently raised to the peerage as the first – and last – Baron Knightley of Fawsley. The Tories turned to the other great political family of South Northants, the Cartwrights of Aynho. Both the name and the personality of their candidate, Thomas Robert Brook Leslie Melville Cartwright, exemplify the difficulties facing the old order when it tried to accommodate itself to 'democracy'. The Tory candidate was the grandson of W.R. Cartwright and nephew of the Colonel Cartwright who had figured so prominently in the Brackley Workhouse Scandal.

Described by Adkins as 'A Pillar of the Primrose League', Cartwright did his best, letting it be known that people were welcome to call him 'Tom' Cartwright.[23] He thought this would qualify him as a man of the people, quite different from his elder brother, the scholarly and cultivated Cornwallis Cartwright, MP for Oxfordshire. He attempted to make rousing speeches, generously interspersed with his favourite war cry of 'Tory-up!' But even the charitable Adkins found it hard to enthuse about Cartwright. He was 'far from being a bad candidate' – hardly ecstatic praise. On one occasion, he 'made an excellent speech at Towcester', but that leaves us wondering what the others were like.[24] Above all, Adkins suggests that the 'hail fellow, well met' style was false and that the real Cartwright emerged too often – cold and remote from ordinary voters.

Try as he would, Cartwright could not make himself liked. He was 'without fascination of manner' and did not 'excel in those magnetic qualities which give men more popularity than they deserve'.[25] It might have been better not to attempt the impossible. Perhaps Cartwright should have campaigned, in the old Knightley fashion, as 'an upright and honourable country gentleman'. Cartwright had already given an unwise hostage to fortune by insisting that the Primrose League was not a party association. Judge attacked this as a lie and went on to describe the League as 'a shrine before which snobs, toadies, parasites, sycophants, and hangers-on might worship and it toadied to the worst phases of human nature … The tyranny and despotism exercised was as bad as that of Russia.'

Cartwright was not helped by the decline of his class. It was a sign of the times that at Aynho itself, the 'capital' of the old 'Cartwright corner', a wretched farm labourer had the temerity to have his wheelbarrow painted bright red (at the substantial cost of 4s) as a sign of his Radical sympathies.[26] Colours acquired an extraordinary significance and, in some Tory gardens in Brackley, red flowers were rooted up to avoid any hint of Radicalism. But, to return to 'Tom' Cartwright, it is hard to disagree with Adkins' assessment:

It may however be remarked that the high and dry Toryism and brand new Tory democracy do not unite easily in one personality, and there is a world of truth in the parable which foretells sad results when new cloth is sewn upon old garments.[27]

We learn that, if Cartwright was 'Tom' on the hustings, he was always 'Melville' in gentry circles.

---

23 Ibid., p.65.

24 Adkins, *Our County*, p.66.

25 Ibid., p.67.

26 Howarth, Janet, 'Politics and Society in Late Victorian Northamptonshire', *Northamptonshire Past and Present*, Vol. IV, No. 5 (1970–71), p.272.

27 Adkins, *Our County*, p.66.

The Liberals had a better candidate than in 1886 in the shape of David Charles Guthrie. Unlike previous Liberal candidates, Guthrie, aged 31 in 1892, was not a complete outsider. It is true that he was a Scotsman, the son of James Guthrie of Craigie, Forfarshire. But he had been educated in England – at Eton and Christ Church – and had served as Secretary to the Liberal statesman, Lord Ripon. More important, Guthrie had links with Northamptonshire. He was adopted as Liberal candidate as early as 1889 and understood the significance of the recent Reform Act. In a speech at Middleton Cheney on 27 March 1889 he declared, 'The great battle now-a-days is between two orders of working men – Conservatives and Liberals – although I do not see how a working man can be a Conservative'.

In 1891 Guthrie married Mary Low, a Northamptonshire girl, and the couple lived at East Haddon Hall. Guthrie was accepted into county society and the account of his funeral in *The Times* of 15 January 1918 describes him as 'a leading member of the Pytchley Hunt'. Thus, Janet Howarth is not strictly accurate in her claim that, in South Northamptonshire, 'All the Liberal candidates were carpet baggers'. Indeed, the example of the brewer, Pickering Phipps, also casts doubt on her assertion that 'all the conservatives came from the local landed gentry'.[28]

Medical issues – going right back to the Workhouse Scandal of 1840 – were a potent source of discontent in Victorian Brackley. Brackley had acquired a Cottage Hospital in 1876, well in advance of other market towns in the area. But there were several occasions when overzealous adherence to 'professional ethics' may have cost a patient his life. On Friday, 13 March 1885, John Greenwood was injured in a shunting accident at the LNWR station. He died of lockjaw on the following Thursday. Greenwood was a member of a 'club' whose doctor was Mr Farmer. Farmer was away at the time of the accident but the Matron of the Hospital, Mrs Watton, would not let another doctor attend to Greenwood on the grounds that he was Farmer's patient. Rightly or wrongly, some people felt that Greenwood might have survived if he had been attended to at once.[29]

In 1888, a woman from Radstone complained that she had been given inadequate food while in the Cottage Hospital and that the newly arrived doctor, George Nicholson Stathers, had given her insufficient medical attention.[30] But another 'medical' issue aroused even stronger feelings: compulsory vaccination against smallpox, which Guthrie made much of in his campaign. The Vaccination Act of 1871 (prompted by a recent epidemic) set up a system of Vaccination Officers throughout the country. Their task was to ensure that every child was vaccinated by the age of three months, regardless of parental wishes or the child's state of health. Sadly, there were some instances when complications following vaccination resulted in death. Even when one of their children died after vaccination, parents were still forced to have any other children vaccinated. Those who refused were fined.

On 28 February 1887, *The Brackley Observer* carried an account of what was clearly a tragic case:

28   Howarth, Janet, 'The Liberal Revival in Northamptonshire', op. cit., p.84.

29   Smith, Donald, *Brackley Cottage Hospital*, op. cit., pp.29–31.

30   Ibid., p.40.

VACCINATION NEGLECT AT BRACKLEY
Petty Sessions, Wednesday 16th February

Joseph Taylor, Brackley, was charged with neglecting to have his child, 16 months old, vaccinated. Mrs Taylor appeared – John Barrows, Vaccination Officer, proved the case – Mrs Taylor said they had had two children vaccinated, were ill afterwards and both died. She and her husband had fully made up their minds not to have another child vaccinated. One of their children was never well for a day after it was vaccinated. An order was made to have the child vaccinated, and the defendant to pay us 6d costs.

There were many who opposed the legislation and Banbury was regarded as 'the home and headquarters of anti-vaccination agitation'.[31] One Brackley man, William Freeman, was sent to prison for twenty days for failing to have his child vaccinated. On his release, a wagon awaited him at Brackley Station, together with a welcoming group of members of the Banbury and Bicester Anti-Vaccination Leagues. There was a brass band and the procession moved to the Town Hall where Judge addressed a crowd of several hundred people and lauded the example of a man who was prepared to lose his liberty 'to protect his beloved little ones from a great evil'.

An anti-vaccination demonstration, on lines similar to the earlier Reform demonstrations, was held in the Market Square on 19 June 1891. Once more Thomas Judge took the Chair and was joined on the wagonette by Mr J Swindell of London, Mr George Knight (Manager of the Co-operative Stores) and Mr Ambrose Jelleyman. Judge described a recent speech by Cartwright on the subject as 'all humbug' and claimed that the enforcement of the vaccination legislation was 'hellish and infernal'. Mr Knight proposed the formation of a Brackley Anti-Compulsory Vaccination League and some fifty-five people joined at once. No fewer than eleven vaccination cases from Brackley had been heard at the Magistrates' Court held earlier in the day. Those convicted were Austin Springwell, Timothy Howard, Ambrose Jelleyman, Andrew Knibbs, Richard Neath, Walter Whitehead, Thomas Rawlins, Albert Paxton, Charles Hagram and John Lathbury.

There were wider implications to the vaccination issue. The 1871 Act appeared to infringe liberty and, according to RM Macleod, vaccination seemed 'the embodiment of impersonal and uncompromising government interference'.[32] Many believed that the real cause of smallpox was poor housing and bad sanitation; in order to escape their obligations, the ruling classes were resorting to 'quackery'. The debate acquired religious and moral overtones and one Northampton Radical urged his audience 'to fight the battle of pure blood against experimental butchery upon the defenceless little ones'.[33]

Those who opposed compulsory vaccination called themselves 'anti-contagionists' and local campaigns were often led by Nonconformist ministers. Tom Cartwright, however, was an uncompromising supporter of compulsory vaccination. He was a member of the Brackley Board of Guardians which – despite the objections of Judge and Curtis – implemented the law vigorously. He was also a magistrate and, as the *Northampton Mercury* commented, 'there seems to be a lot of persons who have been sentenced by Mr Cartwright for sticking to their principles on this matter'.[34]

---

31 Trinder, Barrie, *Victorian Banbury*, p.151.

32 Macleod, RM, 'Law, Medicine and Public Opinion: Resistance to Compulsory Health Legislation 1870–1907', *Public Law* (1967), p.107.

33 Ibid., p.112.

34 Howarth, Janet, 'Politics and Society in late Northamptonshire', op. cit., p.273.

Tories ridiculed the campaign against compulsory vaccination as an example of Liberal 'faddism' or a tendency to embrace a ragbag of vaguely left-wing causes of little interest to the general public. Henry Rider Haggard's novel, *Dr Therne* (1898), took up the theme of 'faddism' and linked the 'anti-contagionists' with opponents of vivisection and tied cottages and with the advocates of graduated income tax, old-age pensions, Disestablishment of the Church of England and the payment of Members of Parliament.[35]

But 'anti-contagionism' was not a marginal issue in South Northamptonshire. Together with other resentments building up over the years, it produced a desire for change. The mood was reflected in the election result. Guthrie obtained 3,930 votes and Cartwright 3,882. It was noted that those sentenced by Cartwright for refusing to allow their children to be vaccinated had been among the first to vote.[36] It was only a majority of forty-eight and a swing of 2.3 per cent compared to 1886, but at least Guthrie had done it. In the country as a whole, the Liberals obtained a working majority of about forty. Some historians see this Liberal victory as the British equivalent of the 'New Course' proclaimed by Caprivi in Berlin when he replaced Otto von Bismarck as Chancellor of Germany in March 1890.[37]

So, it looked as if Brackley would have its 'New Course' and that the Liberals and Nonconformists had emerged as the winners as the agricultural depression eroded the power of the squires and parsons. Despite the temporary importance of the vaccination issue, the depressed state of agriculture was the underlying reason for the Liberal breakthrough. As Haggard noted, there were now fewer resident landowners in the south of the county. One of the largest, the Duke of Grafton, was resolutely 'non-political' and refused to allow his name to be used in elections.[38] The result was a kind of 'vacuum of influence' which had been filled by rustic demagogues like Judge and his Silverstone counterpart, John Denny, the Methodist School Master, 'said to unite for his beloved village the power of an Irish priest and a French *Maire*'.[39]

But the outcome in 1892 disappointed the Liberals; they had expected a landslide but had won by only the narrowest of margins. Judge thought that 'aristocratic influence' had prevented a more convincing victory. In January 1888, when Parliamentary boundaries were being reviewed, Judge urged Earl Spencer to press for Wolverton to be transferred to the Towcester Division. He obviously calculated that most of the men employed at the carriage works would be Liberal voters, even though he accused the Tories of 'jerrymandering'. Spencer would have none of it; if he supported Judge's plan, he would be accused of trying to deprive the Buckingham constituency of a large Liberal vote. He would actually be guilty of jerrymandering himself. In any case, if the principle of keeping constituency and county boundaries in line was broken, that would only encourage those who wanted to transfer Grimsbury to the Banbury constituency, a move which would damage the Liberal cause in the Towcester Division.

Spencer was probably right when he said that the issue raised by Judge was extremely difficult and involved 'all manner of interests and sentiments'. For Spencer, Judge was simply too preoccupied with politics, 'You are so keen a Politician that you bring, it seems to me, Politics into regions where I am unable

35   Macleod, op. cit., p.115.

36   As Note 34.

37   Stone, Norman, *Europe Transformed*, p.74.

38   Howarth, Janet, 'The Liberal Revival in Northamptonshire', op. cit., p.91.

39   Ibid., pp.91–92. Adkins, *Our County*, p.116.

to take them'.[40] One can see Spencer's point, but his comments seem strange from a man who himself came close to becoming the leader of the Liberal Party.

In the event, Brackley's New Course was short-lived. David Guthrie's record was disappointing and an examination of Hansard reveals that he never spoke in Parliament. This, coupled with the general disenchantment at the seeming ineffectiveness of the Liberal Government, resulted in his defeat at the General Election of 1895. The Tory, Hon. Edward Sholto Douglas-Pennant of Sholebroke Lodge, Towcester, won by the unusually large margin of 1,229 votes on a turnout of 86.2 per cent.

Towcester Division Elections 1885–1895

	1885	1886	1892	1895
Liberal	4,012: 49.6%	3,687: 48%	3,930: 50.3%	3,324: 42.2%
Conservative	4,074: 50.4%	4,003: 52%	3,882: 49.7%	4,553: 57.8%
Percentage of Electorate Voting	83.9	79.8	84.4	86.2
Swing For/Against Liberals	–	−1.6%	+2.3%	−8.1%

Yet the New Course did have one tangible result for Brackley. One of the few important measures carried by the Liberal Government was the Local Government Act of 1894. This Act removed the non-elected ex officio members – always the toughest – from the Board of Guardians and put an end to the property qualification for elected Guardians. According to one critic, the way was now open to 'a demagogic dispensation of relief'. In Brackley it was hardly likely to amount to that, although circulars from central government now recommended such unheard-of luxuries as a provision of toys and books for children and tobacco or snuff for the old people.

The last meeting of the old-style Brackley Board of Guardians was held on 24 December 1894. The Chairman, JL Stratton suggested that the occasion might be marked by planting ornamental shrubs and flowers in front of the Workhouse; there would still be plenty of room for vegetables. Probably not seriously, Judge put forward another idea. The front garden should be turned into a tennis court for the use of the elderly inmates! Despite further changes, the Boards of Guardians themselves were not abolished until 1929.

40   Spencer to Judge, 3 January 1888. Letter shown to me by Mrs Pat Phillips.

Brackley Temperance Hotel. (NRO)

The Billiard Room, the Manor House.

The Manor House courtyard.

The Manor House, east front.

Church Schools, St Peter's Feast, 1893.

Toll Gate, Oxford Road. (NRO)

Wood & Co.

Chapter Nine

FORWARD WITH THE
GREAT CENTRAL?

The New Course represented the triumph of an 'alternative', or Radical, vision of Brackley personified by Tommy Judge. In many ways, it is astonishing that it happened at all. The New Course flew in the face of a well-established trend towards hierarchy and deference. The trend may have culminated in the Thicknesse Revolution of the 1870s, but, in one form or another, things had been moving in an elitist direction ever since the Cartwrights decided to impose 'stricter discipline' on the people of Brackley at the end of the eighteenth century. In short, the New Course stands as a remarkable testimony to the personal charisma of Tommy Judge, coupled with clever exploitation of the crisis of the old order.

Yet the New Course rested upon insubstantial foundations – in that it ignored national trends pointing to the eventual demise of Liberalism and also bore little relation to social reality in the Brackley area. By 1895, reality was reasserting itself once more. Was it likely that grocers and elementary school teachers would replace the gentry and clergy as the dominant element in local politics and society? As Janet Howarth argues:

'The socialization of politics' in the country meant fetes and garden parties, dances and smoking concerts, and the Liberals could not hope to compete with the Primrose League in providing entertainments of this kind … The reason for the weak organization of rural Liberalism was simply that the Conservatives had after 1885 the overwhelming support of those classes in Northamptonshire country society which had time and money at their disposal and a tradition of political activity. The gentry, the larger tenant farmers, the parsons and the publicans – these were the people with the best opportunities of patronizing and proselytizing the rural electorate.[1]

1   Howarth, Janet, 'The Liberal Revival in Northamptonshire', op. cit., p.96.

Edward Sholto Douglas-Pennant's impressive victory at the 1895 General Election ushered in a new period of Tory dominance. Douglas-Pennant retired in 1900. At the 'Khaki Election' (so called because it was held at the height of the Boer War), he was succeeded by his nephew, Captain Hon Edward Algernon Fitzroy, who held the Towcester Division for the Tories with a majority of 1,088 over the Liberal, Thomas Grove.

But if the future was to be Tory, what would be the nature of that Toryism? There were two possibilities. Although defeated in 1892, it was not out of the question that the old-style Toryism of the squires and parsons would make a comeback, though doubtless covering itself in a slightly populist veneer to take account of the larger electorate. Despite the Thicknesse Revolution, followed by the coming of partial democracy in the 1880s, there was still much of the 'Sleepy Hollow' about Brackley. To outsiders, it seemed a town forgotten by time. In 1947, the *Brackley Advertiser* carried an article by Luther Brailsford on his impressions when he arrived as a printer's apprentice in 1895.[2] He found elderly women still making pillow lace and the Town Hall bell still ringing for the curfew at 8 p.m., for Church services and in case of fire.

For traditionalists, Douglas-Pennant and Fitzroy were reassuring figures; both were related to one of the great noble houses of the area and Fitzroy actually carried the same family name as the Dukes of Grafton. After the disappointments of the New Course, such a community might well have welcomed a return to 'old-style Toryism'.

Emigration patterns point to the same possibility. A disproportionately large number of those leaving Brackley were Nonconformists and their departure certainly delayed the completion of the new Methodist Chapel. The *Methodist Recorder* of February 1904 admits that 'the removal of young men and women' from Brackley had been on an unusually large scale. The article tries to put a brave face upon what was clearly a serious problem; Brackley's loss has been other places' gain and 'happily, they [the Nonconformist emigrants] have carried with them not only vigorous constitutions and energetic business habits, but piety and devotion to Methodism'. Despite these consoling thoughts, the reality was that fewer Methodists meant fewer Liberal voters.

The possibility of an aristocratic/gentry revival becomes even more plausible in the light of economic trends. Landowners and tenant farmers are notoriously adept at pleading poverty and some of the Northamptonshire informants who complained so bitterly to Rider Haggard may have exaggerated. By the turn of the century, the very worst of the agricultural depression was over. Prices, which for some commodities had fallen by as much 45 per cent since 1873, began to edge up again. Thus, a quarter of grain, which cost only £1 6s in 1898, rose to £1 18s by 1914.[3] The agricultural recovery may be one of the reasons why the late-Victorian decline in Brackley's population was halted, albeit temporarily. Despite the loss of many young Methodists, numbers actually rose from 2,487 in 1901 to 2,633 in 1911.

Yet it would be unwise to suppose that the revival of agriculture necessarily led to a revival in the power of the old gentry and clergy. The depression had taken a heavy toll and some estates had passed to other owners – about whom more later. Most of the benefits of the higher prices went to the tenants and labourers rather than to landowners. In any case, despite the improvement in prices, there was no return to the 'glory days' of the early 1870s; even in 1914, prices were still some 20 per cent below the levels of 1873.

---

2   Brailsford later worked as a compositor in Banbury where he was Treasurer of the Trades and Labour Council in the early 1920s. Hodgkins, *Over the Hills to Glory*, p.179.

3   Stone, Norman, *Europe Transformed*, p.75.

In Brackley, at least, the influence of the Church of England went into sharp decline. In part, this was due to personal factors. By any standards, Brooke de Malpas Egerton and his predecessor, Francis Thicknesse, had been men of outstanding abilities. Perhaps it was too much to expect that every Vicar of Brackley would be of the same stature. Egerton left Brackley in 1894. He had been on the point of departure in 1891, but the warmth of the tributes paid to him and Mrs Egerton persuaded him to stay. An illuminated address was presented to the Egertons, expressing 'our great feelings of gratification that you remain at Brackley'.

Egerton had incurred financial loss by declining preferment but:

It is a great gain to us, for we felt that in losing you, we were parting with not only an excellent Pastor, but with most kind friends; for you have both endeared yourselves to all classes during the time you have lived amongst us.

The signatures, appropriately headed by those of Egerton Ellesmere, Katherine Ellesmere and their daughters Mabel, Alice and Beatrice, numbered 958. Those signing included the Chapel School Headmaster, Robert Aldous.

By the early 1890s, levels of literacy were quite high and only a small number were reduced to making their 'mark', although many of the signatures are obviously in the same hand. Those making a mark included John Tuckey, Sarah Tuckey, Hannah Tuckey, Henry Lathbury, George Humphries, Caroline Makepeace, Maria George, Edward Makepeace, Sarah Jeacock, Caroline Bishop, Sarah Freeman, James George, Ann George, John Jeacock, Clara Gaskyns, William Gaskyns, Mary Ann Waddup, Charlotte Jones, Elizabeth Jeacock, Robert Lucas and Eliza Lathbury. Some of the younger signatories such as A.E. Sawford – his beautiful handwriting unchanged over seventy years – were well known to me in my childhood.

Of course, illiteracy could have serious disadvantages. In the late 1880s and early 1890s, my great-great-grandmother lived in a small cottage at the top of Buckingham Road and there she brought up my grandfather, Walter Gibbard. She was old – so old that she could remember the days when stagecoaches passed through Brackley – and she was poor. In order to keep herself and her grandson from the Workhouse – there were no old-age pensions then – she took in washing from Magdalen College School. She was virtually illiterate and thus could not read the newspapers when, in 1890, it was announced that the government had finally abolished the fees charged for pupils at elementary schools. The fees were only a few pence a week, but even that must have been a lot for a poor old lady. She continued to give my grandfather the money for his fees but he took it for himself as 'pocket money'. When she finally discovered what had happened, she gave him a sound thrashing; in later life he admitted that he had deserved it.

On 8 June 1894, Egerton was presented to the living of St Mark's, Peterborough. Mrs Egerton died in 1913, but Egerton himself proved even more long-lived than Frank Thicknesse. In 1937, at the age of 92, Egerton became 13th Baronet of Grey-Egerton (created 1617) – both of the 12th Baronet's sons had been killed in World War I. Brooke de Malpas Egerton died, aged 100, on 5 November 1945, to date, Brackley's only centenarian Vicar. I would have loved to have overlapped with Egerton. As it was, this great Victorian figure died only just over a year before I was born.

Egerton's successor, Walter Basil Broughton, served from 1894 to 1927. By definition, as Vicar, Broughton was an important figure in the town. Brailsford's account of Brackley in 1895 suggests that most social as well as religious activities were still centred on places of worship. Broughton figures prominently in Brailsford's list of the 'leading lights':

147

College Chapel
Rev Isaac Wodhams

St Peter's
Vicar: Rev WB Broughton
Churchwardens: John Allen   J Richardson
Sidesmen: WH & GW Hawkins   C Wright   Robert Gibbard

St James
Churchwardens: H Bedford   GS Broughton.
Sidesmen: J Smart   E Bartlett   JG & JW Clarke

Congregational Chapel
Pastor: Rev W Whiting
Deacons: Thomas Curtis   W Glenn   Charles Gardner

Old Wesleyan Chapel
Minister: Rev G Dixon
Active Members: John Webb   J Jeacock   F Whitlock   Arthur Haynes   F Tibbets   Mr R Aldous

The Salvation Army had recently appeared in Brackley. One of its most enthusiastic supporters was Bandsman Ward – a brilliant performer on the cornet and euphonium. The presence of the Salvation Army, in addition to the older traditions of Methodism and Congregationalism, suggests that Brackley was becoming a place of religious pluralism. This may have been inevitable but it was a development that would have horrified Thicknesse and Egerton. Both had striven to ensure that the Church of England was the Church of the entire community. They had never been completely successful but, at least compared to the 'bad old days' of Sage, they had come a long way.

Now Broughton effectively abandoned his predecessors' policy. He assumed an attitude of stony hostility to all but the most regular Churchgoers. Some thought that he positively turned people away from the Church. Those who came only occasionally were made to feel uncomfortable and unwelcome. Understandably, many chose not to repeat the experience. Egerton's practice of holding services in the 'slum' Yards was quietly dropped.

Broughton was sometimes accused of being a snob. It is true that he usually addressed his male parishioners by their surnames – without any 'handle'. Yet, to working men like my grandfather, Walter Gibbard, then a young carpenter who did attend regularly, he was a kind and sympathetic friend. Unfortunately, this good side was seen by few. Broughton's standards of attendance were exacting. He had a short temper and was capable of administering a stinging rebuke in public. On one celebrated occasion, the rising builder and property owner, William Judd, a member of the choir, appeared in the Vestry after missing Church for a couple of Sundays. Broughton came out of the Vicar's Vestry and, in front of the rest of the choir, shouted, 'Judd, you ought to be ashamed of yourself!' It is hard to imagine either Thicknesse or Egerton demeaning himself in such a way. Judd's reaction is even more interesting. According to one eyewitness, he grinned and replied, 'And so ought you'. In the past, not even an out-and-out Nonconformist would have 'cheeked' the Vicar like that.

Perhaps in Judd's response we can see a resemblance to the Aynho labourer who painted his wheelbarrow red at the 1892 Election. Although Judd's remark was non-political – he was a Tory – both he and the Aynho man were being impertinent to their betters. We have seen it before; impertinence was the characteristic of local lower-class behaviour that had so distressed Thomas Mozley back in the 1830s. The triumph of deference symbolised by the Thicknesse Revolution was fading. In some ways, the mood of late-Victorian Brackley had more in common with that of the early-Victorian age than with that of the middle period. Perhaps there was a common cause, to be found in Thomas Hobbes's explanation for most heresies: 'unpleasing priests'.

Walter Basil Broughton must have reminded old people of Charles Arthur Sage. By his 'tough' policy on attendance, Broughton was unconsciously echoing the behaviour of the Chapels. But there was a difference. Chapels imposed regular attendance through peer pressure; worshippers were not treated as second-class citizens by haughty ministers. Broughton was giving the Church most of the disadvantages of a sect without the corresponding advantages.

In Brackley, as elsewhere, Church congregations were ceasing to reflect the age and sex balance of the population as a whole. Increasingly they were dominated by three groups – children, women and the elderly. Broughton was not well equipped to deal with any of these elements. If anecdotal evidence is correct, his normal way of dealing with children was to administer a sharp slap around the ears, often for no good reason. The cultivation of the important women's constituency was usually regarded as the special responsibility of the Vicar's lady, but although Mrs Broughton came to Church, she sat as far away from the rest of the congregation as possible and had little do with Church activities. She always dressed in the height of fashion, which some considered inappropriate in a clergy wife.

Nor were things any better with the elderly. In some ways, Broughton was a thoroughgoing modernist. He was openly contemptuous of old wives' tales and legends, such as the story of the tunnel between the Church and the College Chapel, which elderly people loved to recall. He also upset many old people by his advocacy of cremation, going so far as to express the conviction that it would not be long before a government had the sense to make burials illegal. He argued that they were a menace to public health and, in any case, graves took up too much space.

Yet Broughton had some High Church leanings which also provoked controversy. He had served as a Curate at the decidedly Ritualist Tewkesbury Abbey in Gloucestershire. When he was Vicar of Brackley, he proposed to put more candles on the altar. At this, the entire Parochial Church Council rose as a body and walked out. One member commented, 'He'll want incense and confession next.'

Liturgically, Broughton tried to steer a middle course, but that only antagonised supporters of the High and Low extremes. In the past, whatever their private opinions, Brackley Anglicans had had no alternative but to attend St Peter's. Now greater mobility, first in the shape of bicycles and later motor cars, meant that they could go to neighbouring churches where the services were more to their taste. Some Low Church people went to Croughton, those who liked good sermons went to Turweston and the small Ritualist minority went to Kings Sutton where, as they said, 'things are done properly'. There was no corresponding influx of 'refugees' coming to Brackley from other churches. It is a measure of what was happening to the Church that, while the Methodists were pushing ahead with their plan for a Chapel on the High Street, Broughton' s main building initiative, the Church Institute, was to rise in Cross Lane.

Of course, there are excuses for Broughton. Unlike the wealthy Thicknesse and the comfortably off Egerton, he had no private means. Mrs Broughton's haute couture wardrobe must have been expensive. The large Vicarage, an important feature of the Thicknesse Revolution, became more of a burden than an asset to a poor clergyman. Some of the criticism of Broughton was mischievous and unfair.

During World War I he was sometimes abused because his son had not joined the forces – but the young man was sickly and a virtual invalid. When every allowance has been made, however, it is hard to deny that things might have been better if Egerton had stayed.

While Broughton may remind us of Sage, in other respects, late-Victorian Brackley was the exact opposite of the town in the 1830s. Then the economy had stagnated, but now there was excitement in the air. It was not just the result of the partial recovery of agriculture; the real cause of the buzz was a new railway. The Great Central (GCR) or, more strictly, the Manchester, Sheffield & Lincolnshire Railway, was coming. The name was actually changed to Great Central while the line was under construction, but to avoid confusion, here we will use 'Great Central' throughout in connection with Brackley.

As with Thicknesse's departure in 1879, we may wonder about the real reasons why Egerton left. Perhaps we should think of the town's appearance and the values thus represented. Despite its reputation for unruly impertinence, pre-Victorian Brackley had been dominated by the symbols of clerical and, to a lesser extent, aristocratic power: the two churches, Magdalen College School and the College Chapel, the Tithe House and the Town Hall paid for by the Earl of Bridgewater.

Despite the loss of St James's Church in the 1830s, this physical dominance had been massively reinforced by the Thicknesse Revolution: the new Vicarage, the Church School, the restored College Chapel and the new Manor House. Although the architectural balance of power would be altered if the Methodists ever managed to build their new Chapel, the change would be slight. Egerton is unlikely to have welcomed the prospect of the new Chapel, but he was not the man to flee his beloved Brackley for such a trivial reason. But supposing the physical transformation of Brackley was to be on a truly massive scale, what then? Brackley might almost cease to be Brackley and Egerton may have concluded with genuine humility that he was not the right man to lead the Church into an entirely different age.

That a change was coming, there could be no doubt. The forces behind it were neither Anglican, nor aristocratic or even Dissenting. They were commercial and the work of a company. By the time Egerton decided to move on, the surveyors were already planning the route of the Great Central Railway. Enough was known of the project for it to be clear that it would be nothing like the modest Banbury Branch of the LNWR. The LNWR line was unobtrusive, seeming to defer to God and Nature by keeping close to the floor of the Ouse Valley. The Great Central would have to defy Nature and perhaps God by carrying its line over the Turweston Brook Valley on a massive viaduct of twenty-three arches.

As he looked out from the upper floors of his Vicarage, over the roofs of the Old Town and on towards Turweston, Egerton must have tried to imagine what the view would look like in a few years' time. In its own way, the viaduct would be even more of a piece of architectural megalomania than Thicknesse's Church Schools – but it would be devoted to Mammon, not to God. Brackley Viaduct, soon to be the most impressive feature of the town, was constructed for a company whose motto was 'Forward'. There were some in Brackley who embraced the slogan wholeheartedly; others did not.

If election results suggested that the future would be Tory, the plans for the viaduct could be seen as an indicator that it would also be secular. This possibility increased when Broughton was revealed as a lesser man than Egerton and Nonconformist support was eroded by emigration. It is hardly surprising that the railway project proved divisive. But it was a division unlike earlier ones. In the past, the great divide had been between Church and Chapel, Tories and Liberals – such was the order of nature. Now the division over the railway cut clean across the traditional boundaries; there were pro- and anti- lobbies in both Church and Chapel. It was as if the railway project was bisecting the old natural categories exactly as the viaduct would bisect the hitherto tranquil Turweston Valley.

There were various reasons why people had reservations about the railway. There was the obvious aesthetic dimension. Although Brackley Viaduct turned out to be a brilliant feat of engineering of which later generations could be justly proud, it is understandable that many were shocked by what was undoubtedly a massive intrusion on the landscape. Others were motivated by more delicate considerations. Once it became known that a new station was to be located at the northern end of the town, at the top of Top End, people started to refer to it as 'the Top Station'. That did not pose a problem but how should one then refer to the old LNWR station? Vulgar people might call it 'the Bottom Station', but persons of quality and gentility knew that it was social death to say 'bottom' – under any circumstances. Mercifully, the blushes were spared and soon 'Brackley etiquette' had decreed that the branch line station must be called 'the Lower Station'. This brilliant euphemism was surely a worthy successor to an equally binding decision in the eighteenth century that the actual names, 'Egerton' and 'Humberstone', were never to be mentioned – the first was too sacred and the second too subversive.

At first sight, it may seem surprising that some Nonconformists should have opposed the railway project. But how could straight-laced Chapelgoers, many stern teetotallers, welcome the prospect of an invasion of railway navvies – and the viaduct alone would bring a whole army – when navvies throughout the country had an awesome reputation for drinking, fighting and getting country girls into trouble? The line would give Brackley direct access to London in not much over the hour – far quicker than the LNWR route to Euston which often involved changing at both Verney Junction and Bletchley. The new proximity of London might tempt more young Methodists to leave. For those who remained, Brackley would be only a cheap excursion fare away from a world of brightly lit pubs, music halls and painted women. The railway threatened to contaminate rustic virtue with metropolitan vice.

Some Nonconformists probably suspected that the railway itself, with its plans for grandiose stations and soaring viaducts, was close in spirit to the flamboyant Imperialism that seemed to be carrying all before it. A new religion of jingo-patriotism, in which men put their trust in battleships and colonies rather than in the Lord, was even more distasteful to the old Chapelgoers than traditional Anglicanism at its most arrogant and patronising. The new religion already had its own 'bible' called the *Daily Mail*. The paper was founded in May 1896 and, alarmingly, proved an instant success in Brackley. Not the least of the worries about the Great Central was the knowledge that it would bring in even more copies of the dreadful jingo rag.

Although not teetotallers, much of this analysis was shared by old-style Anglicans, especially by Squire Stratton of Turweston, Brackley's County Councillor and long-serving Mayor. But with this group there was an added dimension. As long ago as 1838, when Dr Arnold, Headmaster of Rugby School, had first seen the London & Birmingham Railway, he had declared, 'I rejoice in it because it will mean the end of feudalism'. But that was precisely the reason why, fifty years on, Stratton still opposed the Great Central. He regarded feudalism' as a very good thing indeed.

Although he could not prevent the arrival of the new railway, Stratton was able to limit its impact. At one stage the Great Central wanted to build a large engine shed, wagon repair works and marshalling yards at Brackley. This would have required a lot of land, some of which was currently owned by Stratton himself. Although a sale would have been to his financial advantage, Stratton rejected all approaches from the GCR. Such a development would ruin the appearance of Brackley and, incidentally, destroy the view from Turweston House. The town would be covered in smoke and soot. It would not be just a matter of the engine sheds and yards; the railway workers would need rows and rows of back-to-back housing. And who would those workers be? Not many of them would be locals. Most would probably come from the North of

England where the company was already well established. They would speak in horrid accents. Hardly any would be Anglicans, some might be Dissenters – hardly a recommendation – but worst of all, large numbers might be totally 'Godless'. If the railway works came, Brackley would be condemned to the equivalent of a permanent occupation by the navvies. It was a prospect not to be tolerated and Stratton stopped it.

In the end the company gave up and located the engine sheds a few miles up the line at Woodford Halse. The Woodford of my childhood gave an impression of what might have happened to Brackley. In its speech, its attitudes and its appearance, the village seemed like an outpost of the industrial North set in the fields of Northamptonshire.[4] The debate on whether Stratton had been right to stop the railway works was still raging in my childhood. Some thought he had been right. When as a young railway enthusiast, I remember saying to an elderly relation that it was a pity that Brackley had not got its engine sheds, that it had not become more like Woodford, it would have been ideal for a train spotter, the old lady was not impressed and observed darkly, 'You know, John, Woodford is such a filthy place – *in every sense of that word*'. At the time, I did not know what she meant, but I think I do now. Perhaps the ultimate vindication of Stratton came when the Great Central closed on 3 September 1966 – *infelix atque infaustum iter* – less than a lifetime after it opened. The engine sheds would not have brought prosperity to late-twentieth-century Brackley. After the closure, Woodford became a ghost village.

Yet, both in the 1890s and later, there were many who thought that Stratton had been wrong – although they were grateful that he had not been able to stop the line itself coming to Brackley. There were even some traditional and historical reasons for welcoming the railway. Would not the line reinforce Brackley's curiously close and long-standing relationship with the North-west? Had not the Blencowes originally come from Cumberland in the fifteenth century and the Crewes and Egertons from Cheshire in Elizabethan and Jacobean times? The Great Central already served Manchester and that would make it convenient for the Earl of Ellesmere. The Egerton properties in Lancashire, once as remote as the moon from Brackley, would now be only a few hours away. Brackley had only recently succeeded in 'capturing' the Earl of Ellesmere; the new line would surely help to keep him. Thus, the Great Central would symbolise not the negation but the fulfilment of the Thicknesse Revolution.

There was a comforting sense that Brackley would soon be nearer to the heart of 'Egerton land'. There was a fashion for naming new houses after places owned by the Earl in the North, hence Walkden Place, the row of stone-fronted houses on the corner of Cross Lane and High Street. The compliment was returned when it was announced that a large coal mine under development in Lancashire was to be called 'Brackley Colliery'. In the past, it had been à la mode in Brackley to burn coal from the Baddesley Colliery between Coventry and Nuneaton: 'I never have anything but the *best Baddesley* in *my* grates, my dear'. Baddesley coal came on the LNWR, but the new line would bring 'Brackley coal' to Brackley. Egerton loyalists promised to buy it for its name and out of respect for the Earl, thus further swelling Ellesmere's already ample coffers. Sadly, when it came, 'Brackley coal' proved a disappointment. It left too much ash and clinker and 'Baddesley' regained its social pre-eminence until the days of central heating.

Yet the real argument for the railway was economic. In retrospect, it seemed obvious that the main reason why Brackley had stagnated, almost 'missing out' on the nineteenth century, had been its poor position on the railway network. Now that the century was drawing to its end, Brackley would finally catch

4   See Anscomb, JW, 'Woodford Halse: The Village with a Heart of Steam', *Northamptonshire Past and Present*, Vol. VI, No. 6 (1982–83) pp.341–50. In contrast to the falling numbers in Brackley and most of the surrounding villages, the population of Woodford increased from 527 in 1891 to 1,220 in 1901.

up with it. A new century was just around the corner, but it was expected to be like the previous one – only more so. Few doubted that the line would be profitable. Reliable motor cars were some years in the future and it was taken as read that railways would be the dominant mode of transport in the new century as in the old.

On the face of it, the Great Central's 'London Extension' possessed a sound economic rationale. The 'gathering grounds' of the railway were in the industrial and mining regions of Lancashire and Yorkshire, with links to the agricultural districts, ports and resorts of Lincolnshire. The original lines carried large amounts of traffic, especially coal. The main problem was that much of this coal had to be transferred to the tracks of other companies, such as the Midland or the Great Northern, for transit to the south and London. It was calculated that, for every pound in traffic receipts, the old Manchester, Sheffield & Lincolnshire Railway (MS&L) had to give 13s 4d to other companies, because, on average, coal destined for London travelled on its metals for only 16 miles.[5] The arrangement was particularly unfair because the early stages of the journey south, involving the collection of wagons from collieries and marshalling them into trains, was by far the most costly part of the entire operation.

The answer was to 'hang on' to the coal trains for more of the journey to London – and that meant extending the MS&L's own tracks southwards. There were encouraging precedents. The Midland Railway, now consistently the most profitable of the major companies, had once been in a similar situation, but had made a successful push to London in the 1860s. Initially, the MS&L proceeded in easy stages. Thus, in 1889, it obtained an Act of Parliament enabling it to construct a line from Sheffield to Annesley in Nottinghamshire – adding another 28 miles before the coal trains had to be transferred to the Great Northern. In 1891, however, it decided to go the whole hog – a through route to London of its own which would enable it to retain all of its freight revenue.

To this end, a Bill was prepared seeking Parliamentary approval for a line – 94 miles in length – from Annesley to Quainton Road. This was the line that would pass through Brackley. At Quainton Road it would join the tracks of the Metropolitan Railway, whose Chairman was also Sir Edward Watkin. The new line would share the Metropolitan's tracks into North London, but there would be a separate final stretch leading to a new terminus, to be named Marylebone. Understandably, the other railway companies, especially the Midland, opposed the scheme.

Many directors of railway companies sat in Parliament, but opposition was not confined to this group. Cricket enthusiasts were appalled by the thought that the last stretch of the proposed line would desecrate their 'Holy of Holies' – Lords. Others objected to destruction of 'large and valuable residential properties' in St John's Wood. Mr James, Member for Gateshead – significantly a director of the North Eastern Railway – thought that Watkin already had too much power in the business world. In addition to his Chairmanship of the MS&L and of the Metropolitan, he was also Chairman of the South Eastern Railway. He owned Snowdon, was prospecting for coal in Kent and was 'the parent of the Channel Tunnel scheme and of an Eiffel Tower in London'. James went so far as to quote Shakespeare, comparing Watkin to Julius Caesar:

He doth bestride the narrow world
Like a colossus.

5   'The Great Central Railway: a short account of its early days and growth and London Extension', supplement to the
     Railway News, 1899, p.xvii.

Watkin was a Liberal and Member of Parliament for Hythe, Manchester. The Bill was discussed by a Parliamentary Committee that met on 17 April 1891 and the hearing lasted for fifteen days. The Committee could not agree upon a recommendation and so the Bill lapsed. A revised scheme, making important and expensive concessions to the cricketers, was accepted by the Committee in April 1892 and a Bill authorising the construction finally received Royal Assent on 28 March 1893.[6]

In September 1894 contracts for the sections between Charwelton and Brackley and between Brackley and Quainton Road – a total of 40 miles – were awarded to Sir Walter Scott & Co. Shortly afterwards, the MS&L became the Great Central. Some Brackley people were so carried away with enthusiasm that they rushed to buy Great Central shares. They should have listened to the cynics who made play with the company's old and new initials. The MS&L had often been close to bankruptcy and, at its best, had never declared a dividend of more than 3.5 per cent – compared to the Midland's steady 6 per cent. So MS&L really stood for 'Money Sunk & Lost'. But the change of name to Great Central would only make matters worse. 'GC' would probably turn out to mean 'Gone Completely'.

But whether or not the line proved profitable, it did promise economic advantages to various sections of the community. A few locals might be employed at the station; a job with the security of railway service was much sought after. But the indirect benefits would be more widespread. The expected army of navvies would buy food from local shops. George Gibbard, now the rising grocer, liked to cultivate a 'genteel' air but would not object to the extra business.

Navvying was thirsty work and that was good news for the publicans and the brewers – the Blencowes and the Hopcrafts. It was soon to be Hopcraft & Norris. Somehow, a fairly humble local boy, Walter Norris, managed to win the heart of the wealthy Miss White from Hampshire. The Whites were willing to help Norris set himself up in business. A share in a Brackley brewery seemed an excellent idea. It was not long before the couple were able to move from the Old Hall in Brackley to Steane Park – though reduced from its former glory it was still a country seat.

And after the beer came the gas; indeed, wags claimed that the two were sometimes mingled. If the nineteenth century was the 'Age of the Railway', it was hardly less the 'Age of Gas'. The two went together, with the railways carrying the necessary coal and coke and lighting their stations with gas. Gasworks were almost always located near to railway stations; the one at Brackley, built in the 1850s, was adjacent to the LNWR station. Even in the 1890s, the future of gas lighting seemed as secure as that of rail transport. The new Great Central station at Brackley would surely be gas-lit.

There was no more enthusiastic advocate of the Great Central than John Goffe Clarke, the leading ironmonger in Brackley and one of the chief shareholders in the Brackley Gas Company. Clarke actually went to London to argue the merits of the railway before the Parliamentary Committee, taking the opposite line to his fellow Anglican, John Locke Stratton. The belief that gas would illuminate the twentieth century as it had the nineteenth is evident in a contract made between the Great Central and the Brackley Gas Company. The terms were favourable to the gas company. The Great Central agreed to light its station with the company's gas for an incredible period of 100 years, during which it undertook not to install any other form of lighting. One begins to see why Clarke was so keen on the railway. Astonishingly, the contract survived the railway grouping of 1923 and the nationalisation of both the gas and railway industries after World War II. The Top Station remained gas-lit to the end in 1966. In the 1950s, when young men, whose interests included such things as rock and roll and motorcycles, came to work at the

6   Anscomb, 'Woodford Halse', op. cit., p.341.

station, they could barely keep a straight face when they were told in all solemnity, 'You'll never make a Goods Clerk Mr … until you can change a gas mantle'.

It was appropriate that Clarke should have been the mayor who took Brackley into the twentieth century. He served from 1899 to 1901. The *Northampton Herald* describes him as 'of an enterprising disposition' and comments that his 'business-like qualities and grasp of affairs' made him 'a very esteemed public man'. It is striking that Clarke was the first overtly 'commercial' mayor of the new Corporation. He symbolises a new class in Brackley, one that had been a long time coming – a self-confident bourgeoisie. If Stratton represents old-style Toryism, Clarke represents the new.

Another new man was James Smart, the printer. Both Clarke and Smart were Sidesmen and both were Tories who broke new ground. In the past, Anglican masters had preferred to employ Anglicans or, at any rate, made it clear to any Nonconformist employees that it would be better for them to change their allegiance. Smart imposed no such conditions and it was he who employed the young Methodist, Luther Brailsford. Again, like Clarke, Smart would derive advantage from the Great Central. He perceived that better rail communications would enable him to gain more access to 'leisure markets'.

Smart had two main specialties, both linked indirectly to the new cult of Imperialism. The first involved printing catalogues for stamp dealers and albums for collectors. Smart undoubtedly knew that he was serving the needs of a hobby. But did this Church Sidesman ever wonder whether hobbies, even such seemingly innocuous ones as stamp collecting, might take up the time and energy formerly devoted to Church- and Chapelgoing? Stamp collecting often focused on stamps produced for the growing number of British colonies and dependencies. It was thus an ideal recruiting sergeant for the new 'religion' of Imperialism. Smart's other line also had a hidden Imperialist dimension. He produced school magazines, not only for Magdalen College School Brackley, but also for a range of minor public schools. Amid the accounts of cricket matches and academic achievements, one of the most common features of these magazines were the summaries of talks, usually given by bronzed old boys who had returned to their alma maters, telling the present pupils about the wonders of the Empire and the great opportunities that awaited them if they would only 'take up "the White Man's Burden"'. It is hardly surprising that most of Brackley was to be so keen on the Boer War. In its own way, Mr Smart's business was every bit as 'secular' as Brackley Viaduct and even more Imperialist.

Even Magdalen College School, once a bastion of the 'old order' gave tacit support for the railway. It would bring more boarders to the school and more boarders would mean more fees. More pupils would mean more school uniforms to be purchased from the draper and outfitter Edward Bartlett (Mayor of Brackley 1901–04). He too supported the railway. It was a sign of the times that Edward Chapman, a Fellow of Magdalen College, a man who took considerable interest in the school, was also Deputy Chairman of the MS&L. Chapman clearly had a decidedly railway-orientated view of Brackley's future. After laying the foundation stone of the new South Wing building at the school on 18 February 1896, Chapman declared that he 'hoped that Brackley meant to import excursionists and export scholars'.[7]

Although Wodhams and his successor, Rev William Wyatt Holdgate (1899–1910), were both clergymen, it is hard not to detect a more secular tone in the curriculum which corresponds closely to the mood of the 'Age of Imperialism'. Wodhams himself introduced chemistry, astronomy, botany, physical geography,

---

7   Forrester, Eric, G., *A History of Magdalen College School, Brackley*, p.123.

bookkeeping and shorthand.[8] Holdgate had been Senior Science Master at Trent College before coming to Brackley and his greatest achievements were the chemistry and physics laboratories opened in 1904. Perhaps even more significant for the future was the formation of a Cadet Force in 1905.[9]

Only one of the 'Brackley entrepreneurs' was actually known to me. He was William Judd. I knew him when he was a very old man of over 90, who burned his slippers by the fire as his daughter, Pearl, gave me my piano lessons. Judd was also the most controversial of the group. Unlike Norris, George Gibbard, John Goffe Clarke and James Smart, Judd had few pretensions to gentility – though this was more than compensated by Mrs Judd whose theatrical manner and cut-glass voice formed the basis of many a Brackley story. Behind a veneer of slightly cynical good humour, Judd was an exceptionally astute businessman. He perceived that, if Brackley became more prosperous, there would be a demand for a different kind of working-class housing. Skilled workers at Smart's or Clarke's, even the new railway workers, would not be content with the tumbledown cottages which had housed the Brackley poor for so long.

Judd had very humble origins. His family came from Croughton and he began life as a pedlar taking a pack of ribbons around the villages. He then moved to Brackley and opened a boot and shoe shop. This venture failed and Judd went bankrupt. While the railway was being built, Judd and his wife scavenged woollen socks discarded by the navvies. These they washed and repaired and then sold. Somehow or other, Judd managed to set up as a speculative builder and property owner. By the time of his death in 1955 he owned nearly 100 houses. Established builders mocked Judd's cheapskate methods and dubbed his houses 'Colander Rows', because the roofs were always leaking. Judd always replied to critics that the houses would 'see me out', and they did, even though he lived to a great age. Most are still standing.

In reality, Judd was a benefactor to the people of Brackley – although not many of them gave him credit for it. He provided affordable housing which, if not meeting the highest standards of craftsmanship, certainly offered far more hygienic and comfortable accommodation than the old cottages. Some of Judd's tenants did not go to Church or Chapel, but many read the Daily Mail. In some households there were young wives who had been to London and to the Music Hall. As they hung up their washing, they laughed at Mr Broughton and Squire Stratton before launching into the latest song –TA RA BUM DE AY, TA RA BUM DE AY. Old-style Church and Chapel alike was shocked, but William Judd did not mind. He joked and chaffed with the young wives as he came to collect the rents – after all he too had his reservations about Mr Broughton. As he left, old Brackley people would say 'There goes a chap that's fond of siller' [silver = money].

Another 'entrepreneur' who scorned 'gentility' was the 'cheap' or 'slop' draper, Tommy Kibble. Kibble gave great offence to polite society by the eye-catching posters he displayed, first on his market stall and later in his shop window on the Banbury Road. One of them read 'Kibble's trousers down again'.

Appropriately, the 'Congregational Entrepreneur', Charlie Gardner assumed a more sombre air. Unlike Judd, Gardner was not a builder although he did own quite a lot of cottages. As he came back with his rents in his pony and trap, he always sang the words of the Harvest Hymn – 'All is safely gathered in, free from sorrow, free from sin'. Gardner was a great one for hymns and later led community singing in the town. The words were so familiar to him that he tended to run them together – so that 'Oh God

8   Ibid., p.106.

9   Ibid., p.177.

156

our Help in Ages Past, Our Hope for Years to Come', became 'Oh God our Relp in Ages Past, Our Rope for Years to Come'.

Of course, the 'entrepreneurs' were a mixed bunch and there was a huge gulf between the brewer Norris – who now moved on the edge of gentry circles – and the former pedlar, William Judd. But they had a lot in common. With the exception of Gardner and the solicitor Mr Law, they were Tories and Anglicans, but their Toryism inclined to the Imperialist variety and their Anglicanism accommodated itself easily to an increasingly secular world. They were not excessively deferential to their betters. When William Judd built his first row of 'villas', he made no reference to the possessions of the Earl of Ellesmere; he proudly called his houses 'Juddville Place'. One thing united them all; every one of them, from Walter Norris to William Judd, hoped to make a killing from the coming of the railway.

But it seemed that the killing would be a little delayed and that God and Nature still favoured the 'Old Order' and Squire Stratton. The first workmen had barely arrived when an unusually severe winter descended. The early months of 1895 were so cold that construction had to be suspended. The navvies were laid off and many were left destitute. Soup kitchens were opened in Brackley for their benefit. (On a lighter note, the Hinton Brook was flooded to provide a skating rink – and skating enjoyed a great popularity.)

When work resumed it was discovered that geological conditions in the Turweston Brook Valley were much more unstable than expected. If the viaduct had been built to the original plans it might have been unsafe. Extensive and expensive changes had to be made. But the forces of Mammon persisted.

As expected some of the navvies turned out to be boisterous and crude. They sang a *very* rude song about the girls of Brackley. It began:

Oh! Brackley girls are pretty,
You ought to see them dance.
They cock their legs right over their heads
And show ...

Even in these degenerate and permissive days, it would not be proper to continue. Yet, on the whole, the navvies and brickies were not as bad as people like Stratton had feared. There were even fewer of them than expected. This was because the Great Central London Extension was the first major civil engineering project in this country in which machinery was employed on an extensive scale. Traditionally, railway cuttings and embankments were created almost entirely with picks and shovels. Walter Scott & Co. used huge steam-driven excavators.

Although the navvies working on the Great Central enjoyed better conditions than the men who had built the first railways, there were still serious accidents. Thirteen navvies were admitted to the Cottage Hospital in the course of 1895 and two died. There were several fractures and a number of amputations. Since the hospital had a very small staff and no proper operating theatre, 'the enterprise takes on heroic proportions'.[10] Some of the navvies attended Mission Services, which were held in prefabricated 'tin-tabs'. These could be dismantled and then reassembled on other sites as the work progressed. One of these 'tin-tabs', however, stayed behind and can still be seen as the Church at Halse.

10   Smith, Donald, 'Brackley Cottage Hospital', op. cit., p.43.

Whatever their faults, the men who built the Great Central were good workers and they had the benefit of superb materials. The red and purple bricks were slightly glazed and proved so resistant to weathering that, to the end, the Top Station, designed by Alexander Ross, had a new, slightly raw look about it.[11] Ross (1834–1925), a Scotsman from Inverness, had travelled extensively in Europe and the Middle East. His station buildings for the GCR at Brackley and elsewhere have a definite Continental feel, perhaps reflecting Watkins's Channel Tunnel project. They are certainly less English than the stone gables of the old Bottom Station.

The Borough Council, dominated by Squire Stratton, was able to make one final difficulty. Like all of the stations on the London Extension, the Top Station had an 'island platform' with the tracks passing on either side. Here there were the waiting rooms and other facilities to serve the needs of passengers for both 'up' and 'down' trains. While this avoided the duplication of the facilities inherent in the usual two-platform pattern, it did create problems of access from the road. When the station was in a cutting, as at Brackley, the obvious solution was to build an entrance on the bridge taking the road over the line. Steps would then lead directly down to the island platform. But Brackley Council would not agree that their road bridge should be used in this way – citing likely traffic congestion. Given the sparse road traffic of the time, this was nonsense, but the Great Central had to agree to bear the extra expense of building a special approach road. Furthermore, because the entrance hall housing the Booking and Station Master's Offices would now be at the side of the island platform rather than directly above it, a footbridge for passengers and luggage had to be built over the line. One strange feature of the Top Station was a dummy platform which was installed in the expectation of traffic growth in the future, probably for trains that would serve a branch line to Northampton. The branch was never built. The dummy platform was a symbol of the Great Central's ambitions, ambitions that tended to run ahead of reality. We begin to see why the original estimates were so far exceeded.

Finally it was all ready. The first passenger train arrived on 15 March 1899. Photographs taken at the time illustrate the divisions that the railway had caused. One youngish woman is waving her umbrella and literally jumping for joy. The black-coated and hunched figure of Squire Stratton seems to be turning away from the train.

11   Rolt, LTC, *The Making of a Railway* (London: Hugh Evelyn, 1971) p.114.

Charlie Tugwood, Brackley blacksmith shop.

Brackley Town Hall, later nineteenth century: note the closed arches.

The Hopcraft & Norris Brewery workforce.

Building the viaduct.

Building the viaduct.

Steam excavator.

Brackley Top Station, Great Central. (NRO)

The first train.

Local worthies.

Brackley Council, 1902. (A.A. Green Collection, Brackley Library)

Chapter Ten

THE IMAGE OF WAR

The arrival of the Great Central gave Brackley a psychological boost and created a spirit of optimism not seen for centuries. The town was smartening up its appearance and presenting a more attractive face to the world. The achievement is summarised in the *Methodist Recorder* of February 1904:

> Brackley in late years has been greatly improved, although the population has not greatly increased. By the creation of a Local Board, authority was given for new developments, a system of drainage was introduced, water works were built at a very considerable cost and the entire town is flagged. By the rebuilding of the manor house, by the residence of the family there, a new class of society has been brought into the neighbourhood. A good deal of old property, formerly thatched and antique, has been rebuilt. The lines of trees on either side of the street, so conspicuous a feature of generations past, have been continued from one end of the town to the other, giving it the appearance rather of a boulevard than a mere straggling street.

The smart new Brackley with its 'boulevard', its viaduct and large station, epitomised the confident spirit of the Imperialism that was a candidate to take over as the new religion in a more secular age. This Imperialism found expression in the Boer War. Although some Chapelgoers had their doubts, most people supported the war. Egerton loyalists were thrilled to learn that the Earl of Ellesmere's son and heir, the appropriately named Viscount Brackley – who had actually shown worryingly little interest in the town – was serving in South Africa as ADC to Major General Sir WG Knox. A few volunteers came forward and subscriptions were raised to present them with field glasses for use on the veldt. Although essentially a 'spectator sport', the Boer War left a deep impression in Brackley. As a child, I asked one old lady who she thought had been the worst man of all time. I expected that she would name Hitler or perhaps the Kaiser, but she said, 'Oh, I think he must have been "Oom Paul"'. This was a reference to the Boer leader, President Paul Kruger of the Transvaal. One local boy had the misfortune to be nicknamed 'Kruger' by his fellows. It stuck and may have blighted his life. Sixty years later, 'Kruger' still had a miserable, hangdog look about him.

But would Imperialism carry all before it? Beneath the glossy surface of Imperialism, a darker side was emerging – tales of military incompetence (Sir WG Knox included) and horrifying stories of the mistreatment of Boer women and children in concentration camps. Did Brackley resemble Imperialism in this respect as well? All might be fine along the boulevard, but what of the Brackley of the Yards?

In 1910, Dr WWE Fletcher produced a Report for the Local Government Board on the state of Public Health in Brackley. Fletcher notes that, in 1908, the total rateable value of the town is £12,012, producing an income of £9,050; there is an outstanding debt of £12,830 that has been incurred for 'sanitary purposes'. Fletcher concedes that there are admirable features. The quality of the water supply is good and, when he visited the Sewage Farm, 'no nuisance was observed'. There is a larger proportion of good-sized residences than usually met with in towns of a similar size and the 'dwellings of the working classes' are generally well built and in good repair. The facilities for the collection of refuse and ashes are excellent.

Despite these good points, Fletcher finds much to criticise. Water is still scarce in outlying cottages and 'the Council appear to be unwilling to take any action in this matter'. There are many cottages which suffer from damp – in some because the floors are below the ordinary ground level, in others through the soil resting against the outer walls to some height above the floors, and again, in others, through defective roofs and spouting eaves. There have been some improvements and the poor cottages near the Church and on the site of the new Methodist Chapel have recently been demolished; the 'unfit housing' in Nicholls's Yard, though still standing, is unoccupied.

Examples of bad houses still survive in Halls Lane and in Barretts Yard (off Church Lane) and in New Road. In many instances, sanitary arrangements remain deplorable:

> In the case of cottage property, the water closets which are situated outside the dwellings are seldom provided with flushing cisterns and, as a result, many of them are in a neglected and filthy condition. In the country part of the borough, cesspit privies, ashpit privies and pail closets are in use.

Fletcher is appalled at the conditions in the four registered slaughterhouses – with floors of broken bricks and fastening pens inside the actual slaughterhouse. The Council has obtained a bye-law prohibiting the keeping of pigs within 100 feet of a dwelling, but this law is widely ignored. The conclusion is damning:

> The Council has failed to provide an efficient disinfecting apparatus and hospital accommodation for persons suffering from infectious disease; dwelling houses have been allowed to remain in dilapidated and insanitary conditions; and the repeated complaints of the medical officer of health with respect to such dwellings have been ignored. The Council also appears to be very lax in dealing with nuisances arising from the keeping of pigs and fowls in filthy conditions.

Fletcher believes that these problems must be blamed upon the councillors themselves rather than upon the Borough officials – the Medical Officer of Health, Dr John Fenton, and the Inspector of Nuisances and Borough Surveyor, Mr Arthur Abraham Green. He describes Green as 'a capable and satisfactory officer'. Green came from Peterborough and, as a boy, had sung in the Cathedral Choir.

Perhaps Fletcher was being unfair to the Council. We should remember that it had the ratepayers to think about. Furthermore, attempts to enforce the bye-law on pig keeping would have probably been unpopular. Pigs formed an important addition to the lower-class diet and, as Flora Thompson's *Lark*

Rise to Candleford suggests, a pig killing was a major social event, much enjoyed by children. When every allowance has been made, however, it looks as if the Council was more concerned with appearances than with the fundamentals of public health. The priority was with the boulevard; for the rest of the town it was probably a matter of 'out of sight, out of mind'.

The impression given by Fletcher's report, is reinforced by the recollections of Fred Turvey (1898–1984) who, towards the end of his life, was interviewed by the local Oral History Group. He described sleeping conditions in his parents' cottage in the Old Town – he slept with his brothers 'three in a bed and one across the bottom'. We begin to suspect that, despite the Thicknesse Revolution and the more recent Municipal Revolution, conditions in the Yards may have been no better than when Rev Smith wrote his gloomy report for Sage back in 1865. Of course, the changes had been more than cosmetic and there were fewer people now living in really dreadful conditions – emigration and rebuilding had seen to that – but the numbers affected were still significant.

But it was not just a matter of physical conditions. In addition to the very poor and disadvantaged, others were becoming discontented with the petty class distinctions that still played an important part in Brackley life. It was easy to identify members of the lower orders. The Vicar addressed the men by their surnames alone. If they went to Church they were expected to sit in one of the side aisles. The women should curtsey to those reckoned a notch or two higher in the social scale. They bought their clothes from Tommy Kibble rather than Edward Bartlett. They still believed in 'old wives tales'. They used the local accent rather than 'speaking nicely'. They burned cheap coal – certainly not best Baddesley. They said 'Bottom Station', not 'Lower Station'. Perhaps most significantly of all, they were expected to use the Back Way (Manor Road) and not show themselves too often in the High Street.

Some people seem to have regarded the layout of the town itself as similar to that of a gentleman's residence, though on the horizontal rather than the vertical plane. The High Street or 'boulevard' corresponded to the 'front stairs' – to be used mainly by the gentry and 'better sort' – while the Back Way was the equivalent of the narrower and more utilitarian servants' stairs, *quite* good enough for the lower orders. They had no need of tree-lined avenues and should not presume to disfigure them by their inelegant presence.

There were still timid old ladies in the Brackley of my childhood who admitted to feeling 'uncomfortable' if they had to go into the High Street and actually took detours to avoid it. Even in the early 1900s, however, many found such taboos ludicrous, offensive or simply incomprehensible. In other words, the old class distinctions were being challenged. Soon, new catchphrases like 'fed up' and 'browned off' were heard in Brackley – though we may doubt if such vulgar expressions ever came to the ears, much less passed the lips, of the Earl of Ellesmere.

Trouble was coming, but would it resemble the short-lived and fairly feeble New Course of the early 1890s or would the mood be closer to the more dangerous and Radical, even violent, mid-1860s? Sober reflection might have suggested the latter. We may wonder if, around 1905, some of the successful entrepreneurs or their betters were ever troubled by the thought that they might soon be haunted by the 'Ghost of 1867'. If they had such thoughts, they would have known that, this time, the Church of England could not save them. Broughton was no Thicknesse and even the Earl of Ellesmere seemed to be spending more time away from Brackley.

The similarities with the 1860s are striking. Methodism was more vigorous than at any time since the arrival of Francis Thicknesse. In some ways, the coming of the Great Central helped the Methodists. A few of the men who had worked on the line married and settled down. Some became stalwarts of the

Chapel; one such was the bricklayer 'Dickie' Law who set up a successful building business. Perhaps more important, at the very time that the Church of England was going into decline under Broughton, the Methodists acquired an outstanding minister in Rev John Osborn. Appointed in 1900, Osborn put new life into the flagging project for a new Chapel, commissioning plans from the Birmingham firm of Messrs Ewen Harper & Brother. Osborn held a public meeting to launch a fundraising campaign on 11 June 1903. Although Methodist rules stipulated that a minister should move after three years, an exception was made for Osborn.[1]

Local and national trends coincided. A great Nonconformist revival was taking place throughout the nation and this fed through to a corresponding revival in the Liberal Party. But – and this was very worrying – the Liberal Party had moved much further to the Left during its long years in opposition and now presented the electorate with plans that would do something for the very poor. There was a real possibility – indeed, it actually happened – that a new Liberal Government would bring in measures like old-age pensions (removing the spectre of the Workhouse), Workmen's Compensation, more rights for Trades Unions, sickness and unemployment pay. The just society which the Evenley strikers of 1867 had glimpsed – and been mocked for even thinking about – appeared to be at hand. At very least, these proposals were more exciting than the emphasis on Irish Home Rule and Welsh Disestablishment, the causes that had dominated the Liberal agenda in the 1890s.

There was another difference from 1892. Locally, the Liberals had a better candidate than the ineffective David Guthrie. Depending on one's point of view, the hopes or threats of 1867 would find their fulfilment in a great Liberal victory at the polls.

Thomas Newcomen Archibald Grove had lost to Fitzroy in 1900. Although essentially a 'carpet bagger' – he had served as Liberal Member for West Ham, London, from 1892 to 1895 – at least Grove had 'stuck with' the Towcester constituency. Now aged 50, he was hardly a man of the people. He was wealthy and well connected – his mother was a Ponsonby – and he lived in some style at Pollards Park, Chalfont St Giles. Of course, this meant that he could come to Brackley on the Great Central from Amersham or from Chalfont & Latimer. Curiously, Grove had been at Oriel College, Oxford, once Rev Thomas Mozley's college. But the Liberal-inclined Oriel of the 1870s – when Grove was 'up' – had been a very different place from the clerical Oriel, dominated by John Henry Newman, of Mozley's time in the 1830s. Grove used some of his private means to found, edit and support a Radical journal called the *New Review*. At the 'Liberal Landslide' Election of January 1906, Grove obtained a majority of 322 over the Tory, Charles Douglas-Pennant – eight times the size of Guthrie's victory back in 1892.

For a while, the future did seem to lie with Radicalism and with Methodism. Yet it was not to be and, despite the great achievements of the Liberal Government, Brackley's second 'Liberal interlude' proved hardly more substantial than the New Course. In 1910, Grove stood down and Fitzroy returned as the Tory candidate. There were two elections that year. In January, Fitzroy defeated FG Kellaway by 610 votes and, in December, he defeated AA Thomas by 513. In the event, Fitzroy was to retain the seat until his death on 3 March 1943 – having served as Speaker of the House of Commons since 1928.

So, what had gone wrong? In a small community, personalities matter as much as broader trends. Brackley Liberalism had long 'punched above its weight' because of the personal charisma of Thomas Judge. But Judge was mellowing. It is hard to imagine the young Radical of the 1860s seeking a public

1   *Methodist Recorder*, 4 February 1904.

honour for 'the Compleat Squire' (Adkins's description), John Locke Stratton of Turweston.[2] But in 1898 that is precisely what Judge did. He wrote to Sir Michael Hicks Beach, Chancellor of the Exchequer in Lord Salisbury's government, suggesting that Stratton should be knighted. He may have been influenced by the fact that Hicks Beach was Stratton's nephew, the son of his sister, Harriet. But the reply from the Treasury, dated 8 February 1898, makes it clear that Hicks Beach regarded Judge's suggestion as ludicrous. He was sure that Stratton did not want a knighthood and, even if he did, 'I could not obtain it for him'. Stratton's public service, as a magistrate, on the Board of Guardians and on the County Council, was no different from the work done by many country gentlemen without the least thought of reward. It was only as Mayor of Brackley that Stratton had done work that was occasionally rewarded with a knighthood. But such recognition was confined to the mayors of large cities:

> I do not wish to underrate the importance of Brackley. But it is so small a town, that the grant of a knighthood to its mayor as such would undoubtedly be felt as a slight by many towns in the country who would be much offended at its being preferred to them. For this reason, I am sure that Lord Salisbury would not comply with any request of the kind.[3]

Although Judge had many contacts with national politics, it seems that, in his heart of hearts, he still regarded Brackley as the centre of the universe. Hicks Beach's thinly veiled contempt for the town must have hurt him.

One might have expected that Judge, the brains behind the Evenley strike, would have been ecstatic at what Campbell Bannerman and later Asquith secured in the face of the unremitting hostility of the Tories and the House of Lords. Yet Judge was less than enthusiastic. Shortly after the 1906 election, he suffered a stroke. He recovered sufficiently to make it clear that he had no time for many of the Liberals' measures. He particularly disliked the Workmen's Compensation Act, which he considered unfair to employers. Judge's Radicalism was always essentially individualistic rather than collectivist. He probably still subscribed to the line taken by Henry Vincent, the Chartist candidate for Banbury at the 1841 election: 'I have always told you that the interests of the middle and working classes are one and the same. Both are interested in having good and cheap responsible government'.[4] As the *Banbury Guardian* noted in its obituary of Judge:

> Of late years, his former ardent Liberalism had somewhat moderated, as is often the case with men as they advance in life, and who find the views and enthusiasms of their youth somewhat illusory when they reach riper years.

Even so, when Judge died on 23 February 1910, still a Brackley Alderman and still a County Councillor, local Radicalism was left with a gap which has never been filled.

Then there was 'the trouble at the Chapel' which, even after two world wars, my Churchgoing parents and grandparents still chuckled about in the 1950s – even though they warned me never to mention it to

2   Adkins, *Our County*, p.122.

3   Letter shown me by Mrs Pat Phillips.

4   Hodgkins, *Over the Hills to Glory*, p.17.

our neighbours, (Mr and Mrs Morgan), nice Methodist 'immigrants' from South Wales.[5] By 1910, the old Anglican jibe that Methodist Ministers were mere 'homemade uns', was no longer valid. The new Methodist Ministers had been to theological colleges and were properly trained professionals. While this gave them some advantages, it also created the danger of a gulf opening up between the minister and ordinary Chapelgoers. More and more, Methodist Ministers seemed to be modelling themselves on their Anglican opposite numbers, becoming almost indistinguishable in appearance with their black suits and dog collars. Some tried to acquire greater control over what happened in their Chapels – and that caused a major row in Brackley.

What was true of the ministers was also true of the Chapel buildings. In a sense, by seeking to have their Chapel on the boulevard, the Methodists were turning their backs on the side streets and poor cottages. As the new Chapel arose – it was finished in 1911 – the message became even clearer. The new Chapel with its Gothic tracery windows and little tower looks a bit like an Anglican Church. The Chapel's impressive appearance could be taken as a sign that Methodism had really 'arrived', yet, by entering into a kind of architectural competition with the Church of England, the Chapel was in danger of losing touch with the very poor. Some of those who lived in the Yards probably found the new Chapel intimidating, like the boulevard in general. It would never be *their* Chapel in the way that the old one had been; it certainly never flourished to the same extent. Ordinary Methodists could be forgiven for wondering what was the real significance of the tower and the Gothic windows. If Anglicans speculated that Mr Broughton would want incense and confessions next, would a Methodist Minister soon suggest bells and surplices? Perhaps the Chapel was being taken over by 'Broughtons in disguise'.

Although the Chapel might look a little like a Church, it could never be mistaken for a *real* Church. At best it was an imitation. Arguably, the Methodists were getting the worst of both worlds. If they truly wanted their Chapel to be indistinguishable from a Church they made a grave error. Perhaps in their eagerness to establish a presence on the boulevard with an appropriately impressive entrance – at least as grand as that of the College Chapel – they forgot the fundamental difference between the two sites. The College Chapel is on the east side of the High Street; its entrance is at its west end and its altar and sanctuary at the liturgically correct east end. The Methodist Chapel, however, is on the west side of the High Street. Its High Street entrance is at its east end and its Communion table is at its liturgically incorrect west end. The Anglican critique of the Chapel's deficiencies was summed up by one Church stalwart, who delightedly told the Vicar that the 'long eared uns' had 'got it all arse about face'. I have been informed that Broughton quite properly reproved the man for his unseemly language, but allowed himself a rare smile before passing on.

The opening of the Chapel turned out to be a disaster because it raised the central question of authority. The minister insisted that the dedication stones should be laid by visiting Methodist grandees and not by local people who had worked so hard to raise the money. A group, led by the butcher, Billy Winkles, took umbrage and decamped for the Church of England. At least Broughton had the sense to give Winkles a warm welcome and even to hide his distaste for the butcher's ignorance of Anglican forms – evident in his habitual reference to the Lady Chapel as 'the Ladies' Chapel'. Winkles eventually became a Churchwarden and used his fundraising skills, developed when working for the new Chapel, for the benefit of St Peter's.

---

5   In the late 1930s, Mr Clifford Morgan succeeded AA Green as Borough Surveyor.

There can be no doubt that the 'Methodist schism' dealt a tremendous blow to the Chapel and helped to arrest the decline of the Church of England – though it strengthened the Low Church element there, and hence caused problems for the High Church Vicar Danter in the 1930s and later. The situation appears deliciously paradoxical. The Chapel is copying the Church and the Church is copying the Chapel – and both are 'losing out' as a result. Winkles's defection for essentially 'democratic' reasons raises the intriguing possibility that Church and Chapel were on the point of changing roles. Of course, that was impossible – or at least it was impossible with the autocratic Broughton as Vicar. Church could never be Chapel, any more than Chapel could be Church. But the crucial point is that neither Church nor Chapel were truly 'popular' religions any more – and much the same could be said of the Congregationalists, led by the entrepreneur Charlie Gardner. Now the only 'popular' religion in Brackley was the Salvation Army, but despite Bandsman Ward's virtuoso performances on the cornet, Salvationism never really took off.

It is hard to escape the conclusion that, even in Brackley, Victorian values were being challenged or discarded. In February 1911, Miss June Long, the Matron of the Hospital, was found dead in suspicious circumstances. Although the Inquest verdict was 'Misadventure', rumours were rife that Miss Long had committed suicide by taking an overdose of chloroform. The Curate, Rev CB Shapland, publicly rebuked 'the disciples of Satan in this town' who 'were not able to allow her memory to remain untarnished but started a rumour that she had made away with her life in order to hush up some private trial or trouble'.[6]

It looked as if the 'religion of the future' underpinning the Tory victory in 1910 would have to be a secular 'religion'. As we have seen, at the turn of the century, Imperialism looked a promising candidate. But the electorate had rejected Imperialism in 1906 and even in 1910 did not seem very keen. If there was a symbolic connection between Imperialism and the Great Central, the future did not look bright, witness the low price of Great Central shares: 'Gone Completely' had proved spot on. In reality, the line had been a huge, expensive mistake, costing over £11 million, or about four times the original estimate. Time had shown there was not enough traffic between London and the North for yet another company to muscle in successfully. Sir John Clapham was later to describe the whole project as 'a belated and almost entirely superfluous product of the original era of fighting construction'.[7]

In relation to the revenue it produced, the Great Central had been grotesquely overengineered. In particular, it was obvious that the section through Brackley, through the thinly populated countryside of Northants and Bucks, would never pay its way. The commercial implications of Haggard's telling phrase, 'lonesome as the veldt', were hardly encouraging.

The large gas-lit Top Station had been built on the wrong technological assumptions. Electric light was coming and so too were motor cars. By 11 June 1903, only just over four years after the first train arrived at the Top Station, Captain Fitzroy was speaking in Parliament in support of a Bill for the registration of motor cars. Fitzroy admitted that some people had a deep-seated antipathy to motor cars. But he was not one of them, 'he believed that motor cars were an invention of great importance and had a great future before them for the public good'.

Given the problems of Church and Chapel, the failure of Imperialism, even the death of Tommy Judge, was there any other creed that would provide the basis for Brackley's new 'religion'? I believe there was. In a more industrial setting it might have been Socialism; in Brackley, it was hunting. Of course, there

6   Smith, Donald, *Brackley Cottage Hospital*, op. cit., pp.52–54.

7   Quoted in Rolt, LTC, *The Making of a Railway* (London: Hugh Evelyn, 1971) p.13.

is much about hunting that reminds us of a religion. It certainly has spectacle and ceremonial. Arguably it even has a theology – with the sacrifice of the fox and the 'blooding' of young hunters comparable to the Mass. It differs from Christianity in some important respects. The relationship between hunters and their horses and hounds, perhaps even with their quarry, makes them doubt the Christian doctrine that animals have no souls.

Loyalty to a particular Hunt can be as intense as to any Church. Despite David Guthrie's enthusiasm for the Pytchley and the existence of an earlier Liberal ideology of hunting, expounded in some of the novels of Anthony Trollope, the political implications of hunting were now essentially Tory. In terms of conventional religion, hunting posed more of a threat to the Chapels than to the Church. Traditional Chapelgoers were usually indifferent or hostile. It may be that a love of hunting was a factor in Winkles's move from Chapel to Church. After his 'defection', he actually composed a song entitled 'Hurrah for the Hounds of the Bicester!'

In the past there had been many foxhunting parsons in the area – not least Francis Litchfield – but these days were gone. Few Anglican clergymen now had either the money or the inclination to go hunting – another point of convergence with their Methodist counterparts. Hunting met the essential requirements identified by the old Roman Emperors for keeping the people quiet: it offered both 'bread' and 'circuses'. The circuses came in the spectacle of the Meet and the Chase – at which foot followers were welcome. Such spectacles were perhaps more exciting than services in either Church or Chapel. Further, despite the coming of the Great Central, the spectacles of hunting were more accessible to Brackley people than the spectacles of Imperialism – military bands in London and the fleet lit up at Spit Head.

Hunting also provided 'bread'. In 1910 a large number of Brackley men were employed as grooms of one sort or another. Of course, grooming was dusty and hence thirsty work – and that meant profits for tavern keepers and brewers. But there was much more to it than that – work for saddlers, blacksmiths, tailors, fodder merchants and vets. The dinner parties and general socialising that went with hunting brought good business to grocers and wine merchants. One way or another, hunting did far more for Brackley than any of the benefits conferred by the GCR.

There is much about Brackley's economy in the years before 1914 to remind us of that of Melton Mowbray – the 'capital' of English fox hunting. The dominance of the Hunt was exemplified in the somewhat unconventional banking arrangements when the Grafton met at Brackley – usually a Saturday in November. The ladies and gentlemen would knock on the windows of Gilletts' Bank (later Barclays) with their riding crops. The Manager, Mr Greening, would then send out a junior clerk to collect their cheques and take them their money.

With the exception of Norris, none of the Brackley entrepreneurs went hunting themselves. George Gibbard was no Mr Jorrocks. But without the Hunt, it is doubtful whether the entrepreneurs could have flourished as they did, much less guaranteed Brackley's Tory future in a secular age. Another element was needed, more powerful and wealthy than they, to fill the gap left by the wreck of the squires and the failure of the Radicals and Nonconformists. It was the hunters themselves.

Of course, some of the old squires continued to hunt, but they were finding it difficult to sustain. To be successful and smart, Hunts needed really wealthy backers, and the squires no longer had that kind of money. Given the still-depressed state of agriculture, the support could only come from non-agricultural, essentially urban sources. We must return to Haggard; we begin to see the significance of Sir Charles Knightley's comment that, without hunting, there would be 'nobody in the district' and of Sir Hereward Wake's remark that, with such rents, agricultural estates had become merely 'beautiful toys' for rich men.

The decline of the squirearchy was not just a matter of the agricultural depression. Political and social influence is determined as much by will and by culture as by economics. The mainstay of the old order had been an almost fanatical dedication to the preservation of family estates over the generations. This had been rational to the extent that the possession of land had been the best guarantee of wider influence in politics and society. But once that guarantee disappeared, much of the attraction of land went with it.

There had always been a high price to pay. From the middle of the seventeenth century onwards, landowners had forced themselves to submit to 'Strict Settlements'. These settlements made the actual landowner no more than a 'life tenant' or trustee for generations yet unborn. It was virtually impossible for him to sell the family lands in his lifetime and even his freedom to determine who should inherit it after his death was severely restricted. Everything had to be preserved in the interests of a single male heir and his heirs. Thus, landowners had to sacrifice their own comfort and convenience for the future and, in the process, could make little provision for younger sons and daughters.

The Strict Settlement weighed particularly heavily on those without direct male heirs of their own. They might be required to stint themselves for the benefit of some distant male cousin, perhaps hardly known or even intensely disliked. Quite apart from political considerations, the traditional self-sacrifice for an extended family was hardly in accordance with Victorian notions of individualism, still less with the Edwardian trend to hedonism. Perhaps the time has come for historians to look more carefully at the little known and – at the time relatively uncontroversial – Settled Land Act of 1882, which abolished life tenancies and gave landowners greater freedom both to sell their lands and to bequeath them as they wished.

The Brackley area was being invaded by a new race, one that had made its money elsewhere but was now prepared to use its wealth to acquire a house in the country as a basis for the pleasures of the chase. In a word, the newcomers were nouveau riche, not an aristocracy or a squirearchy, but a plutocracy. They came in all shapes and sizes. There were the Whiteleys of Mixbury and Tingewick, who had made their money from a London department store. In Brackley itself there were the Campbells of Market House and, above all, the Allens. Local gossip had it that the Allens had made their money from making hats, though in reality they had an engineering firm. They displaced the Pierrepoints from Evenley Hall and the Cartwrights from Brackley House.

To begin with, some of the newcomers were regarded as a bit vulgar. William Allen, the founder of the fortune, who acquired Evenley Hall as early as 1887, may have had a few rough edges, but they soon became accepted and acclimatised. William Allen's two sons – Harry and John – had beautiful manners. Even in the 1950s, John Allen was held up as the perfect gentleman, so delicate indeed that he would never use that vulgar expression, 'good afternoon'. With John Allen, it was always 'good morning' before 3 p.m. and 'good evening' afterwards.

Acceptance of the newcomers was easier because they went to Church – the Campbells paid for the restoration of the Lady Chapel at St Peter's. They were generally enthusiastic Tories and they gave their servants better pay and conditions than the old squires could afford, or even consider seemly.

Of course, as with the Earl of Ellesmere, there were always fears that the newcomers would not stay. It was worrying to learn that the Allens had an estate on the Isle of Gigha off the west coast of Scotland. Indeed, in the event, most of the newcomers left after a couple of generations, with the Allens leaving at the end of the 1930s. Yet, for the time being, it looked as if they were putting down roots, even marrying into the old squirearchy.

In 1910, Harry Allen married Louisa, widow of EI Stratton of Heathfield, Oxon. John Allen went furthest of all to present himself as the successor of John Locke Stratton. He joined the Borough Council in 1896 and served as Mayor from 1904 to 1909 – the first mayor not to have been a member of the original 1887 Council. The *Northampton Herald* of 22 September 1911 praises John Allen to the skies. It dwells on the 'considerable value' of his estate and stresses that his knowledge of engineering has made him an invaluable member of the Water Works Committee. Allen is 'highly popular amongst all classes for his generosity and good nature'. An active Conservative, he has always been 'to the fore' in political battles and 'in pushing forward the Constitutional cause'. He has put a field at the disposal of the Rifle Club and donated butts. Mrs Allen is 'also held in high esteem in the town by all sections of the community and is especially kind and generous to those in needy circumstances'. If it was not quite feudalism à la Stratton, at least it was feudalism of a kind.

Yet the element of permanence was missing. The newcomers were not motivated by the same sense of dynastic ambition that had been so strong among the old squires. The change is summed up by Sir John Habakkuk (in *Marriage, Debt and the Estate System*, 1994), who speaks of:

> … an increase in the purchasers who regard an estate as a species of property, with particular advantages it is true – as a source of social status and a base for an attractive style of life, and latterly also as a tax-efficient method of holding wealth – but not as a trust to be handed on to their posterity and the foundation of an enduring landed family … There was an increase in the number of owners who bought without a firm intention of holding beyond their own lifetime.

Many of the hunting 'set' clearly never intended to settle down in Brackley at all, although they still provided good business and employment during their stay. They tended to lease a Hunting Box for a season or two; one such was Viscount Brackley's brother-in-law, Toby Lambton. The Lambton connection, with its Northern associations, must have been alarming; Viscount Brackley bought the large Mertoun Estate in Berwickshire in 1912. Would that mean that he would not live in Brackley when he succeeded?

Some of the hunters were not really resident at all. Here the Great Central's true role was revealed. The swift communication with London meant that it was now possible to come to Brackley for a day's hunting with the Grafton, the Bicester or the Whaddon Chase. Even those who took a house locally could easily go up to Town for business or pleasure. The old hunters had hated railways with their Town associations, the smoke, the danger posed by trains to a pack in full cry. Of course, the Great Central had done its best to meet their fears, adding to its costs by building bridges and culverts for the special convenience of the hunters. Indeed, by facilitating communication with London, the railway actually helped to keep hunting going.

With the institution of the Hunt Train, the synthesis was complete. Far from marking the end of feudalism, the Great Central helped to perpetuate it in a new form. The wealthiest of all the 'Great Central hunting plutocrats' were the Rothschilds, who became so powerful in the Whaddon Chase that it was referred to as 'the Jewish Pack'. One wonders what the anti-Semitic Francis Litchfield would have said about that. Although the Rothschilds did not acquire land in the immediate vicinity of Brackley, they were well established up the line in Buckinghamshire, even having a special station called Waddesdon constructed for their guests.

It is striking that, at the time of the Parliamentary debates on the London Extension, the most enthusiastic local MP had been Baron Ferdinand de Rothschild, who represented Aylesbury. Knightley and later Guthrie were completely silent on the matter. On 17 March 1891, Rothschild had told Parliament:

Passenger traffic is slow and inconvenient with constant delays and stoppages and the cost of goods traffic is exceptionally high. We have heard a good deal about the agricultural labourer and only the other day, we passed the Second Reading of a Bill to enable him to have small holdings; and I am convinced that no scheme can be of more advantage to the agricultural labourer in Bucks than to secure the advantage of direct railway communication.

Given his family's sense of social responsibility, it would be unfair to suppose that the Baron's concern for the agricultural labourer was a sham, but we may suspect that the Great Central's advantages for London-based hunters also figured in his calculations.

The connection between the Great Central and the Rothschild plutocracy is well illustrated in a story told by my other grandfather, Charlie Clarke. Shortly after the turn of the century, he was at Marylebone Station late one night. A group of gentlemen in evening dress came into the deserted booking hall and inquired about the trains for Waddesdon. When they were informed that the last train had already gone, one of them took out his pocket book, pushed a handful of notes at the clerk and said, 'Well, then get us one'. It was a gesture worthy of Phileas Fogg. Within a few minutes an engine and a coach appeared and off they went to Waddesdon. They probably did not want to miss hunting the next day. Of course, they could afford it, but perhaps the Great Central itself, like the agricultural estates through which it passed, had become something of a rich man's toy.

Between 1910 and 1914, we have many photographs of well-attended meets of the Grafton Hunt in Brackley. The Market Square is filled with riders and horses surrounded by admiring locals. In 1913, however, the picture changes, if only slightly. Again, the square is filled with horses and riders and admiring locals and with black and white photography the difference is barely perceptible; if there had been colour photographs then it would have been clearer. Instead of Hunting Pink, the dominant colour would have been khaki, because the men on horseback are soldiers. Brackley was one of the chief centres of extensive army manoeuvres; although the country as a whole did not realise it, war was not far away.

The summer of 1914 marked a great turning point and it was not just the war. *The Times* of 14 July carries an item headed 'Death of a Notable Sportsman'. It is the obituary of the Earl of Ellesmere; the Earl had led a fortunate life and he was surely fortunate in the hour of his death. The most important symbol of the Thicknesse Revolution was no more. In 1915, it was announced that the new Earl did not require the Manor House and the Brackley Estate was put on the market.

But in another way, the change was more gradual. To begin with, the war still seemed all about horses. On August Bank Holiday, my mother, then a little girl of 6, was attending a horse show. In the middle of the show, soldiers appeared with orders to commandeer the horses for military purposes. The hunters went off to France – and so did many Brackley men. Many of the horses and many of the men did not return. One lucky survivor was a horse called Bella; she lived in a field behind The Bell until the late 1920s – she had had an ear shot off in France.

Thus, hunting foxes turned into hunting Germans. The link had been observed before. RS Surtees's foxhunting grocer, Mr Jorrocks, had lauded hunting as providing 'the image of war, without the guilt and with only five and twenty per cent of the danger'. Now the image of war was turning into the reality, and proving to be rather more than four times more dangerous than hunting. In the process, Brackley achieved a unity through suffering and hatred of Germans that had eluded it in the past; the Kaiser did what Thicknesse, Egerton, Tommy Judge, the Great Central Railway, the Imperialists and the fox hunters had all only achieved in part. At the end, in November 1918, they hanged the Kaiser in effigy in Brackley Market Place. Brackley had finally caught its quarry.

John Allen, JP. (NRO)

Harry Allen. (NRO)

Church Lads' Brigade.

The Tennis Club. (NRO)

The opening of the Methodist Chapel, 1911. (NRO)

Brackley football team.

The Brackley Parade.

The Church Lads' Brigade.

Capt. Amos   Fireman Wright   Engineer Blaby   Fireman Jones   Engineer Wodhams

Brackley Fire Brigade, 1906.

Brackley Wool Fair, 1913.

Fire at Alcock's, April 1911.

The Grafton Hunt, 1912.

Army manoeuvres, 1913. (NRO)

Belgian officers in Brackley, November 1914. (NRO)

What happened to the KAISER and LITTLE WILLIE at
BRACKLEY.
NOVEMBER 11, 1918.

'Hang the Kaiser', 1918.

BIBLIOGRAPHY

Archive Material

Northamptonshire County Record Office
Brackley Borough Papers
Brackley Guardians' Minute Books
Brackley Parish Papers
Cartwright Papers
Ellesmere Papers

Newspapers & Periodicals

Banbury Advertiser
Banbury Guardian
Bicester Herald
Brackley Parish Magazine
Methodist Recorder
Northampton Herald
Northampton Mercury
The Times

Printed Books & Journals

Adkins, WRD, *Our County* (London: Elliot Stock, 1893).

Anon., 'Alexander Ross Obituary', *Journal of the Royal Institute of British Architects*, Vol. 33 (1926), p.64.

Anon., *Northamptonshire Leaders, Social and Political* (Exeter: 1898).

Anon., *A Short History of the Brackley Feoffee Charity* (Brackley: 1889).

Anscomb, JW, 'Woodford Halse: The Village with a Heart of Steam', *Northamptonshire Past and Present*, Vol. VI, No. 6 (1982–83) pp.341–50.

Arch, J, *Joseph Arch: The Story of His Life. Told by Himself* (London: 1898).

Bamford, TW, *Thomas Arnold* (London: 1960).

Banks, SW, and MJ Garrett, 'Hunting by Train', *Brackley Observed*, Vol. I, No. 1 (1986), pp.14–21.

Burns, JG, 'Report on Northamptonshire', in the *Second Report of Children's Employment Commission*, P.P. Vol. XIV (1843).

Cartwright, J (ed.), *The Journals of Lady Knightley of Fawsley* (London: Murray, 1915).

Chandler, K, 'Morris Dancing at Brackley', *Brackley Observed*, Vol. I, No. 1 (1986), pp.22–35.

Clarke, JC, *The Book of Brackley* (Buckingham, Barracuda Books, 1987).

Clarke, JC, 'Rev Francis Litchfield and the transformation of Farthinghoe', *Brackley Observed*, Vol. I, No. 3. (1989), pp.23–30.

Clarke, JC, *Yesterday's Brackley: From Restoration to Reform* (Buckingham: Barracuda Books, 1990).

Clarke, JC, 'Northamptonshire in 1857', *Brackley Observed*, Vol. II, No. 1 (1994), pp.3–18.

Clarke, JC, 'Early Victorian South Northamptonshire', *Cake and Cockhorse*, Vol. XIII, No. 3, pp.77–88.

Cooper, N, *Aynho: A Northamptonshire Village* (Banbury: Leopard's Head Press, 1984).

Cowley, R, *Policing Northamptonshire 1836–1986* (Studley, Warwickshire: Brewin Books, 1986).

Currey, WE, 'Report on the Schools of Northamptonshire 1875'. Contained in *Report of the Committee of Council on Education*. P.P. 1876. Vol. XXIII.

Dow, G, *Great Central* (London: 1959).

Forrester, EG, *A History of Magdalen College School, Brackley, Northamptonshire 1548–1949* (Buckingham: E.N. Hillier & Sons Ltd, 1950).

Gordon, P, *The Red Earl: The Papers of the Fifth Earl Spencer 1835–1910*, Vol. 1: 1835–85 (Northampton: 1981).

Gordon, P, 'Lady Knightley and the South Northamptonshire Election of 1885', *Northamptonshire Past and Present*, Vol. VI, No. 6 (1981–82), pp.265–73.

Gordon, P, 'A County Parliament: The First Northamptonshire County Council', *Northamptonshire Past and Present*, Vol. VII, No. 3 (1985–86), pp.188–95.

Greenall, RL, *A History of Northamptonshire* (London: Phillimore & Co., 1979).

Greenall, RL, 'Parson as a Man of Affairs: The Rev Francis Litchfield of Farthinghoe (1792–1876)', *Northamptonshire Past and Present*, Vol. VIII, No. 2 (1990–91), pp.121–35.

Habakkuk, J, *Marriage, Debt and the Estate System: English Landownership 1650–1950* (Oxford: Clarendon Press, 1994).

Haggard, H Rider, *Rural England*, two vols (London: 1902).

Harrison, B, 'For Church, Queen and Family: The Girls' Friendly Society 1874–1920', *Northamptonshire Past and Present*, No. 61 (1973).

Healy, JMC, *Great Central Memories* (London: Baton Transport, 1988).

Horn, P, 'The Evenley Strike in 1867', *Northamptonshire Past and Present*, Vol. IV, No. 1, pp.47–50.

Horn, P, 'Child Workers in the Victorian Countryside: The Case of Northamptonshire', *Northamptonshire Past and Present*, Vol. VII, No. 3 (1985–86), pp.173–85.

Howarth, J, 'The Liberal Revival in Northamptonshire 1880–1895: A Case Study in Late Nineteenth-Century Elections', *The Historical Journal*, Vol. XII (1969), pp.78–118.

Howarth, J, 'Politics and Society in Late Victorian Northamptonshire', *Northamptonshire Past and Present*, Vol. IV, No. 5 (1970–71), pp.269–74.

Lenton, JM, 'Brackley Wesleyan Day School', *Brackley Observed*, Vol. I, No. 2 (1987), pp.4–7.

Linnell, JE, *Old Oak* (3rd Edition, Northampton: The Burlington Press, 1984).

Litchfield, F, *County Police and Prevention* (Northampton: 1849).

Longden, H Isham, *Northamptonshire and Rutland Clergy from 1550* (Northampton: Archer Goodman, 1938–52).

Macleod, RM, 'Law, Medicine and Public Opinion; the Resistance to Compulsory Health Legislation' in *Public Law* (1967).

Marx, K, *Das Kapital* (translation, London: Everyman, 1962).

Mozley, T, *Reminiscences. Chiefly of Towns, Villages and Churches*, two volumes (London: Longmans, Green & Co., 1885).

Norman, FH, 'Report on Northamptonshire' contained in *First Report of the Royal Commission on the Employment of Children, Young Persons and Women in Agriculture*, P.P. 1867–68, Vol. XVII.

Pearson, BE, *Local Gleanings II: The Town Hall* (Brackley: James Smart, 1881).

Pelling, H, *Social Geography of British Elections 1885–1910* (London: Palgrave Macmillan, 1967).

Phillips, P, *Thomas Judge: The Demon Grocer of Brackley* (Buckingham: Phillips Print, 2000).

Pringle, R Hunter, 'Report on Beds, Hunts and Northants' in *Reports from the Assistant Commissioners on Agricultural Depression with Statistical Returns 1895–96*, P.P. Eng. 1895–96, Vol. XVII.

Robb, JH, *The Primrose League 1883–1906* (London: 1968).

Rolt, LTC, *The Making of a Railway* (2nd edition, London: Hugh Evelyn, 1971).

Saint, A, 'Charles Buckeridge and his Family', *Oxoniensia*, Vol. XXXVIII (1973), pp.357–72.

Shorthouse, RW, 'Justices of the Peace in Northamptonshire, 1830–1845, Part I', *Northamptonshire Past and Present* Vol. V, No. 2 (1974), pp.129–40.

Shorthouse, RW, 'Justices of the Peace in Northamptonshire, 1830–1845, Part II', *Northamptonshire Past and Present* Vol. V, No. 3 (1975), pp.243–51.

Simpson, B, *The Banbury to Verney Junction Branch* (Oxford: Oxford Publishing Company, 1977).

Smith, D, 'Brackley Cottage Hospital, 1876–1966', *Brackley and District History Society Occasional Paper 2* (1996).

Taylor, AM, *Gilletts: Bankers at Banbury and Oxford* (Oxford: Clarendon Press, 1964).

Thompson, F, *Still Glides the Stream* (London: 1977).

Thompson, F, *Lark Rise* (London: 1993).

Tregarthen, W F, 'Report on Schools in Northamptonshire', contained in *Report of the Committee of Council on Education*, P.P. 1867, Vol. XXII.

Trinder, B (ed.), *A Victorian M.P. and his Constituents: The Correspondence of H.W. Tancred, 1841–1859* (Banbury: 1967).

Trinder, B, *Victorian Banbury* (Chichester: Phillimore & Co., 1982).

Turner, JD, 'The Education of the Poor in Brackley during the Nineteenth Century', *Brackley and District History Society Occasional Paper 1*, n.d.

Whellan, W, *History, Gazetteer and Directory of Northamptonshire* (London: 1849).

White, IE, 'Report on Northamptonshire', contained in *First Report of Children's Employment Commission*, P.P. 1863, Vol. XVIII.

White, IE, 'Report on Northamptonshire', contained in *Sixth Report of the Children's Employment Commission*, P.P. 1867, Vol. XVI.

Wright, T, *The Romance of the Lace Pillow* (Olney: 1919).

Young, GM, *Portrait of an Age: Victorian England* (London: 1973).

INDEX

Hirons, William 43—47, 75
Hopcraft & Norris Brewery *160*
Hunting 171—175
    Hunt Train 174
    Rothschild, Baron Ferdinand de 174, 175
Hunts
    Bicester 174
    Grafton 131, 172, 175, *182*
    Pytchley 127n, 172
    Whaddon Chase 174
Inns
    The Bell 175
    The Cross Keys 20
    The Crown 43, *79*
    The George 20
    The Greyhound 14
    The Horse and Jockey 20
    The Locomotive 71
    The Plough 120
    The Reindeer 20
    The Wagon and Horses 20
    The Red Lion 22
    The Wheat Sheaf 130
    The White Lion 52
Jakeman, William (Billy) 26, *34*
Jones, Pryce Rev 39—47
Judd, William 12, 148, 149, 156, 157
Judge, Thomas 12, 67, 67n, 68, 68n, 69, 71, 73, 76,
    83, 85, 86, 96, 107, 108, 110, 112, 113, 116, 117,
    121, 127, 130, 131, 132, 135, 137, 138, 139, 145,
    168, 169, 171, 175
    Brackley Temperance Society 68
    Bright, John 71, 73
    Disraeli, Benjamin 73, 105, 109, 109n, 118
Kaiser Wilhelm II 165, 175
    'Hang the Kaiser' *183*
Kibble, Tommy 156, 167
Knightley, Sir Charles 36, 37, 50, 123, 172
Knightley (née Bowater), Lady Louisa 90, 90n, 92,
    92n, 105, 105n, 106, 108n, 109, 109n, 110, 111,
    111n, 112, 112n, 113, 114, 117, 118, 118n, 121,
    126
    Girls' Friendly Society 111, 111n
    Primrose League 112, 112n, 127, 132, 135, 145
    Cartwright, Beatrice 111, 132
Knightley, Sir Rainald 90, 107, 108, 108n, 109, 110,
    111, 112, 113, 118, 123, 124, 135, 174
Labouchère, Henry Du Pré 107
Lace Making 28—31, 71, 146
    Baysley, Mrs *65*

Langley, J B 49, 70, 76
Leapor, Mary 85
    Artemisia: A Dialogue 85, 85n
Liberal Candidates
    Carmichael, Sir James 124, 127
    Fitzgerald, Sir Maurice 109, 110, 117, 118
    Grove, Thomas Newcomen Archibald 146, 168
    Guthrie, David Charles 136, 138, 139, 168, 172,
    174
    Kellaway, F G 168
    Thomas, A A 168
Litchfield, Rev Francis 35, 35n, 36, 36n, 37—40, 42,
    44, 45, 49, 50, 51, 54, 55, 56, 69, 72, 74, 75, 76,
    83, 88, 172, 174
Lock, James 19, 20
Magdalen College, Oxford 59, 60, 67, 89, 110, 133
    Bulley, President 59, 60, 88, 89
Magdalen College Chapel 12, 59, 60, 88, 89, 90, 92,
    97, 98, 116, 150, 170
Magdalen College School 12, 14, 57 58, 59, 59n, 60,
    88, 89, 90, 92, *97*, 115, 116, 116n, 127, 127n, 131,
    147, 149, 150, 155, 155n, 170
    Ashwin, Rev Robert 14
    Buckeridge, Charles 12, 88, 89, 89n, 90, 91
    Falkner, Rev F B 60, 115
    Holdgate, Rev William Wyatt 155, 156
    Russell, Rev Thomas 60
    Wodhams, Rev Isaac 12, 60, 115, 116, 116n, 117,
    120, 127, 155
Manor House (formerly Tithe House *98*) 12, 88, 92,
    94, 95, *100*, 103, *140, 141*, 150, 165, 175
    Brailsford, Luther 94, 146, 146n, 147, 155
Mobbs, John 94
    See 3rd Earl of Ellesmere
Marx, Karl 76, 76n
Methodist Chapel 12, 14, 25, 26, 27, 35, 68, 88, 92,
    108, 133, 134, 146, 149, 156, 166, 170, 171, 172,
    178
Methodist Chapel School 28, 55, 56, 57, 94, 129,
    138, 147
    Aldous, Robert 147
    Browton, John 57
    Clark, Mrs 57
    Osborn, Rev John 168
Methodist Recorder 24, 25n, 26, 26n, 56, 57n, 134n,
    146, 165
Mozley, Thomas 28, 29, 29n, 31, 31n, 32, 32n, 36,
    36n, 61, 62, 84, 149, 168
National School 55—57
New Review 168

SUBSCRIBERS

Mrs Absalom

Dr H.J. Apel, 37th Lord of Brackley

Pam & Graham Archdale

Jane Atkins

Anthony & Kareen Bagot-Webb

Kate Bartlett

Robert Beckingham

Helen Berry

Beverly Bigmore

Caryl Billingham MBE

Janet Blencowe

Joan Boatwright

Margaret Bolton

Cllr Jim Broomfield

Denis Cannings

Cantor & Nissel Ltd

Anne Carter

Cllr Chris & Jane Cartmell

Barbara Clarke

Connie Coleman

Donald G. Cox

Linda Daniels

Gerald Davis & Francoise Szigeti

Robin Digby

Janet & Michael Dingvean

Elaine Dixon

J.T. Dobson

Diane Dotterill

Kathleen Draper

Judith Dunn

Tim East

Joy Eastwood

Rosalyn Fowler

Max and Janet Garratt

Karen Gees

Carol Gilbert

Jennifer Griffiths

Phil & Mary Hawkins

Deborah Hayter

Theodora Hayward

R.W. Houghton

Carolyn Hunter

Mr & Mrs G. Johnson

Marion Kapusniak

Joyce King

Jill Knight

Rosemary Leeper

Lesley Lenthall

Mr Nick Lewis

Roger Lewry

Martin Lucas

Richard & Erika Lumb

Mrs Diane Lumbard
Ben Macintyre
Philippa Macmahon
Wendy Manley
Josine Martin
Manuela G. Mera
Gerry & David Mico
Rosemary Miles
Dave Morris
Richard Murdin
Brenda Nutting
Helen and Brian Pacey
Joanna Pajor
Pam Pell
Judith Perkins
Steve & Jane Pope
Sandy Prentice
Shirley Pryce
Peter Rawlinson
Gwen Rhys
Norma Root
Barbara Saunders
Anne Seckinton
Cllr Sue Sharps

Joao Maia e Silva
Martin Sirot-Smith
Colin R. Smith
Karrol Smulovic
Walter & Lilian Stageman
Blake Stimpson
Jan & Alan Thompson
Margaret Tanner
Charles and Jean Teague
Cecil Thompson
Mrs E. Torrance
Cindy Turvey
Mrs Hilary Watts
Terrance Warren
John Webber
Linda Williams
Ian Wilmot
Michael Wilmot
Tony Wilmot
Wendy Wilmot
Mrs E. Wilson
Paul Wiltshire

Remaining names unlisted